AMERICAN UNIVERSALISM

Its Origins, Organization and Heritage

Elmo Arnold Robinson

AN EXPOSITION-TESTAMENT BOOK

Exposition Press   *New York*

EXPOSITION PRESS INC.

50 Jericho Turnpike   Jericho, New York 11753

FIRST EDITION

To the memory of my father

EDGAR LEWIS ROBINSON

and of my mother, born

MARY BARTON ARNOLD

*onetime members of Universalist churches in
Portland (Maine), Rochester and Canandaigua (New York),
Oak Park (Illinois), and Pasadena (California),
in appreciation of
their character and influence*

Contents

Part III

EPILOGUE: THE HERITAGE

Preface

"Have you anything on Universalism in Indiana?" I asked the librarian in the State Library at Indianapolis. It was, as I recall, August 27, 1915.

"No," she replied. "Why don't you write something?"

Ever since, off and on (more frequently off), I have been writing "something" about Universalism. And now more than a year of intensive work has been devoted to this book.

Why have I done it? The story of the birth, life, and transmigration (rather than death) of the Universalist Church is a choice bit of Americana and an important strand in the development of American religion. Many have never heard of it. Even members of Unitarian Universalist churches sometimes ask, "Who were these Universalists? I know a little something about Unitarianism. But Universalism? What was that?"

Moreover, this is a thank-you offering. I am grateful for my Universalist ancestry and for the contribution which the denomination has made to my life.

I first became acquainted with Universalist clergymen during my youth, and in 1912 I joined their ranks. Among those I remember are the following men and women of patriarchal standing: C. Ellwood Nash (born 1855), George L. Perin and Gideon I. Keirn (1854), Sara L. Stoner (1853), Edwin D. Sweetser and Anson Titus (1847), William G. Tousey (1842), Ezekial Fitzgerald (1840), Isaac M. Atwood (1838), Robert T. Polk (1837), Marion D. Crosley (1835), Henry Blanchard (1833), and Lucinda ("Auntie") Brown (1822). I think that I recall Gerherdus L. Demerest (1816). Many of the memories are very dim. But these men and women and many others born since 1860 serve, not as source material but as emotional links to the days of denominational beginnings.

For twenty years I was closely identified with the work of the denomination, and for forty more I have been on the sidelines. I write, I hope, objectively, yet for some items, the Winchester Profession of Faith for example, I have deep veneration. And to me Universalism has come to imply much more than it seems originally to have signified. What this is I shall suggest in the final chapter. Meanwhile I have tried to be factual and impartial, permitting myself only occasional value judgments.

I have limited the story to organized Universalism in the United States. But the idea of universal salvation is ancient. It certainly can be found among the radicals of the Reformation. Earlier still it was taught by some neo-Platonic Christians. Universalists have asserted it to be a biblical doctrine. But I hardly touch on such matters.

This is not a complete history even of American Universalism. There is little here about auxiliary organizations for women, for men, for youth, for Sunday-school workers. There is little about our several state conventions, associations, churches, and societies. There is little biography, little discussion of theology, little about practical efforts at service and reform. I leave to others unused opportunities for those essays, dissertations, and books which I have not attempted to write.

What this purports to be is a general survey of American Universalism seen chiefly from the central position of one of the two participants in the merger with the American Unitarian Association, the Universalist General Convention, or as it came to be known, the Universalist Church of America.

Many topics here neglected are discussed in Clinton Scott's *The Universalist Church of America* (Universalist Historical Society, 25 Beacon Street, Boston), which interested readers should consult.

Some material from the historical chapters is scheduled to appear in the forthcoming issue of the *Journal of the Universalist Historical Society.*

—E.A.R.

Los Alamos, New Mexico
January 1, 1970

ACKNOWLEDGMENTS

I am grateful for the warm encouragement, helpful hints, and valuable bits of information which I have received, not only from friends but from persons whom I have never met. Careful reading of much of the manuscript by Dr. James D. Hunt, Mrs. Jasper (Betty) Jackson, and Mrs. Guy (Gloria) Elliott eliminated many unfortunate expressions and misleading approaches. Miss Charlotte Irwin assisted in checking some of the references. The manuscript was typed by Mrs. Douglas (Pat) Rodgers. Encouragement from my wife, Elizabeth, has made this book possible.

The following, among others, have kindly replied to my inquiries concerning specific matters:

Mrs. Maude Banks, Mount Ida, Ark.
Miss Georgene E. Bowen, Philadelphia
Dr. Foster S. Brown, St. Lawrence University
Mrs. John Buwalda, Pasadena
Harry Carey, Jr.
Dr. Ernest Cassara, Goddard College
Dr. Robert Cummins, Bowdoinham, Maine
Dr. Carleton M. Fisher, Freeport, N. Y.
Dr. Harmon M. Gehr, Pasadena
Dr. Brainard Gibbons, No. Kingston, R. I.
Dr. Philip R. Giles, Towson, Md.
Elizabeth Gourley, Santa Paula, Cal.
Mrs. Beatrice T. Greene, Millbourne, Fla.
Mrs. Charles Hartshorne, Austin, Tex.
Dr. Winthrop S. Hudson, Colgate Rochester Divinity School
Dr. James D. Hunt, Shaw University
Miss Charlotte Irwin, Cambridge, Mass.

Constant H. Jacquet, National Council of Churches of Christ

Neil R. Jordahl, Meadville Theological School, Lombard College

Dr. Max A. Kapp, Unitarian Universalist Association

Harold S. Latham, Kearney, N. J.

Walter MacPeak, No. Brunswick, N. J.

Louisa L. Magraw, Quincy, Mass.

Dr. Stanley Manning, Avon, Ill.

Dr. Leonard C. Mead, Tufts University

Dr. Hermann Muelder, Knox College

John Mullane, Cincinnati

Henry A. Niven, West Dennis, Mass.

Dr. Harold Ostvold, California Institute of Technology

Lois M. Sargent, Montpelier, Vt.

Dr. Clinton L. Scott, Tarpon Springs, Fla.

Alan Seaburg, Boston

Carl Seaburg, Medford, Mass.

Dr. Dorothy Tilden Spoerl, Unitarian Universalist Association

Elmer T. Stevens, Chicago

Haynie Summers, Turin, Ga.

Dr. Malcolm R. Sutherland, Meadville Theological School of Lombard College

David W. Veit, Cleveland

Charles N. Vickery, Unitarian Universalist Service Committee

Dr. John C. Weigel, Joliet, Ill.

William Woodward, Claremont, Cal.

Mrs. Robert Zwirner, Windsor, Conn.

DEFINITIONS OF TERMS

For the benefit of those who may be unfamiliar with the terminology employed, I offer these working definitions.

Universalism. The doctrine that ultimately all men will be saved from sin and misery.

Ultra universalism. The doctrine that salvation for every man occurs as he enters into heaven at death. There, no longer exposed to temptation, he will cease to sin.

Restorationism (sometimes called Universal Restorationism or Restitutionism). The doctrine that punishment for sin continues after death but that it is remedial and therefore not endless.

Orthodoxy. The traditional Christian doctrinal system involving the literal inspiration of the Bible, the virgin birth, the deity of Jesus, the natural wickedness of man, the vicarious atonement, and the endless separation of the saved from the lost in heaven and hell.

Partialism. The name given by Universalists to views of their orthodox opponents for teaching that part, not all, of mankind will be saved.

Trinitarianism. The doctrine that God comprises three persons—Father, Son, and Holy Spirit.

Unitarianism (the meaning has changed during two centuries). Generally: the denial of the doctrine of the Trinity. More specifically: the affirmation of God's unity, and thus the affirmation that Jesus was a human being (either with or without special mission and powers)

Establishment (sometimes referred to as the Established churches or the Standing Order). Churches supported by public taxation. In colonial days, in several colonies, there were established churches, including Episcopal and Dutch Reformed. South of

New England, after the Revolution, taxation gave way to voluntary support. In New England the Establishment continued for a few years, finally disappearing in Massachusetts in 1833. The group of churches which took the name Unitarian in 1825 already had a long history as part of the colonial Establishment. After 1800 some New England churches gradually became Unitarian; others remained Congregational. Universalist churches were rarely eligible to receive tax support.

Separatist church. In New England, any church group which withdrew from the traditional establishment to form an independent or "gathered" congregation with voluntary support. Early Baptist, Methodist, and Universalist societies are included.

Theism. A general term for various doctrines about God, usually those taught by orthodox Christians.

Deism. The doctrine that God exists, that He can be known through human reason, and that revelation is unnecessary. Hence orthodoxy is rejected.

Atheism. Formerly a term thrown at an opponent who held any theory about God other than that held by oneself. Now, a badge often worn to proclaim one's nonconformity.

Transcendentalism. The doctrine that ultimate truths are not gained through the senses, nor provable by experience or reason, but are known directly by the mind.

Revelation. A form of communication from God to man, other than by sense experience or reason, by which the truths of man's salvation are made known. Orthodox Protestantism holds that this revelation is found in the Bible.

Part I

PROLOGUE:

BACKGROUND OF CHALLENGE—
VOICES IN PROTEST

"There was not a sermon preached that represented God as a good being; but on the contrary, he has invariably been pictured as the most malicious, partial and unjust being imaginable."

ANONYMOUS

"I have been preaching on the everlasting punishment of the wicked in hell, and I had a glorious time."

Quoted by G. A. GORDON

"I imbibed a different idea of the Deity, from what I had before entertained. I understood all those expressions in Scripture which represented him angry to be figurative. I considered all the wrath, enmity, and discord to be wholly in creatures and never in the essence of the Deity."

WALTER FERRISS

CHAPTER 1

A Persistent Theological Nightmare

It was a fitful dream, terrifying, hypnotic in its horror. The first quotation on the previous page is too sweeping, too unjust; nevertheless, it does mirror the religious atmosphere as it appeared to some critical minds. It seemed to them that for forty years and more prior to the Revolution large numbers of American colonists had been sleepwalking in a theological nightmare. After the Revolution, as population moved westward, many took their nightmare with them.

To represent the gospel as it was often preached I have drawn upon two sermons by Jonathan Edwards. Edwards did not always preach in this way, and these sermons were not an immediate cause of Universalist organization. But their message, repeated by many a lesser evangelist, was widely heard and accepted by the laity. It was a challenge to which varied protests responded. One such response was Universalism.

Let Edwards be my first witness. I call him, as it were, from the spirit world. Hear him speak to you in his own words.

JONATHAN EDWARDS (1703–1758)

My name is Jonathan Edwards.[1] Born in 1703, I lived much of my life in Massachusetts, where I was pastor of the church in Northampton. Your author asks me to explain to you the fate of those who die unconverted to the Christian religion. I respond by quoting condensed passages from one of my sermons, "The Portion of the Wicked."

"The soul, when it is separated from the body, shall be cast down into hell. The soul of the wicked man will then see how terrible God is, he will see how holy a God he is, how infinitely he hates sin, how dreadful is his displeasure. Then shall the soul come naked with all its guilt, and in all its filthiness, a vile, loathsome, abominable creature, an enemy to God, a rebel against him, before God as its judge. This will fill the soul with horror and amazement. Then its misery will begin. It will that moment be swallowed up in despair; the great gulf will forever shut up, the irrevocable sentence will be passed."

Then I go on to describe the prison in which the soul will be confined until the Day of Judgment. "They are there in extreme and inconceivable misery. They have no rest nor comfort. God there executes wrath upon them without mercy. Those wicked men who died many years ago, their souls went to hell, and there they are still. And those who went to hell in former ages of the world have been in hell ever since, all the while suffering torment. They have nothing else to spend their time in there, but to suffer torment, no friend, no love, no pity, no quietness, no prospect, no hope.

"When the Day of Judgment comes they shall rise to the resurrection of damnation. It is always a doleful time in hell, but when the news is heard that the day appointed for judgment is come, hell will be filled with louder shrieks than ever before. The last trumpet will sound. Then the sentence of condemnation will be pronounced by the Judge upon them: 'Depart from me, ye cursed, into everlasting fire, prepared for the devil and his angels.' Then the sentence shall be executed. That great company of devils and wicked men must then enter into those everlasting burnings to which they are sentenced.

"In this condition they shall remain throughout the never-ending ages of eternity. They will dwell in a fire that never shall be quenched. Here they must wear out one thousand years after another, and that without end. There is no reckoning up the millions of years or millions of ages. All arithmetic here fails. No rules of multiplication can reach the amount, for there is no end. And they shall never have any rest, nor any atonement. Their torments shall never grow any easier by their being accustomed to them. They shall never have done with the ages of their torment."

Many of you have heard of another of my sermons, "Sinners in the Hands of an Angry God," which I preached at Enfield on July 8, 1741. I began by pointing out that God has no want of power to cast men into hell. Men deserve to be cast there. They are already under a sentence of condemnation, are already objects of God's anger. The devil stands ready to seize them whenever God permits. There is no escape from this fate for those who reject Christ. God is under no obligation to save them. And now I quote from that sermon.

"The use of this awful subject may be for the awakening of unconverted persons in this congregation. The world of misery, the lake of burning brimstone, is extended abroad under you. There is the dreadful pit of the glowing flames of the wrath of God; there is hell's gaping mouth wide open, and you have nothing to stand upon, nor anything to take hold of. There is nothing between you and hell but the air. It is only the power and mere pleasure of God that holds you up.

"Your wickedness makes you, as it were, heavy as lead and to tend downwards with great weight and pressure towards hell. If God should let you go, you would immediately sink and swiftly descend and plunge into the bottomless pit.

"The bow of God's wrath is bent, and the arrow made ready on the string, and justice bends the arrow at your heart, and strains the bow, and it is nothing but the mere pleasure of God, and that of an angry God, without any promise or obligation at all, that keeps the arrow one moment from being made drunk with your blood. Thus all of you that never passed under a great change of heart, by the mighty power of the Spirit of God upon your souls; all you that were never born again and made new creatures are in the hands of an angry God.

"The God that holds you over the pit of hell, much as one holds a spider or some loathsome insect over the fire, abhors you. You have offended him. Yet it is nothing but his hand that holds you from falling into fire every moment. It is to be ascribed to nothing else that you did not go to hell last night, that you were suffered to awake again in this world after you closed your eyes to sleep. And there is no other reason to be given why you have not dropped into hell since you arose in the morning, but that God's hand has held you up. There is no other reason to be given why you have not gone to hell since you sat here in the house of God, provoking his pure eyes by your sinful wicked manner of attending his solemn worship. Yes, there is nothing else to be given as a reason why you do not at this very moment drop down into hell.

"O Sinner! You hang by a slender thread, with the flames of divine wrath flashing about it, and ready every moment to singe it, and burn it asunder. You have nothing to lay hold of to save yourself. There is nothing that you have ever done, nothing that you can do, to induce God to spare you one moment."

COMMENT

It would be unfair to Edwards to judge his character and ability from these extracts, for he is now regarded as one of America's important early philosophers. When he wrote philosophy, he did not write in this style. But when he preached, he could certainly plead for conversions by arousing fear and dread. About 1740 his influence, together with that of others, among whom was George Whitefield, one of the founders of Methodism, aroused throughout the colonies a wave of religious feeling which has come to be called the Great Revival or the Great Awakening.

In certain respects it was an awakening whose results Universalists may find commendable. Church life in the colonies had been largely formal, with some one denomination established as the official religion to be supported by public taxation. Church attendance was looked upon as something expected, but this did not imply that the individual was deeply involved. The effect of the revival was forcefully to remind him that religion was fundamentally a highly personal affair, embedded in each man's feelings and convictions. Moreover, it opened the way for the preaching of Universalism, a gospel very different in content but one which spoke directly to the heart of the hearer.

In other respects the revival was harmful, as Universalists see it, for the doctrine of everlasting punishment of the non-elect in the torments of a fiery hell brought terror and misery to men, women, and children in hundreds of congregations. For their admonition the entire universe was described as being under the inescapable control of an angry, revengeful God, whose love (if His better nature might be called love) was extended to but a small portion of the race. Such doctrines were not new, but they were being proclaimed so vividly and so effectively by preachers influenced by Edwards, and the group mind had become so widely susceptible, that instead of deserving to be called the Great Awakening the movement might better be called the Great Nightmare.

Acceptance of the revival varied with geographical region and among different classes. Some Boston clergymen, for example, did not welcome it; their opposition was a phase of the preparation for the later Unitarian development. But on the whole acceptance by religious leaders was widespread. When the Ohio Valley and other parts of the Middle West began to be settled, this was the dominant form in which Christianity was taught. The Kentucky revival and the spreading popularity of prolonged camp meetings were characteristic of this era and region. American church historians distinguish several waves of revivalism, and the movement still finds expression in the twentieth century.

One liberal Boston clergyman of the Establishment who opposed the revival was Charles Chauncey. In his sermon "Seasonable Thoughts on the State of Religion in New England" (1743) he declared, "They have thundered out Death and Damnation in a manner more fit for the Stage than the Sacred Desk. . . . Religion, of late, has been more a Commotion in the Passions, than a change in the Temper of the Mind."[2]

Supporting Witnesses: Joseph Priestley (1733-1804)

In an address at the Universalist Church in Philadelphia in 1796 Joseph Priestley defended universal salvation. "The doctrine of eternal torments is altogether indefensible on any principles of justice or equity." It is only an inference from certain Bible passages and is not fully treated either by Jesus or elsewhere in the Bible. "No human beings can be so depraved as it shall not be in the power of proper discipline to reclaim them, so as to make them valuable characters." He quotes with approval a phrase from Hartley: "ultimate unlimited heaven to all."[3]

P. T. Barnum (1810-1891)

A crusading Universalist of a later generation was P. T. Barnum of circus fame. "I was educated," he says, "in the strictest so-called 'orthodox faith.' When I was from ten to fourteen years of age I attended prayer meetings where I could almost feel the burning waves and smell of sulphurous fumes. I remember the shrieks and groans of suffering children and parents and even aged grandparents. I would return to my home and with the utmost sincerity ask God to take me out of the world if He would only save me from hell."[4]

Harriet Beecher Stowe (1811–1896)

One evening when Harriet Beecher was a little girl her father was reading to the family Edwards' sermon on sinners and an angry God. Harriet was watching her mother. "She saw an expression of horror and abhorrence on her face—a bright red spot every moment growing redder." Rising, her mother swept from the room, saying as she left, "'Mr. Beecher, I will not listen to another word! Why, it is horrible! It is a slander on the character of my Heavenly Father! I will not hear it!'"[5]

Even in 1930 a writer could recall from his painful childhood: "My good mathematics teacher seemed to feel it her religious duty to perpetually remind us of the awful and unending torture to be inflicted on the so-called unsaved."[6]

HORACE MANN (1796–1859)

In a letter to a friend Horace Mann offered his description of the religious situation. "The pastor of the church at Franklin . . . expounded all the doctrines of total depravity, election, and reprobation, and not only the eternity, but the extremity, of hell-torments, unflinchingly and in their most terrible signficance. . . . A certain number of souls were to be forever lost, and nothing—nor powers, nor principalities, nor man, nor angel, nor Christ, nor the Holy Spirit, nay not God himself—could save them; for he had sworn, before time was, to get eternal glory out of their eternal torment. But perhaps I might not be one of the lost! But my little sister might be, my mother might be, or others whom I loved. And I felt that, if they were in hell, it would make a hell of whatever other part of the universe I might inhabit; for I could never get a glimpse of consolation from the idea that my own nature could be so transformed, and become so like what God's was said to be, that I could rejoice in their sufferings. . . .

"To my vivid imagination, a physical hell was a living reality, as much so as though I could have heard the shrieks of the tormented, or stretched out my hand to grasp their burning souls, in a vain endeavor for their rescue. . . . I could see the burning lake filled with torments, and hear the wailing and agony of its victims. . . .

"Often, on going to bed at night, did the objects of the day and the faces of friends give place to a vision of the awful throne, the inexorable Judge, and the hapless myriads, among whom I often seemed to see those whom I loved best; and there I wept and sobbed until Nature found that counterfeit repose in exhaustion. . . . All these fears and sufferings . . . never prompted to a single good action, or had the slightest efficacy in deterring me from a bad one."[7]

WILLIAM A. VENABLE

Venable describes his youth in Ohio. His parents tended somewhat towards Universalism, but at the time neighborhood orthodoxy was a more powerful influence. Writing in the third person, he says of himself: "The boy was brought up in conformity with Presbyterian traditions modified by the plain and direct simplicity of the teachings of William Penn. He was taught to say his prayers, to read the Bible, and to remember the Sabbath day and keep it holy in a certain perfunctory manner. There was no Sunday School for him to enter, but he was permitted and encouraged, though not urged, to attend whatever religious service was accessible to him. Any form of worship was regarded as better than none.

"It may well be doubted whether so much religious liberty was a blessing or a bane, in his case, considering that he was keenly alive to exciting influences, and that to his susceptible mind an admonition to a spiritual duty, a half-comprehended sermon, or even a threatening phrase of Scripture, often brought painful disturbances.

"He was, as he conceived, unquestionably a sinner—the chief of sinners;—he had every symptom of total depravity. He was one of those whom he had heard described from the pulpit, as being 'hair-hung and breeze-shaken' over the mouth of the bottomless pit. The worst of his misery was that he could do nothing to avert his doom, however correct and virtuous his outward behavior, for, as his Baptist aunt told him, by grace and not by good thoughts or good deeds he must be saved, if saved. Yes, he was lost. John Bunyan, in his darkest hour, never waded in such blackness as surrounded this lonesome farmboy's spirit. The fear of hell gat hold on him, the wrath of God pursued him."[8]

COMMENT

It was in such a nightmarish environment that Universalism arose in America. To those in the grip of evil dreaming it addressed itself. Some there could pass the matter off lightly. When young Andrew White gave expression to his fears, he was told by a female relative, "Well, sonny, there is of course some merciful way out of it." But this did not satisfy White, who rejected religion until at Yale he listened to the preaching of Unitarian Parker, Congregationalist Beecher, and Universalist Chapin.[9] It is unfortunate that the term Great Awakening has already been appropriated, for if ever there was a great religious awakening in America, it came about through the ringing Universalist message.

"At this day," wrote Hosea Ballou 2nd in 1848, "we can hardly conceive the sudden change of view, from a God of infinite wrath, and the world of eternal sin and torment, to a Father in heaven, who had secured, in his unerring administration, the final welfare of his entire family. . . . How many agonies of despair, how many helpless wrestlings with horror, were changed into boundless trust and joy! How much anguish of soul for kindred, or friends, or mankind at large, into the peace of God which passeth understanding!"[10]

Even more difficult is it, in a period when belief in any future life at all has been cast off by so many, to understand the appearance and the popularity of the Universalist movement. One must apprehend the religious climate of years long gone. To such apprehension this chapter has been devoted. In the next we shall hear from some of those who, shaking off the nightmare, were partly responsible for the gathering of Universalist societies.

These two chapters of the Prologue do not pretend to offer a complete historical account of the preliminary period. They attempt rather to communicate the opposing moods of those who cherished a belief in endless fiery punishment of the wicked and those who denied it in favor of universal salvation.

CHAPTER 2

Awakening: A Few of the Early Voices (1740-1800)

Many attempts were made to awaken the victims of this disturbing dream from their slumber. Voices were heard in various localities and at various levels of society. Among them were voices of those influential in the movement whose history we are to sketch in later chapters. Let us listen to some of them.

The method followed in this chapter resembles that followed in the preceding. In trying to reproduce the spirit and mood of those days, I have somewhat fictionalized history by using paraphrase and imagination. Several characters will present themselves as if speaking to you directly. My object is to represent their attitudes, even though direct quotations are few.

"The wind will never change, sir, until you have delivered to us, in that meeting-house, a message from God."[1]

Those surprising words were spoken to me by a total stranger. In deep depression I had sailed from England in July, 1770. Through a series of circumstances which I, John Murray, believe to have been providential, I found myself strolling ashore on the Jersey coast near Barnegat Bay.

Born in England in 1741, the year of Edwards' famous sermon, I grew up with little formal education in an intensely and genuinely religious family. In early maturity I became a zealous teacher and preacher of Methodism, acquainted with and sometimes associated with John Wesley, George Whitefield, and other pioneers of that movement. But through the influence of James Relly of London, at first unwelcome and resisted, I became a Universalist. Reluctantly, somewhat fearfully, but soon joyously, I accepted this new gospel.

I had attained some modest success in business, had married, and was the father of an infant child. Then came a series of blows. Wife and child died. Prosperity turned into failure. I was imprisoned for debt. By the time I was released I was despondent. Resolved to bury myself in the wilderness of America, never to preach again, I came to your new land. On the afternoon when I stepped ashore in New Jersey, I was in charge of a small vessel, under promise to sail her to New York as soon as the wind would permit.

The stranger from whom I heard that surprising weather prediction was Thomas Potter, a settler in that region, and a man with religious convictions unique among his neighbors. With faith he had constructed a meetinghouse, but no clergyman to suit him had ever appeared. As soon as I began to inquire about purchasing some fish for the crew of my little ship, he pronounced me his long-awaited preacher. Imagine my surprise! At first unwilling, I was finally persuaded to preach on Sunday, if the wind did not change.

The wind did not change. I preached. It was September 30, 1770. In the congregation were persons probably influenced by reports of Universalism brought to this region some years earlier by Dunker missionaries from Ephrata. Members of my crew were there also. They were responsible for the fact that soon after arriving in New York my services were in great demand. This was not so much on account of a new doctrine, for I preferred for some years to proclaim my Universalism cryptically. Nor did I pretend to be a scholar or an original thinker. But it is not immodest to tell you that I was looked upon as an able man, a fluent speaker, and one well versed in the Bible.[2] Perhaps history was on my side.

Invitations soon poured in from New York, the Jerseys, Philadelphia, and even Gloucester, where some sailor had already brought a copy of James Relly's book, which had aroused the thinking of a small group. Except at Gloucester, in all the years of my early itinerant preaching among the coastal towns from Baltimore to Portsmouth, I met no Universalists. After considerable urging I allowed myself to accept an invitation from Gloucester to settle there. Here I married a second time. My wife was Judith Sargent, member of a prominent Massachusetts family. Here I continued as clerk, or as you would say, minister, for twenty years.

It was my early custom, both at Gloucester and as an itinerant, not to permit or accept financial contributions. But legal complications forced me to modify this rule. For my parishioners were taxed by the town for the support of the Congregational minister and church. From this they could not escape unless I would bring suit to have their share of the money paid to me. After delays and appeals the case was decided in my favor. Thus a precedent was established which could be used by other non-congregational churches until Massachusetts abandoned its church tax. On another occasion it was necessary to petition the legislature to establish my right to perform marriage ceremonies.

As Universalists of Boston increasingly requested my services, arrangements were made for me to spend some Sundays there each month. In 1788 these Bostonians generously paid for a trip back to my homeland. On the return voyage I met future president John Adams, with whom I enjoyed a long friendship. In 1789 the Philadelphia society invited me to be their minister, at a price of $1,000 a year and house rent for life, a salary said to be equal to that of any clergyman in the country. Although I was earning not more than five dollars a week, I declined the offer. In 1793, however, I was induced to move to Boston, where I found living expenses very high. I had to pay $400 a year for rent.

With this group, the First Universalist Society in the town of Boston, I remained for the rest of my life. In retrospect I see that I was never an enthusiastic leader of the Universalist denomination. In fact, I was often at odds with what was going on. Sensitive to the theological differences between me and other Universalist preachers, I found their criticisms hard to take. Sometimes I wish that I could have been more active in the General Convention which they organized.

*"I was condemned to the scaffold. . . . The executioner bound
my hands, and while he was employed in so doing, a courier
arrived from Louis XV, the King, with a reprieve for me."*[3]

John Murray was not the first to preach the liberating doctrine on your continent. I was here first; in fact, in 1741. My name
is George de Benneville. Unlike Murray, I was a scholar, and a
participant in many adventures. Indeed I was something of an
internationalist, for I was born in England, where my Protestant
French parents, members of the nobility, had been invited by
William III and his queen, Anne. After my parents' death the
Queen saw to it that I, her godson, at the age of twelve, was
appointed a midshipman in the navy. Thus I enjoyed a voyage to
the Barbary States. The University of Padua gave me a good
education. At seventeen I became a convert in France to my own
brand of religion. Later I was a medical practitioner and a writer
in the German states.[4]

The religious views which I held and preached were sufficiently
unconventional to bring about imprisonment. But this did not
stop me from preaching. My life was not unlike that of your
agitators for peace and civil rights. The final charge against me,
treason, brought the death penalty, but at the last moment I was
reprieved.

When at the age of thirty-eight, and at the invitation of Christopher Sower, Universalist Quaker, I came to America, booksellers
in Philadelphia were already displaying Universalist books. Near
Reading I established a home of my own, one room of which I
used both as chapel for a congregation of fifty and as a day
school. Later I moved to Philadelphia, where I taught, wrote,
opened an apothecary shop, practiced medicine, engaged in correspondence, conducted an occasional ministry to the Indians, and
devoted some weeks each year to a preaching tour among English
and German residents in nearby Pennsylvania, Delaware, Maryland, and Virginia,

In Europe I had been associated with the more liberal sects
of Protestantism, some of whom were disciples of Jakob Boehme,
the mystic. From these groups two books appeared: *The Everlasting Gospel* by Paul Siegvolck and the *Berlenburg Bible* by a group

of scholars. Some friends, familiar with these works, had preceded me to Philadelphia. Here I associated myself with Christopher Sower in printing and distributing these same books, and even in translating of *The Everlasting Gospel* into English. In this way I helped to spread Universalist ideas in that part of America.

I had some acquaintance with another Philadelphia Universalist, Dr. Benjamin Rush. He was an eminent physician of his day, a member of the medical-school faculty, an advocate of Sunday schools, occasionally a public official, and later a signer of the Declaration of Independence. In my day two other members of the medical faculty were Universalists, but I am afraid that none of us ever took an active part in organized Universalism. I regret to confess that in the Philadelphia region the movement was organizationally less effective than in New England.[5]

"How dreadful the thought that God should punish his creatures to all eternity without having the least design for their good or happiness. Can a wise and good God punish for no purpose, but merely to satisfy what they call vindictive justice, which they say can never be satisfied to all eternity? Endless misery seems to reflect upon the character of God, and for that reason I cannot believe it to be true."

These convictions I did not arrive at until I was nearly thirty years of age, and then only gradually. My name is Elhanan Winchester.[6] Unlike John Murray and George de Benneville, I am a native-born American, indeed almost a native Bostonian, for I was born in Brookline in 1751. Even in childhood I was blessed with an unusual memory which enabled me at the age of five to read any book I came across in the English language, and later to acquire a fluency in Greek, Hebrew, and French. As a man I read the Bible through several times a year.

At the age of eighteen I became a preacher of the Baptist persuasion with a growing preference for a modified Calvinism, and with an ability to conduct successful revivals. In spite of travel difficulties in those days, I made journeys to South Carolina and Virginia. In one community I converted a number of

Negro slaves, who had never before been addressed by a preacher.

The change in my theological views came slowly. At first the ideal of universal salvation, as set forth in the *Restitution of all Things* by George Stonehouse, seemed an ingenious hypothesis but not one deserving serious consideration. But later *The Everlasting Gospel* led me to reflect more deeply concerning the meaning of many biblical passages with which I was already familiar.

In 1780 I was persuaded to accept the pastorate of a Baptist church in Philadelphia. This gave me an opportunity to become acquainted with Dr. de Benneville. Presently the conservative members of my church forced me into a public avowal of my new faith, which I called Universal Restorationism. They also forced me out of the church. With the support of my followers we started a new society, over which I ministered for about six years. Among my friends and supporters were Dr. Benjamin Rush and his teacher, Dr. John Redman, first president of the college of medicine. In fact, Dr. Redman jokingly used to call me "our theological Newton."

During this pastorate there were opportunities for trips to New York and New England. So convincingly did I preach my Restorationism in Attleboro that the established Congregational First Parish became a Restorationist society. In the city of Providence also I had many friends and followers.

One summer day in 1787 I chanced to be walking along a Philadelphia dock where a ship was being prepared to sail for England within three or four days. Almost immediately I decided that my wife and I should embark as passengers. Quickly resigning my pastorate, obtaining letters of introduction from Dr. Rush, and getting in hand a small sum of money, we left America for England, a country where we knew no one. But I soon succeeded in securing opportunities to preach which enabled me to remain abroad for nearly seven years. Here I became acquainted with Unitarians Richard Price and Joseph Priestley, and developed a close friendship with John Wesley, the Methodist leader. Incidentally, George Stonehouse, whose book had opened the way to Universalism for me, had been a member of the Holy Club at Oxford, made famous by the Wesleys. I think that John Wesley himself became a believer in universal salvation, but hesitated to disturb his young Methodist movement by saying so publicly.

My life was continually saddened by illnesses and deaths in my family. After my return to America, although unable to return to a resident pastorate in Philadelphia, I continued to preach in my old haunts. In 1794 I presided over the Universalist Convention at Oxford. Had a longer life been granted me, perhaps I might have justified the friendly title which Dr. Redman so generously used to bestow upon me.[7]

"Each read, or prayed, or sung, or spoke, as the spirit directed, and all were edified."

It was with some reluctance that John Murray became a settled pastor, and even then he gave only nominal encouragement to forming a general association of churches. Dr. de Benneville had no pastorate at all. Mr. Winchester's settled ministry in America was brief. I feel that I may properly put in a claim for the title which W. S. Balch once bestowed upon me: "the real founder" of Universalism in America.

My name is Caleb Rich.[8] The son of strict Congregational parents, I was born in 1750 at Sutton, Massachusetts. The Baptists were zealous in that region. Well-read in the Bible, opposed to formalism, they by their aggressive methods often divided families. So it was that my father joined them, whereas my mother remained in the village church. Family discussions of disputed doctrines propelled me into years of serious inquiry, with alternating moods of doubt and conviction. Occasional vivid dreams or visions both disturbed and guided me. An experience which I then regarded as conversion led me to follow my father into the Baptist fold.

When I was twenty-one years of age the family moved to Warwick, near the New Hampshire line, where Maturin Ballou was a well-known figure among the Baptists. But some of the Ballous had already accepted the Universalist idea. Although I had never heard a preacher of that sect, tentatively I found the position attractive to the point of sharing it with some of my Baptist friends, who promptly had me dismissed from their church. Thereupon my brother Nathaniel and I, together with Joseph Goodell, legally formed a three-man religious society of our own for further study and discussion, issuing to each other certificates of non-conformity to free us from the obligation of paying taxes to support the Congregational church. During the first year the membership of our society increased to ten.

When the Revolution broke out I arranged a mutually agreeable substitution, taking the place of a hired man on a farm at Oxford. Here and at Sutton I gathered private meetings for Bible study, attended by from thirty to fifty inquirers. The quotation with which I began describes our meetings. Sometimes these were prolonged to midnight or even daybreak. In this way I became a fully convinced Universalist, accepting invitations to speak, but preferring to call myself teacher or Bible counselor rather than preacher. I have been criticized for oversensitivity concerning my lack of formal education and for having too little self-confidence. But I had sufficient persistence to meet the requirements for marriage imposed upon me by my wife-to-be: I converted her parents to the new faith.

Returning to Warwick, I organized a single general religious society for Universalists of Warwick, and in New Hampshire, Richmond and Jaffrey. Friends in Winchester were included. Adams Streeter, an ordained Baptist turned Universalist, ordained me at a service attended by three hundred persons, including David Ballou. Thus I became entitled to perform marriage ceremonies.

For my church I drew up a statement of faith and duties. And I began to give formal sermons, still largely interpretive of biblical passages. Increasingly I was in demand throughout that section of Massachusetts and New Hampshire, where my ideas attracted favorable attention even among the Congregational clergy. An early convert was Thomas Barns, later a pioneer Universalist in Maine. I believe that I also had considerable influence upon

Hosea Ballou. Certainly I was one who strongly urged him to become a minister. Into my hill country came some of the greatest Universalist preachers of those days.

Was it among the seafaring people of Gloucester or among the farmers of the region from Oxford to Winchester that the Universalist denomination was born? Was Murray or myself the founder? Or was it Ballou? It does not matter now. What does matter is that you, our heirs, must not forget the emotional and intellectual struggles, the searchings of the heart and the persistent study of the Book, the bitter opposition and the faithful loyalty engendered in the lives of simple men and women, who found escape from theological nightmare for themselves and sought to rescue others still groping in that dark terror.

"Brother Ballou, I press to your heart the written Jehovah."
Unexpectedly at a meeting at Oxford in 1794 Elhanan Winchester pressed a copy of the Bible to my chest, addressing to me these words. His action I interpreted as ordination.

My name is Hosea Ballou.[9] Universalists of later generations, I am told, have looked back upon me more than upon any other man as their spiritual ancestor. I suppose that they base their opinion upon my historically significant book, my important pastorates, and my leadership in denominational affairs. All this is in contrast to my origin and youthful years.

Richmond, New Hampshire, was my birthplace, in 1771. Here I grew up with a minimum of formal education and in Lincoln-like poverty. My father, Maturin Ballou, was the not quite orthodox Baptist preacher already mentioned by Caleb Rich. Like Mr. Rich I was troubled in adolescence by theological uncertainties. Impulsively I joined the Baptists, but by persistent examination of the Bible I brought myself over to the Universalist position.

After a go at teaching school I tried preaching, but with no initial success. Nevertheless, I devoted myself with increasing facility to the ministry, traveling from Cape May to the Connecticut River and speaking in whatever kind of building I could find listeners, or even in the open. A meeting which I addressed some years later near Utica has been described by a friend of those days. It took place "in the open air, under some trees, on the bank of the Mohawk River. . . . It was a glorious day early in June—the silence of Sunday was around us—the bright blue heavens above us, partly veiled by the branches of a few scattering oaks—the clear quiet river at our side—the ruddy and healthy preacher in all the vigor of manhood before us, and pleading the cause of God and humanity with a group of most attentive hearers."

I read works attacking orthodox theological views and began to put my own ideas into written form. My most important book, *A Treatise on Atonement,* appeared in 1805. My first settled pastorate was at Hardwick, between Oxford and Warwick. My first in a city was at Portsmouth in 1809, with a society which had been incorporated in 1793 and now had a building only two years old. Here I slowly made the difficult transition from living an itinerant life to assuming day-by-day duties with a stable people. It was not easy. Here too I encountered that difficulty so frequently faced by the first settled Universalist ministers: collecting my salary. It was $800 a year.

After Portsmouth I spent two years in Salem, and then in 1817 I accepted a call from the Second Universalist Society in the Town of Boston. Previously I had declined invitations from this society out of respect to Mr. Murray, still preaching for the First Society. But Mr. Murray had now died, and although his successor, Paul Dean, did not welcome my coming, I decided to make the move. Here I continued to serve until my death. The relationship was a success from the beginning. There was time for continued activity in denominational affairs, for reading, writing, revising my *Treatise,* editing hymnals, and establishing a Universalist newspaper. Friendships through our movement multiplied to the extent that in my declining years I became known as Father Ballou.

"The preaching and the conversation of Brother Farwell set my soul as it were on fire. . . . My mind was much and deeply

*exercised for some time afterwards. I considered the state of re-
ligion in my country. I considered my own individual station. I
considered the various leadings of divine Providence with regard to
me for many years past. Every circumstance and every feeling of
my heart seemed to confirm my apprehension that God had made
it my duty to preach the gospel."*

My name is Walter Ferriss.[10] Of Quaker parents residing on
Quaker Hill in Dutchess County, New York, I was born in 1767.
I had three brothers and a sister. Our grandfather was a Quaker
preacher. I learned to read early, and during my childhood I read
much, both about religion and about amusing and trifling subjects. At the last Universalist convention which I attended I was
still seeking more reading material. Perhaps you can call me a
lifelong reader.

My childhood was marked by alternating religious moods and
convictions. In Quaker fashion my parents gave me religious
instruction, from which, unfortunately, I acquired an intense fear
of hell. There was a period when reading Paine and others led
me to classify myself as a deist. At another time I became convinced that the Bible indeed teaches the unbelievable doctrine of
endless punishment and that therefore the Bible is not to be
believed. An unusually vivid dream of the world in flames turned
me back to a strictly orthodox way of living and thinking. I
became piously self-exalted, scorning dancing and music. But
this too wore off.

Growing up, I discovered that there are genuinely religious
people outside the Quaker fold. Slowly I began to think for myself
and to interpret the Bible for myself. By the age of nineteen, without ever having heard a Universalist preacher, I had become a believer in universal salvation.

My friends had expected that my intellectual interests would
lead me into one of the professions, but not so. I preferred farming.
I had inherited virgin land from my grandfather in Charlotte and
Shelburn, Vermont, and it was to the hardships of this new country
that I turned. After clearing the land, sowing wheat, and starting
a cabin in the summer of 1793, I returned to Quaker Hill to marry

a childhood friend on January 3 in the eighteenth year of our American independence. Off the two of us went in a sleigh one hundred miles into the north country. It was a hard life, but it brought no regrets. I interested myself in town business and Vermont politics. We usually attended the Congregational church, for the support of which we paid taxes. Eventually life became easier with modest prosperity coming our way.

In December, 1798, William Farwell, itinerant Universalist minister from Barre, preached in our neighborhood. It was the first time that either of us had heard a Universalist sermon. Immediately I felt the call to preach.[11] Yet I hesitated. I would be preaching an unpopular doctrine. My temperament was diffident and reserved. I was slow at extemporaneous speech, not good at disputation. Nevertheless, in February, 1799, a small group of sympathetic neighbors gathered at the home of Israel Lockwood, where they heard my first sermon, delivered without notes.

Thus was born a Universalist church embracing three communities—Charlotte, Hinesburg, and Moncton—over which I was the settled pastor for the short seven years of my ministry. By this church I was ordained in 1801. Here at least every fortnight I preached, except when on a journey or ill, and sometimes when I was ill. For my services I received no pay. Late in life I wrote a brief autobiography, in which you may find, if you wish, other details of my life. Your author has reserved for a later chapter the account of my chief contribution to the Universalist denomination.

COMMENT

It is tempting to add further details about these men. However, there is little more to be said about Rich; and concerning Murray, Winchester, and Ballou there are biographies, even autobiographies. Ferriss' little-known but fascinating *Notes and Sketches* has been preserved. From it I shall quote later. There is much material about De Benneville, but for an understanding of Pennsylvania Universalism it seems appropriate to mention some of it here.

In 1782 Winchester persuaded De Benneville to write an account of his life, promising not to make it public until after De Benneville's death. A few years later, 1791, Winchester, assuming that De Benneville had probably died, and even if living, would not know about it, printed an English edition for the "benefit of a poor widow." De Benneville became angry, destroying papers which would have made a more complete story possible.

As a youth George lived for fifteen months under the conviction that he was damned, from which condition he was freed by a vision of the risen Christ and into a commitment to preach the "restoration of all souls." This he did briefly in England and for two years in France, especially in Normandy, his ancestral home. Still under twenty-one years of age, he had associated with him several other preachers, who conducted their meetings in mountains and woods, persistently in the face of cruel punishments to themselves or to their adherents.

After liberation from a Paris prison he spent eighteen years in Germany and Holland, acquiring the languages of those countries and preaching among French refugees and members of the native nobility. He also studied medicine and engaged in literary activities with scholarly friends. At Mons a severe illness ended in coma or apparent death for forty-two hours, during which he believed that he left his body for a conducted trip through hell and heaven.

After recovery he came to America, where several groups of friends had preceded him, "leftists" of the Reformation. Among them were those known as Tunkers, Dunkers, German Baptists, or Seventh-Day Baptists, who shared his Universalist views. They were inclined to be ascetic and communal, with separation of the sexes. One of them, Beissel, founded the Ephrata Cloisters. A special friend was Christopher Saur (Sower), exhorter turned printer-publisher.

Part II

THE STORY: ORGANIZED UNIVERSALISM IN THE UNITED STATES

"Every man did that which was right in his own mind."
Book of Judges

"There is no Christianity with a hundred years of history that does not become, to a more or less degree, institutional."
R. A. KNOX

"Rare indeed is he who comes to a matured appreciation of his own religious tradition, seeing both its values and disvalues in reasonable perspective."
FLOYD H. ROSS

CHAPTER 3

Rural Beginnings: Gathering the First Societies and Conventions (1790-1833)

There were other voices.[1] In the first chapter of his *Universalism in America* Richard Eddy lists five channels through which the doctrine of universal salvation was introduced among American colonies:

1. Independent mystics: Samuel Gorton, Sir Henry Vane the Younger, Joseph Gatchell, De Benneville, George Rapp, and others.
2. A group of Dunkers who came to Pennsylvania in 1719, some of whom established a settlement at Ephrata.
3. A group of Moravians who came first to Georgia and then to Bethlehem, Pennsylvania.
4. Some Episcopalians: the Reverends Richard Clarke, Robert Yancy, Jacob Duche, John Tyler, and Dr. William Smith.
5. Some New England Congregationalists: the Reverends Charles Chauncey, Jonathan Mayhew, Jeremy Belknap, Joseph Huntington. Some of these are also regarded as forerunners of Unitarianism.

Although these channels should be duly noted, it should also be said that through none of them did there flow direct contributions to the founding of a new denomination. The individuals and groups mentioned tended to hold quietly and perhaps as subordinate their faith in the final salvation of all men. With but few exceptions they did not arouse strong opposition in their communities. Their influence was in letting it be known among limited circles that able and responsible Christians found it possible to accept an idea commonly regarded as a devilish deception. When the new denomination began to recruit its clergymen from other denominations, the greatest number came from the Baptists.

Nevertheless, there are some interesting items about the Ephrata group. The Dunker creed is long. Their belief in universal salvation, seldom quoted directly, is almost reluctant, almost hidden away. They confess that it is impossible for them to understand how God can save everybody, yet He has promised that "as all are fallen in Adam, so must all be raised up in Christ."[2]

The coastal region of New Jersey was described as heavily timbered, thinly settled, often by squatters who were seldom visited by clergymen. Some called themselves Quakers. There was a Quaker meetinghouse at Tuckerton. Near Good Luck there were Seventh-Day Baptists.

In the autumn of 1744 four "strangely clad men with untrimmed hair and flowing beards" marched silently single-file through these woods. They were on their way from their colony near Reading to visit kindred souls as far east as Connecticut. At Barnegat they had friends, and there they preached. It is believed that their influence persisted and was partially responsible for Murray's favorable reception. Thomas Potter, his host, after serving in the British navy and army, had settled here to farm, to fish, and to operate a sawmill.[3]

THE DEISTS

Elihu Palmer is an example of those who hovered uncertainly between Universalism, Unitarianism, and Deism. He had been associated with Paine. Refused Universalist fellowship in Philadelphia, he ministered to a "Universal Church" in that city, established by John Fitch, credited by many with inventing the steamboat.[4]

For a genuine Universalist of this period to be also a deist would have been impossible. Through French influence deism was widespread among Revolutionary leaders, including some whom we would today call Unitarians or Universalists, and widespread also among students at Yale and Harvard. There was also a native deism, expressed in the writings of Ethan Allen and Thomas Paine. But deism had no organization.

Nevertheless, orthodox leaders were greatly alarmed by its prevalence, attacking it as atheism. Even in my lifetime Paine has been falsely described by one who should have known better as "a filthy little atheist." No; what deists rejected was the alleged biblical revelation. They believed in God but tried to understand His qualities through reason based on a study of nature. They believed in worship, repentance, and the future life. Genuine Universalists of this period could not be genuine deists, because Universalists accepted most of the traditional Christian revelation, while at the same time they rejected a part of it. In undignified moments a Universalist might call a deist an atheist, while the orthodox accuser could classify them together by calling them both atheists.

The deists are worth mentioning for three reasons: (1) The distinction between them and Universalists was not always understood, or at least not accepted. (2) Some early Universalists, Hosea Ballou for example, read Allen's *Reason the Only Oracle of Man*. (3) By undermining traditional orthodoxy, deism opened men's minds to other new departures.[5]

PIONEER UNIVERSALIST PREACHERS

From the biographical sketches in Chapter Two it will be seen that early proclaimers of Universalism were usually men who laboriously read and thought themselves out of orthodoxy into an unpopular faith. There were many others who made a similar transition. From the first preaching of the doctrine by De Benneville in 1741 through the years until 1800 there were at least forty-two men who, for longer or shorter periods, publicly proclaimed the new vision. Of these only two will be named here.[6]

Special mention should be made of Abel Morgan Sargent.[7] About him such widely divergent tales are recorded that it has even been suggested that there were two men with the same name or similar names. At one time he lived in Morgantown, Virginia. Early in life he was a Freewill Baptist preacher. He became a Universalist in 1790. In 1793 he came to Baltimore (and New York?), publishing the first Universalist journal in America, the *Free Universal Magazine*. Publication continued for one year only. About this time he wrote a Universalist creed, Unitarian in content. In that same year he attended the Philadelphia convention. He preached in some of the New Jersey churches. About 1800 he moved to southeastern Ohio. His territory until 1833 was in the area between Marietta and Gallipolis. The churches which he organized there and in western Pennsylvania were called Free churches or Halcyon churches. In fact, they constituted a small sect. If the churhes survived at all, they were absorbed into the Universalist movement. In 1827 Sargent edited the *Lamp of Liberty* in Cincinnati. He had many dramatic encounters with prominent orthodox leaders.

Edward Turner (1776–1853), "the peer of Hosea Ballou," was born in Medfield, Massachusetts, and educated at Leicester Academy. Becoming a Universalist, he began to preach in 1798. His pastorates included Charlestown and Portsmouth. During these years he was the foremost scholar of the denomination. An unfortunate misunderstanding which led to a quarrel between him and Hosea Ballou was an important factor in the Restorationist controversy. It led to his eventual transfer to the Unitarians.

THE BIBLE AS PRINCE CHARMING

These were some of those who awakened increasing numbers of religious people from their dogmatic but restless slumber. How did they go about their task?

One is tempted to say that in 1779 and for some years afterwards everyone in America believed in the Bible. But this would not be quite true. The strong undercurrent of natural religion or deism represented a search for the common essentials of all religions and the rejection of specifically Christian dogmas. But this search was confined to a minority.

Throughout the colonial period the churches had been largely on their own without ecclesiastical supervision from Europe. Maintaining their own societies and controlling their own property fostered an independent spirit and a dislike of bishops. In fact, the fear that the British government might send bishops to assume control is said to have been one of the causes of rebellion. Thus American commitment to political liberty was reinforced by love of religious liberty. Love of liberty in the face of an external threat, supplemented by unifying tendencies of the Great Awakening of 1740, was characteristic of all but the most authoritarian religious groups.[8] The seedlings of early Universalism grew in this atmosphere. In some respects each denomination differed from the others, and Universalists from all of them. And within each denomination, Universalists included, there were internal differences.

The common faith of the time has been described as a dualistic Platonism, a faith in two worlds, the natural world and the supernatural. To the supernatural were ascribed value, reality, and changelessness. The natural world was the locus of creation, history, and redemption. It was regarded as a loose collection of parts. What was more proper than individualistic democracy, congregationalism, and the scheme of salvation by individual conversion? Universalists were just beginning to see the flaws in this accepted world view, but they could not at once escape from it.[9]

Another segment of the common heritage was a general acceptance of the Bible as the one authoritative revelation from God, which set forth all man's religious obligations, the process of salvation through Christ, the impending day of judgment, and the everlasting separation of the saved from the lost. The lost souls, eternally damned, were to undergo never-ending torments far worse than those of any inquisition chamber or concentration camp.

In such an environment it is not surprising that intelligent inquiring minds should examine this allegedly divine plan at its source. And its source was the written word of the Bible. Since this was accepted by them and by their neighbors as the one genuine revelation of religious truth, the decision to study it for themselves came naturally. They differed from some of their neighbors in that they brought to this study their own rational, logical powers, learning to interpret what they read, not in accordance with conventional orthodoxy but as their intelligence directed.

The outcome for those who became Universalists was a rejection of everlasting punishment and a conviction that God's plan is through Christ's divine mission to save all. Such divergence from the usual interpretation was startling—to themselves and to their friends. The dawn of such an idea in the inquirer's mind was often resisted. It might require a considerable period of thinking before he would admit to himself the acceptance of the new gospel. And it often demanded courage to confess to one's family or neighbors the result of the quest.

When such conversions to Universalism were communicated to others, reactions were varied. Some who had feared, yet doubted, the existence of hell, eagerly welcomed the new interpretation of Scripture. Clergy and laiety of orthodox churches usually opposed the venturesome prophet. According to denominational folklore, opposition took many forms. It might be a personally denunciatory sermon. It might be social ostracism, which in minor forms persisted even into the twentieth century. It might be action in the courts. Sometimes Universalists were locked out of buildings to which they had contributed and which had been dedicated as open to all. Once a sheriff with drawn sword guarded the entrance against them. Once it took the approach of a man with an axe to persuade the caretaker to find his "lost" key. Occasionally there was mob behavior. A more mature form of opposition was public debate, which Universalists welcomed.

But whether in private as a lonely seeker or in earnest discussion with friends or in an attempt to persuade a doubter or an opponent, it was the Bible to which appeal was made. Favorable passages had to be found, memorized, quoted. Passages relied upon by the orthodox had to be realistically confronted and re-interpreted in the light of context or other passages. The intellectual battles were magnificent. Not all the doubters were converted. But to those who were, the Bible assumed a new role, a new character. It became a kind of Prince Charming, whose kiss awakened the sleeper from his nightmare and set him about his daily duties with a new peace, a new interest in human affairs of the present life, and a new gospel to share with others.

FAVORITE BIBLICAL PASSAGES

The whole range of the Bible was a field from which Universalists picked favorite passages like flowers. I have selected a few from the New Testament as samples, using the translation available to our pioneers.

. . . The times of restitution of all things . . .—*Acts 3:21*

Therefore as by the offense of one, judgment came upon all men to condemnation; even so by the righteousness of one, the free gift came upon all men unto justification of life.—*Rom. 5:18*

For I am persuaded that neither death, nor life, nor angels, nor principalities, nor powers, nor things present, nor things to come, nor height, nor depth, nor any other creature, shall be able to separate us from the love of God, which is in Christ Jesus our Lord.—*Rom. 8:38, 39*

For as in Adam all die, even so in Christ shall all be made alive.—*I Cor. 15:22*

God was in Christ, reconciling the world unto himself, not imputing their trespasses unto them.—*II Cor. 5:19*

[God] . . . who will have all men to be saved, and to come under the knowledge of the truth. For there is one God, and one mediator between God and men, the man Christ Jesus, who gave himself a ransom for all, to be testified in due time.—*I Tim. 2:5, 6*

> And God shall wipe away all tears from their eyes, and there
> shall be no more death, neither sorrow, nor crying, neither shall
> there be any more pain, for the former things are passed away.—
> *Rev. 21:4*

Longer passages involving narrative were also appealed to.
Especially convincing were the parables of Jesus, notably those
dealing with the prodigal son, the lost coin, and the lost sheep.

The American Scene

In 1790 the United States was a nation of four million people,
living chiefly along the Atlantic Coast.[10] Although there was some
territory disputed with Great Britain, its northern boundary was
approximately that of today. On the south it did not include
Florida nor any of the Gulf Coast. It extended westward to the
Mississippi, but the region between the Allegheny Mountains and
that river was sparsely settled and disputed with Indian tribes.

Concentrations of population were to be found at or near
good harbors, and to a lesser extent at river ports, especially
along the rivers of New England, along the Hudson, and along
other streams to the south. The more favorably situated of these,
already having gathered populations of eight thousand or more,
were classified as cities. Overland travel was difficult. Such roads
as there were, primitive and unpaved, were traversed by peddlers,
farmers, and others, some on foot, some on horseback, some driv-
ing pack trains of merchandise, some moving livestock to city
markets.

Boston's commodious busy harbor was fronted by numerous
wharves, from which streets, often narrow and unpaved, led
gently up to its dwellings, its churches, its schools, its com-
mercial establishments, and its undecorated Beacon Hill. Nearby
towards the north were other prosperous, smaller communities, and
farther away that part of Massachusetts then and until 1820 known
as the District of Maine, where another harbor was facilitating
the development of another city, Portland. Between the two

regions lay part of New Hampshire with its important city and harbor, Portsmouth.

To the south beyond the treacherous seas of Cape Cod and the calmer waters of the Sound was New York City, characterized by the Dutch architecture of its shops and homes and churches but already cosmopolitan in population. Here had been the temporary capital of the nation until its removal to Philadelphia in 1790. Already America had come to be known as the land of speculation, and now New York was challenging its rival, Philadelphia, as a center for trading in investment securities. Its shaded Wall Street was a meeting place for buyers and sellers.

But in 1790 Philadelphia was still the nation's chief city, with its large Quaker population and its various German sects. It had been host to the Continental Congress and was now to be the capital of the new nation until 1800. It was the seat of a university, of academies, and of the American Philosophical Society. Beyond it lay Baltimore, Charleston, and other, lesser centers of urbanity and culture.

These and other port cities along the ocean and rivers were the outgrowth of trade, both transatlantic and coastal. To them came the small groups and the individuals who brought to America their diverse religious teachings, including the doctrine of universal salvation. In them Universalism took root. From them it sent shoots into the surrounding countryside.

From these ports adventurous Americans sent their ships to strange far-off China and even around the world, successfully laying the foundations of fortunes. Although the established Congregationalists and conservative Federalists of New England were concerned over their declining influence and the rising strength of Jeffersonian democracy, nevertheless, as years of national security were achieved the spirit of the country was confidently optimistic. This spirit facilitated the acceptance of an optimistic religion.

Four decades, 1790–1830, brought many changes to the new nation. Some states began to provide for a system of state roads. Even the federal government became a road builder with Cumberland Road, over the mountains into the Ohio Valley and eventually to Santa Fe, then in Mexican territory. Private corporations invested in the building and maintenance of toll roads, sometimes paving them. With roads came ingeniously constructed bridges. Increasingly wagons came into use. Travel by stage coach became more popular. By 1825 there were enough lines in operation to warrant a guidebook. Postal service, at first scanty and unfamiliar, was improved. A letter from Walter Ferriss to his friend, George Shove, in Greenville, south of Albany, was long unreceived, because Shove, expecting it by some traveling Quaker, never thought to go to the post office. But from its original fifty post offices the service had expanded in 1830 to eight thousand.

Travelers sometimes sought lodging in private homes, but as taverns were found to be profitable, the tavern as a social center for local residents was tranformed into what would now be known as a hotel. Indeed, the word *hotel* came into use in 1790, in the cities at first.

Canals gradually supplemented roads. The Erie Canal, built between 1817 and 1825, was an ambitious engineering undertaking, requiring the development of native *ad hoc* ability. It facilitated commerce and travel, brought more business to New York City, and opened up western New York and the country beyond. Businessmen began to think of speculation in western lands. Stephen Barton, father of Clara Barton, returning from the Indian Wars, purchased land near the present city of Rochester, but later sold it as remote and worthless.[11] Other merchants began the fur trade, an enterprise which later helped to bring Oregon into the United States.

Nevertheless, there were years of individual hardship and discouragement. From 1819 to 1822 there was much unemployment and poverty. This gave rise to studies and discussions, like those of our own day, as to what part government should play in remedy and relief. Church leaders in the cities sponsored philanthropic projects. In the southern states anti-slavery societies were formed.

After the Revolution the pressure of population was increased by immigrants. The great tides came later, but lesser waves brought formerly wealthy French from Santo Domingo, high-ranking officials from France itself, Irish nationalist leaders, English artisans, and various groups from Germany and Switzerland, all fleeing from undesirable political or religious or economic conditions, seeking safety and fortune within the new nation, and often establishing racial neighborhoods in the cities or farming areas. Unlike some other religious groups, there was no specifically Universalist Church in Europe from which groups could establish their communities here.

The language of politics was often dirty and slanderous. Nationalism was challenged in several quarters. The War of 1812 was unpopular. New England opposed it. Its ports and Philadelphia were raided by the British. Washington was burned. Everywhere enlistments lagged. Vermont beef was sold to the British army in Canada. Even the "era of good feeling" from 1820 to 1830 was a truce between parties, under cover of which they maneuvered for position. The antagonisms later erupting into the slavery contest were simmering. On the other hand, the special privileges of an aristocratic class had been greatly curtailed. Indentured servitude was eliminated. To labor, even if temporarily as a servant, was respectable.

During the decades now under discussion native craftmanship produced the furniture so highly prized later as antique. Some communities were developing specialized manufacturing: shoes in Lynn, hats in Danbury, muskets in New Haven, clocks in Waterbury, glass in Pittsburgh, textiles in several New England cities. Eli Whitney had invented not only the cotton gin but also the fundamental principles of standardized factory production. Factories were small, employing few workers. Located near waterfalls, they became the nuclei of growing towns. Labor of women and children was often used, with unfortunate social results.[12] Some philanthropists tried to remedy the worst conditions. People were beginning to dream of an ideal community. In 1825 New Harmony, Indiana, was founded on a cooperative basis.

In rural areas the typical farm was about two hundred acres.[13] Log cabins were on their way out, being replaced by frame construction. Some manufacturing was still being done in the home. Farm work was for the entire family, since help was scarce. Much meat was eaten, although the farmer could grow vegetables. Maple sugar was a staple product. Recreation, except in isolated areas, was abundant: husking and other bees, hunting and fishing, skating and sleighing, and dancing. With Boston as a center, sweep a radius from eastern Maine to western Massachusetts; it will cover a territory largely of virgin forest, in which many of the inhabitants lived in pioneer primitiveness. It was into the farming and backwoods settlements of this area that seeds of Universalism were blown.

Isolated homes had to educate their own young. Settlements made schools possible, but an educational system developed slowly. Even public schools were not necessarily free. They were supplemented by private and charity schools. Private academies, forerunners of our high schools, spread widely. Colleges were multiplying rapidly. But outside the established churches few clergymen had much education. If a college education was not available, the only method of training, as it was for medicine and the law, was to study in the home of some professional man. Andover (1808) was the first distinctively theological school; others were opened before 1830. But sometimes a struggling college or seminary would have a faculty of only one man.

Improvements came slowly to the American city, originally filthy and unhygienic. Now cities were more and more introducing street cleaning, public water supplies, public fire departments. Iceboxes were coming into use. New articles of diet appeared: new vegetables, citrus fruit, pineapple. Recreation included group games, foot racing, horse racing. The theater was being increasingly accepted. Amusement parks were springing up. The prosperous had begun to take vacations at ocean beaches and hot springs.

There was both fear and emulation of French life—fear because of the extremes of their Revolution, emulation because of their support for ours. About 1793 many democratic societies were organized under French leadership. French deism excited both support and opposition. By the orthodox, the deists, and along with them the Universalists, were regarded as infidels and were held responsible for a lowering of morality. They were played up as a threat to the stability of the nation.

Periodicals were plentiful. In rural areas and small towns there were singing schools. Congregations sang more hymns. Universalists published their own hymnals and circulated their own periodicals. Literary clubs were popular. Boston after 1815 could look with pride upon its Handel and Haydn Society.

This was the period in which Universalists thoroughly entrenched themselves at least in New England and were preparing to move westward to the interior valleys. One of them, William Brooks, walked from Lewiston, Maine, to Ohio and back in 1813, looking the country over.[14] By the end of this period much of the country east of the Mississippi was well settled.

SOCIETIES ARE ORGANIZED

At first there were itinerant preachers who spread the gospel of universal salvation wherever they could find an audience to listen. Then, if a group of believers accepted the message wholeheartedly, they might organize a Universalist church, or as they preferred to call it, a Universalist society. If they lived in New England, where the Establishment continued after the Revolution, members would need to separate or withdraw from the established church. Perhaps the group would be able to secure only occasional preaching. Perhaps they could contribute to the support of a resident minister, either part time or possibly full time. Along with these arrangements, there might come the erection of a simple building, either for the exclusive use of Universalists or to be shared with others. But in 1800 there were only five exclusively Universalist meetinghouses.

Universalists were not the first to secede from the New England Establishment. The Great Awakening, quickened by Edwards' revivalism, had shattered the hitherto accepted plan of church life. In many communities between 1740 and 1800 splinter churches—"separatist" churches—were formed. Murray's Gloucester society is one example; another is the society at Norwich, Connecticut, which he organized in 1772 after earlier preaching in the Old Church and in Christ Church. Many of these separatist societies took the Baptist name. Maturin Ballou, Hosea's father, was minister of such a church. A few of these Baptist churches, and a few of their ministers, became Universalist. About 1788 and again in 1794 there were noticeable defections to Universalism.[15]

In Chapter Two a few of the early Universalist societies were mentioned. Let us now take a quick run down the coast, pausing at some of these early centers.

Portsmouth. Murray first brought Universalism to this city.[16] In 1793 a church was organized; in 1807 a building was erected. From 1809 to 1815 Hosea Ballou was its minister. When Thomas Farrington King came as pastor in 1828 the church was possibly the largest in the city. The parish included people of wealth, culture, and social influence. In its early days an orthodox Bible society offered to distribute Bibles among Universalists, until a survey of 177 Universalist families disclosed that they possessed 416 Bibles and 202 New Testaments.

Boston. Records do not antedate 1786, but a meetinghouse was purchased the year before. Its owners constituted Boston's twenty-first church.[17] Murray began regular part-time preaching in 1786; full-time in 1790. In 1792 there were about eighty members. Paul Dean became associate minister in 1813 and minister at Murray's death. The Second Society was incorporated in 1816. Dedication of their first building on School Street was postponed one day on account of a cattle show at Brighton. Pews were purchased and were resalable. Pew owners were taxed by the society from $6.76 to $17.16 a year. Hosea Ballou was called and on Christmas Day, 1817, installed. The Charlestown Society was incorporated in 1811, the Roxbury Society in 1820. Hosea Ballou 2nd became pastor at Roxbury.[18] Several other societies eventually appeared within the city. Activities were not limited to preaching services. Universalists of Boston formed a Fire Society. This title had reference not to extinguishing the fires of hell but to mutual assistance at fires in Universalist homes or places of business. Members were to assist in removing goods and furnishings from burning buildings. There were monthly meetings at which the transaction of business was followed by religious discussion and singing.[19]

Gloucester. Under Murray's leadership this society, organized in 1779, took the name Independent Christian Church in Gloucester.[20] At first without officers or funds, it soon succeeded in dedicating a building. In Gloucester occurred probably the first court case testing the right of religious independents to be relieved of tax support of the Congregational Church. In 1804 Murray was succeeded by Thomas Jones. A new building, the present church, was erected in 1806.

Providence. Murray was heard here in a Baptist church in 1772; an informal organization was made in 1785; the First Universalist Society was organized in 1821; and a building was erected the following year. Fayette Mace became the first pastor. The charter provided that "no subscription to any creed, article of faith or covenant, shall ever be required of others by those who may meet for public worship in said house when erected; each individual having free and perfect liberty to give that meaning to the Scriptures of the Old and New Testaments which shall best accord with his or her understanding of the same." Mace was followed by David Pickering (1822-1835) and W. S. Balch (1836-1841). The society supported the adoption of a new Rhode Island constitution with a broader suffrage provision. When the congregation became too large, a second society was organized.[21]

Newport. The chief claim to fame of this small society in 1792 seems to be based on the Boston Society's description of it. "Those that are at Newport join neither with the world nor with each other. They are afraid of months, of days, and of years, and, to avoid being entangled with what they deem a yoke of bondage, they keep from even the appearance of assembling at any time." Thus they set the example for many Unitarian Universalists of today.

New York City.   Murray preached here in 1770. In 1793 a debating society discussed Universalism.[22] In the spring of 1796 three businessmen, Abraham E. Brouer, Robert Snow, and Edward Mitchell, withdrew from a Methodist church because they had become Universalists. They decided to worship together. Others having joined them, in May they became the Society of Christian Friends, with an organization similar to that of the Methodists. Murray declined their invitation to settle there. With a new constitution and incorporation in 1800, Brouer and Snow withdrew, leaving Mitchell to be ordained in 1803 and to serve as a paid minister until his death in 1827. For about two years he was away, serving as Murray's assistant in Boston, whose successor he was expected to become. Invited back to Boston after Murray's death, he declined, preferring to return to New York, where a new building was erected for him on Duane Street.

Mitchell is described as eloquent, sometimes dogmatic. Like Murray, he was opposed to Unitarian ideas. Neither he nor his church ever affiliated with any denominational organization. It is presumably from this society that Thomas Farrington King received his initation into Universalism.

One account has it that a Second Society of Christian Friends on Prince Street (1822) eventually took the name First Universalist Society. Abner Kneeland was once its minister. He favored the socialistic reforms of Robert Owen and others and invited Frances Wright, the radical feminist, to lecture. Many of his people objected and he was dismissed. His later defection from Universalism in Boston disturbed both his followers and his opponents in New York.

Thomas J. Sawyer, young and inexperienced, came to New York in 1832. Apparently only Mitchell's society was still alive, and that about to give up. Sawyer then organized the Orchard Street Society, named (out of courtesy to Mitchell's group) Second Universalist Society in the City of New York. He per-

sonally guaranteed the $1,050 yearly rental for a former Episco-
palian building. Remaining open during the cholera epidemic of
that year, when most churches had closed and most ministers
had fled, it immediately became successful. Succeeding pastors
were Otis Skinner (1846) and C. H. Fay (1849). This church
was instrumental in establishing daughter societies on Murray
Street, Bleecker Street, and Fourth Street, and in Brooklyn and
Williamsburgh.

Philadelphia.   N. Pomp, writing in 1774, affirmed that
Universalism was "never more widely spread than in this country" and "nowhere has the doctrine been more successful and
made greater progress than here in Pennsylvania."[23] Here was a
center of thought more liberal and free than that in Massachusetts.
Here was friendliness from De Benneville, Rush, Jefferson,
Priestley, Franklin, and many other learned and leading men.

Murray spoke in this city in 1771 and 1773. In 1781 Winchester and his followers began to worship in the Hall of the
university, forming the Society of Universal Baptists, which in
1786 purchased a building from the Masonic Lodge.[24] It now
seems unfortunate that Winchester left for England in 1787,
not to return to Philadelphia until 1795, and then in impaired
health. In 1790 during his absence the society changed its name
to First Independent Church of Christ. This was at the time of
the Philadelphia Convention, to be described later. Another group,
the Universal Society, united with this one at about the same
time. In 1793 the lodge was sold and a lot purchased on Lombard
Street, where a building was soon provided. After Winchester
the following men served as pastors: Thomas Jones, Hugh White,
Noah Murray, and George Richards. Finding his flock too un-
democratic, Richards and others set up the Church of the Restitution, but his mental illness and suicide led to its dissolution.
Meanwhile the Lombard Street church dozed until 1816, after
which it had a series of pastors: Ebenezer Lester, David Gilson,
and Abner Kneeland. Ballou delivered twelve sermons there in
1821.

Physical equipment at Lombard Street was scanty and uninviting. The building, eighty by fifty feet, at first without plaster, was cramped. Benches were provided, with perhaps a box for a pulpit. To augment the income, the basement was rented for storage of groceries and liquors. The hall itself was rented for singing schools and lectures. In 1808 funds for purchasing a burial lot were provided by a lottery.

A second church in 1822 obtained property on Callowhill Street, with William P. Morse as minister. Stephen R. Smith took the pulpit in 1825; Abel Thomas (publisher as well as preacher) in 1829. Its members opposed the unsuccessful efforts of Ely to set up an orthodox Christian party in American politics.[25] It supported a move, also unsuccessful, to obtain more liberal civil rights provisions in the Pennsylvania constitution. In 1834 a Young Men's Universalist Institute conducted discussions on public question. At a later date other churches were established.

Turning our view inland, we may note that Thomas Barns (1749-1816) pioneered in *Maine*.[26] [27] A disciple of Rich, he came to Portland to live in 1799, preaching there and at other points. The society in Norway was formed in that year; that in Portland in 1821; that in Lewiston and Auburn in 1828.[28]

In *Massachusetts* Universalists moved inland from coastal towns. The Third Independent Religious Society in the Commonwealth of Massachusetts was organized at Oxford by Adams Streeter in 1785. Fifty-nine persons signed the compact, with an additional sixty-nine from nearby towns. Worcester County communities became known for their Universalist constituency: Milford, Sutton, Douglas, Charlton, and other neighboring settlements.[29] It is said that leading men from the Revolutionary army were influential in establishing societies in these places. And then from these towns Universalists moved northwestward towards the boundaries of New Hampshire and Vermont. The old accounts usually emphasize the religious boldness, outspokenness, and loyalty of these pioneers. A description of a different sort is recorded of a layman of this period: "As to universal salvation, it seems to be his mind, but he don't say so."

In 1828 there were only twelve societies in Massachusetts with their own meetinghouses: Boston (3), Gloucester (2),

Cambridgeport, Charlestown, Haverhill, Lowell, Malden, Roxbury, and Salem. Thirty-four additional buildings were erected in the following thirteen years, but the list was believed to be incomplete.[30]

In *New Hampshire,* in spite of the firm determination of the Establishment to maintain itself, Joab Young was at his task in Grantham, Warner, and Deering. Caleb Rich had assembled a congregation in the Jaffrey-Winchester area. An early preacher in *Vermont* at Clarendon and Pawtel was Michael Coffin. He also visited Whitehall, Granville, and Ballston in eastern New York. The work of Farwell and Ferriss has already been mentioned. The Universalist society in Barre was organized as the First Parish. In *Rhode Island* there were early societies in Pawtucket and Woonsocket Falls. In *Connecticut* there were societies in Norwich, Danbury, Norwalk, New Salem, and Long Ridge. (The last was a part of Stamford.)

In *New York* State, outside New York City, Universalism was first presented by an unknown preacher in 1796 at Amenia, Dutchess County, where there were already a few friendly families. Four years later Noah Murray and Michael Coffin visited this group. Isaac Whitnal preached there in 1812.[31] A more permanent nucleus was to be found at Hudson, where after prior preaching by Kneeland a society was organized in 1817. Kneeland was followed by Joshua Flagg, David Pickering, and Thomas Farrington King. There was preaching in the Poughkeepsie vicinity. Into the Lake Champlain area Edwin Ferriss (1771-1839), a brother of Walter and a disciple of Rich, introduced Universalism in 1802. He preached in the vicinity of Pawlingstown and in Otsego County. Miles Wooley and, more importantly, Nathaniel Stacey were active in these regions. Wooley seems to have organized at Hartwick the first society in this region (1803). Stacey devoted much time to a far-flung itinerary, but at one period served Whiteston (New Hartford) and Hamilton, where the first Universalist building west of the Hudson was built. Paul Dean became a settled pastor over these two churches in 1810. The society at Henderson was formed in 1819.[32]

In 1806 there were four organized societies in upstate New

York, all practicing baptism and all making some provision for the poor. Ballou visited preaching stations in the Utica vicinity in 1808. All these early men, confronted by the aggressive opposition of the partialists, "lived in a state of excitement." Since they were usually Masons, the movement was especially vulnerable to the anti-Masonic agitation of the day. Nevertheless, by 1824 there were forty-five preachers and fifty societies in New York State.

For New Jersey, Maryland, and Pennsylvania, available records are scanty; for Georgia, Alabama, and the Carolinas, even more so. Although Universalism did not take root here as hardily as in the more northerly states, an English journal of 1802 reported gains in this region.[33]

Organizing Groups of Churches

As societies were being formed, it would have been natural for those within easy traveling distance of one another to send delegates once a year to some larger association. With associations as going enterprises, the next step might have been to group a number of them into a larger body. The final step would have been to organize a national convention.

This would have been the logical way to proceed. Actually, events did not follow this neat order. Attempts were made to organize a general convention before there were any state conventions, before much attention was paid to associations, and indeed before there was any large number of societies.

Present-day newcomers to Unitarian Universalist churches sometimes inquire, "Why didn't the merger of Unitarians and Universalists come earlier? Indeed, why were they not one from the beginning?" The second question may be reworded to apply to the period now under discussion: "Why did not these early Universalists, instead of setting up a new denomination, join the Unitarians?" The simple answer is that there were no Unitarians to join. There were individuals, Priestley for example, who called themselves Unitarian. There were others who were thinking in this direction. But an organized Unitarian movement did not then exist. It did not exist as a general body until 1825. Churches that then became Unitarian were still part of the old Establishment. If Universalists were to proclaim and extend their faith, they had no choice. They were not welcome in, or were even excluded from, other churches. They had to start from scratch to form their own organization.

If it now be asked, "Why did not the Unitarians later join the Universalists?" the answer is that there was no reason for the Unitarians to join anybody. The parent Unitarian churches were well-established institutions, some of them two hundred years old, eligible to receive tax money, and with the elite of Massachusetts clergy and laity within their ranks. The most that their leaders could accomplish at first was to persuade them reluctantly to join each other by forming the American Unitarian Association. Any suggestion that they might unite with a new and socially inferior sect, which was challenging the very standing order of which they were a part, would have been regarded as ridiculous.

THE FIRST GENERAL ORGANIZATION (1785)

On July 21, 1785, members of the Second Religious Society in Oxford, also known as the Third Independent Religious Society in the Commonwealth, called Universalist, wrote to societies at Gloucester, Boston, Taunton, Newport, and Providence, suggesting a meeting at Oxford to form an association, and asserting that "our strength depends upon our being cemented together in one united body, in order to anticipate any embarrassment of our Constitutional rights." That meeting was held at Oxford, already a center of Universalism, on September 14. Clerical and lay delegates came from the societies invited, and from Milford, Bellingham, Warwick, and Philadelphia. Clergymen present were Murray, Rich, Adams Streeter, and Winchester, who presided.[34]

What this group called itself is not clear, but it recommended to component societies a charter of compact and the name Independent Christian Society in——, commonly called Universalist. It is doubtful whether this name was widely used. In addition to Universalist, other popular names were Universalian, and Brethren in the Abrahamic Faith from the text in Genesis 12:3, "in thee shall all the families of the earth be blessed." This convention met in Boston in 1786 and in Milford in 1787, after which it disappeared. Its purpose may have been to establish a base for legal recognition of Universalists as a separate denomination. This done, perhaps, no further need was seen for it.

Some varieties of Christianity in America were imported; that is, a community of believers came in a body from Europe, for example the Plymouth colony. Some were the product of activity by official representatives from organized European churches, for example the Roman Catholic Church. Some were native-born. It may be difficult to properly classify some specific bodies, but the Universalist denomination was certainly native-born. It was not the first to appear in this class, for it was preceded by the Freewill Baptists in 1780 and the Methodists in 1784. But at least it was one of the earliest denominations to gather itself above the level of the individual church. It was also one of the most typically American, since its vision of a non-segregated heaven for all was easily compatible with the equalitarian spirit of the post-Revolutionary period.

When the meeting at Oxford was held, there were, in addition to the four men listed, nine known to be Universalist ministers. They were Barns, De Benneville, Evans, Lathe, N. Murray, Parker, Sumner, M. Winchester, and Wright.

The Second General Organization (1790)[35]

As already suggested, Universalism in its beginnings was largely a rural movement. An important exception was at Philadelphia. Here in 1789 some residents believing in the salvation of all men, and others from "Jersey State," discussed the lack of "social union and communion together." At this or the subsequent meeting there were present at least one minister, nine laymen, and seven women. At a second meeting on September 6 a committee of four was instructed to send out a circular letter, inviting "such as hold like faith" to attend a conference in their city. The authorized letter was prepared by William Perkins, James Moore, Arthur Cuthbert, and Israel Israel, and sought an opinion concerning "calling a general convention of Sutable [sic] Persons" for the purpose of adopting "one Uniform mode of Performing Divine Worship and one Method of Obtaining suitable Persons in the Ministry, one Consistent way of Administering the Lord's Supper," and other measures needed "to build on the Broadest Basis of Christian Benevolence."

Favorable response having been received from Boston and elsewhere, the convention met on May 25, 1790, and continued through June 8. Presumably attendance was larger than the ten laymen and seven ministers who were official delegates: four from Philadelphia, two from other Pennsylvania points, eight from Jersey, one from Virginia, and John Murray from Gloucester. The principal business was the composition and adoption of a "Rule of Faith" and a "Plan of Church Government." A century later Hosea Starr Ballou in a General Convention address reported that an autobiographical manuscript by Dr. Benjamin Rush notes that the draft copy of this document was submitted to him for correction and arrangement. Whether Rush attended any of the sessions is doubtful, but the form adopted may well be what he approved.

The Rule of Faith will be reproduced in Chapter Six. Here I shall outline the Plan. There are nine articles. Two of the items mentioned in the call are not referred to: uniform forms of worship and of communion. A church is defined as a self-governing company of believers, united by a covenant in maintaining worship, preaching the gospel, ordaining officers, preserving peace and order among themselves, and relieving the poor. Each church is to worship one day in seven, using such forms of prayer and such hymns as may be agreeable. Those societies who "subscribe our articles of Faith" may be admitted as members, no matter what their views about baptism, communion, confirmation, and other ceremonies. In fact, each church may decide whether to use these ceremonies or not. Each church should maintain a school for the teaching of reading, writing, arithmetic, and psalmody. Poor children should be taught gratis. "As the fullest discovery of the perfections and will of God, and the whole duty of man, is contained in the Bible," our youth should be instructed in it at regular meetings. Societies should send delegates to an annual convention, which should act on common matters, send forth ministers to places where the gospel has not been preached, and thus organize churches. But "each church reserves to itself full and exclusive power to judge of all matters relating to faith and practice."[36]

Attached to the Plan are five recommendations, which may be thus summarized: (1) Although defensive wars are lawful, there is a time coming when universal love of the gospel will put an end to all wars. Hence members should cultivate brotherly love, considering all mankind as brothers. (2) In disputes among members of the same church, "parties" are recommended instead of courts of law. (3) Since slavery is inconsistent with the Saviour's gospel of universal love, total refraining from the African trade is recommended, together with the gradual reduction of slavery and the education of Negro children in English literature and the principles of the gospel. (4) Testimony by simple affirmation, rather than by oath, is recommended on the basis both of Jesus' teaching and of practical results. (5) For the maintenance of order and the support of the government "it is recommended that members offer a peaceful submission to the highest powers" with respect to truth, justice, and the payment of taxes.

The first suggestion for schools for poor children came from the Methodists. The Universalist proposal followed, and may have conveyed the idea to Rush. He supported and broadened the plan, enlisted support of Episcopalians and Catholics, and pushed a citizens' mass meeting to popularize it. Cooperatively the school opened in March, 1791.[37]

The Rule and the Plan were adopted by a few New England

churches, and are suggestive of some early thinking within the new sect. But they were never widely accepted. Subsequent meetings of the convention were held annually for several years, all in Philadelphia. Probably at each meeting a circular letter was ordered prepared and sent to known societies. The minutes mention letters received in return from the First Sister Church in Boston, from Hartford, from the Vermont Universalist Convention [*sic*], from Universalists of New England, and from upstate New York.

In 1791 it was decided to prepare a collection of hymns. Within the year the collection had been compiled, but at the request of the Boston society, publication had been delayed. In 1792 it was decided to proceed with printing. The work appeared as *Evangelical Psalms, Hymns, and Spiritual Songs.* When Morganstown, Georges Hill, and other churches "on account of distances from us" had formed a separate western association, the Philadelphia group expressed rejoicing. Without explanation in the record, the convention apparently held its final session in 1809.

Of the ministers listed earlier in this chapter the following had parts to play in this convention: Timothy Banger, Nicholas Cox, David Evans, Thomas Jones, Noah Murray, Abel Sargent, Artis Seagrave. There was also a Baptist clergyman, William Worth; a layman, Israel Israel; and an unidentified James Moore.

THE THIRD GENERAL ORGANIZATION—THE GENERAL CONVENTION AND ITS FIRST PERIOD (1793-1833)[38]

At that early Massachusetts center of Universalism, Oxford, there gathered on September 4, 1793, "the Ministers, Elders, and Messengers, appointed by the Universal Churches and Societies in Massachusetts, Rhode Island, New Hampshire, Vermont, Connecticut, and New York." Unknowingly, without formal action, without constitution or bylaws, without officers or funds, they laid the foundation of the Universalist General Convention, an organization which continued to function until its merger with the American Unitarian Association in 1961. Apparently transacting little business, they left no enduring minutes of their gathering, issuing instead a "Circular" addressed to "the Brethren in the faith of the Gospel" in those communities where Universalism was known to have established a foothold.

Since in recent years misunderstanding has arisen about this organization, it is important to emphasize that this is the same convention which had its final session in 1961 as it combined with the American Unitarian Association. It was not the New England Convention. It was not the predecessor of the General Convention. It was the General Convention. The names for it used by a succession of secretaries varied. One did write "The Convention Universal of the Four New England States." (Vermont and Maine were not yet states.) At the beginning of the first volume of recorded minutes we find "General Convention of Universalists." In 1804 the official title became "The General Convention of Universalists of the New England States and Others." New York was included from the beginning. To the west there was then little to add. Courtesy required that the Pennsylvania General Convention be given implied recognition, until it became evident that it was no rival. In 1833 there was no obstacle to prevent adopting the name "The General Convention of Universalists in the United States." It met continually in stated sessions from 1793 through 1961, even during the Civil War. Minutes are preserved for every session except those of 1793 and 1798. In the period covered by this chapter sixteen of its forty-one sessions were held in New Hampshire, thirteen in Vermont, seven in Massachusetts, four in New York, and one in Connecticut. Most of these gatherings were in rural communities.

Facilities for Convention meetings varied in different communities. In some there might be a Universalist church building. In others some other public meeting place might be available: the Congregational church at Orange, the Columbia Hotel at Saratoga Springs. Or the business sessions, limited to a council of clergy and delegates, might be held in a private home: Eliam Buel's at Hoosick Falls, Hosea Ballou's at Barnard, Vermont.

The hour of opening the morning meeting varied from six at Strafford to eight at Chesterfield. In the evening religious services were held, often, as at Cavendish, in several meetinghouses in different parts of the township.

Records of attendance are sketchy. About thirty were present at Oxford in 1794. There were sixteen ministers at Chesterfield. On this occasion "it pleased the Lord to send rain gently and steadily, to saturate the thirst of the parched earth." At Strafford in 1802 the audience on both days was "numerous." At Winchester in 1813 the services were "well attended," and the weather remarkably fine. From Charlton in 1817 comes this report: "The serenity of the weather, the plenty of the season, barns and granaries filled with the exuberance of the former harvest, orchards bending with ripened fruit, fields loaded with corn, herds and flocks cropping the flowery food and fattening upon the luxury of the pastures, husbandmen with smiling gratitude surveying the profuse bounties of providence, women who look well to the ways of their households, and children . . . enlivening each mansion and cottage with songs of health, plenty and peace. . . ." At Warner there were "numerous, crowded, and respectable assemblies." At Hartland there were two hundred participants and spectators for the Lord's Supper.

Overnight accommodations were often, perhaps usually, found in private homes. The first mention of hospitality and generous provision for delegates was entered in the minutes in 1807. In 1810 some unrecorded argument led to the vote that delegates were to come at their own expense unless sent by their societies; the host society was to pay for preaching only. The cordiality of the hosts at Barre in 1831 and the singing by the choir were commended; at an earlier session at Clinton a similar note was made of the music of a large choir. At Concord every church building in town was offered for the use of the Convention; many from out of town were entertained in the homes of non-Universalists.

The programs of the earliest sessions were chiefly devoted to religious concerns rather than to business. A first prayer, a sermon, a second prayer, was the order for each of the three daily sessions. Apparently all ministers present expected to preach at least once. Sometimes they drew lots for position on the program. One sermon was often selected to be printed. Based on biblical texts, the elaboration of the Universalist gospel was ever the theme. The style of delivery was such as to kindle the emotions as well as to convince the intellect. Audiences were often deeply moved. During the years, as the amount of business increased, preaching occupied proportionately less time.

From 1794 on, each yearly meeting was an occasion for rejoicing over the widening acceptance of Universalism—sometimes expressed generally, sometimes with specific evidence. It was noted already in 1796 that it was widely spread. Such tidings were gleaned in part from communications with other associations or conventions. In 1800 letters were ordered sent to the societies to the south and to the east. Or the good news might come directly from nearby societies, or by correspondence even from England. In 1801 the clerk was directed "to maintain a brotherly correspondence with all the Churches and Societies in Europe and America, so far as it may be possible." Interrupted by the War of 1812, this foreign correspondence was resumed after the close of hostilities, when Edward Turner reported that "a correspondence had been opened with brethren of like faith in England, which promises happy and beneficial effects." In 1807 the Philadelphians were reported as "shaking themselves from the dust" under the preaching of Noah Murray. An enthusiast of 1817 wrote, "From the banks of the Penobscot to the margin of Ohio; and from the waters of the Tennessee to the shores of the Atlantic our doctrine flourishes." Soon came reports of extensions in Maine and of new societies in Massachusetts.

For many years the Convention appointed someone to draft and send out a circular letter to the several societies. In the absence of a denominational journal these letters were intended as reports of what had gone on at the meetings. Each writer went at his task in his own way, but the earliest communications tended to be very general, perhaps recounting measures voted upon but often largely devoted to enraptured accounts of the spread of Universalist ideas. The language imitated in style the letters of St. Paul. Moral exhortations might be included. "Wives, win your husbands by the charity of your conversation" (1793). As protection against criticism ministers were urged to live righteously and to give no occasion for adversaries; "every member of the body of Universalists is a city set on a hill" (1801). Toward the close of the period the circulars became shorter and less flowery. Eventually they ceased.

What united these people was the common belief in universal salvation. Yet there were different opinions as to how this salvation was to be achieved. These differences were long regarded as of minor significance. Members were urged to avoid "vain disputations on the manner in which Jehovah worketh the council of his will" (1796). Ethical conduct by both laity and clergy was stressed as more important than correctness of belief. Influence upon others, self-satisfaction, and especially example to children were among the motivations to right living (1797). When a group of ministers withdrew to form an independent body, the Convention voted "God speed to the Restorationists" (1831).

Earlier we noted that the laws of the several New England states provided that all residents be taxed for the support of the parish church and that Murray had to bring suit to relieve the members of his congregation. This may have settled matters for Massachusetts but not for New Hampshire. In 1801 a case arose which greatly disturbed Universalists.[39] Christopher Erskine of Claremont, a Universalist since 1796, continued to be taxed by the parish. Upon his refusal to pay, he was arrested. Although a lower court decided in his favor, the Superior Court reversed the decision, on the ground that Universalists and Congregationalists were not different sects within the meaning of the New Hampshire constitution. Differences of belief, the court ruled, were not to be considered; it was identity of mode of government which determined the court's decision. In 1802 the Convention, alerted to the danger to the movement, unsuccessfully memorialized the judges to reconsider. Fearful of similar taxation in other villages, some advocated armed resistance, but the Convention of 1803 advised calm patience while a dispassionate appeal was addressed to the legislature. This body voted a resolution declaring Universalists to be a separate sect within the meaning of the constitution. Similar relief was given the Freewill Baptists and the Methodists. Apprehension that Universalists might be taxed had promoted further organization of local churches, for organization was believed to be evidence of independence.

FELLOWSHIP AND DISCIPLINE OF MINISTERS

In addition to granting fellowship to ordained ministers of other denominations, and issuing temporary licenses to preach, the Convention authorized thirty-five ordinations, most of which were solemnized at a meeting of the Convention itself. Some of those thus honored were inconspicuous, perhaps short-term ministers. Some became denominational leaders: Hosea Ballou, Thomas Barns, Walter Ferriss, Nathaniel Stacey. Then there were Edward Turner and Paul Dean, denominational controversialists; Orestes Brownson, licensed but not ordained (?) by the Convention, and later a famous Roman Catholic; Abner Kneeland, later convicted in Boston of "infidelity"; and Thomas Farrington King, father of Thomas Starr King.

A problem arose early concerning ministerial discipline, a problem which was both theoretical and practical. Theory was involved in drawing up a set of rules to distinguish between proper and improper ministerial behavior and to establish procedures for ordination and possible dismissal. Practical difficulties arose when it was alleged that someone had violated the code. How and by whom should the facts be investigated and judged? What should be done about an offending clergyman? And eventually what criteria should be established in these and related issues? The question of ordination was important to the new denomination to protect churches from being imposed upon by unknown traveling preachers. It was important to the clergyman as being proof that he was legally authorized to conduct weddings.

It was for this reason that Hosea Ballou, concerning whose first impulsive ordination some doubts had been raised, was ordained a second time with Convention authorization and with several ministers participating in the ceremony. This concern was acute, for example, in Vermont about 1803, when a committee was asked to study the legal privileges of newly settled men.

The first specific case of discipline arose in 1800, when an unnamed minister was suspended from fellowship, with the hope that he would return to the Christian life. On this same occasion a committee was asked to visit New Marlboro to investigate complaints, for reasons not recorded, against their minister. Miles Wooley was suspended for a year and then dismissed. Complaints arose against Joab Young and Ebenezer Paine. Young was dismissed for intemperance. As for Paine it was found that the charges against him were not supported, whereupon the society at Washington was asked to explain why they had not defended him. In 1814 the Convention voted disapprobation of Abner Kneeland for leaving the church at Charlestown to devote himself to mercantile pursuits, to which Kneeland objected. Two years later, having returned to a pastorate, he was again in good standing. But in 1830 the Convention believed that it now had full proof "that said Kneeland and Brownson have renounced their faith in the Christian religion, which renunciation is a dissolution of their fellowship with this body."

The simplest approach to dealing with applicants for ordination was by a committee to investigate them; this was done in 1800, with emphasis on the need for conformity of practice among the churches and on regularity of discipline. A plan adopted in 1803 provided that the Convention was the authorized body to examine qualifications and order ordinations. Weary of unbusinesslike methods and of accusations and defenses of ministers, the Convention in 1824 adopted a constitution. It also voted that "in all future difficulties between ministers or between a minister and a church, it is their duty to settle differences by a mutual council from those in fellowship." Still, there was dissatisfaction; two years later a committee was instructed to report on whether additional rules concerning applicants were needed. At the Saratoga Springs session this committee suggested that, prior to Convention sessions, applicants be examined in secular and sacred learning, in literary and theological attainments, and in their talents for sermonizing. Acting on this idea, examining committees were set up for each of four geographical districts. Three of these covered New England; the fourth included New York and Pennsylvania. The only specific book recommended for study was *Greek Lexicon Adapted to the New Testament* by S. C. Loveland. The record becomes confusing as to what specific provisions were adopted, amended, or deleted from the rules, but in 1829 it was voted to print them.

From time to time lists of ministers in fellowship were compiled. Eddy lists 33 for 1800; 40 for 1813. At Hudson in 1821, 23 were reported as present, 56 as not present—a total of 79. Demerest lists 170 for 1830. The lists of societies are less precise, since it is not always clear whether place names designated organized churches or merely communities where Universalism had some kind of foothold. In subsequent years conventions gave fellowship to additional societies. Included among those welcomed prior to 1834 were Haverhill, Brookfield, Dudley, Attleboro, Roxbury, Milford, Cambridgeport, Springfield, Egremont, Scituate, in Massachusetts; Marlboro, Claremont, Wilmot, Newport, in New Hampshire; St. Johnsbury, Whitingham, Strafford, South Woodstock, in Vermont. But this list is not comprehensive. Among unusual names of individual churches are First Christian Toleration Society of Alstead, New Hampshire; the United Christian Friends of Norwich, Connecticut; the Restorationist Society of Royalton, Vermont; the Universal Society of Restorationists of Richmond, New Hampshire; and in New York, the First Society of United Christian Friends, called Restorationists, of Saratoga Springs, and the First Society of Restorationists at Fort Anne.

For several years beginning in 1811 the Convention took upon itself the responsibility of approving the propriety of negotiations which led to the removal of a minister from one church and his settlement in another. Thus the call of Kneeland to Charlestown was approved, as was Dean's to Boston, Bigelow's to Ohio, Wood's to Shirley, Massachusetts, and Streeter's to Boston.

ORGANIZING THE DENOMINATION MORE EFFECTIVELY

As the number of churches increased, groups of them were organized into "associations." Many of these applied to the Convention for affiliation. If no preacher was available for a church the Convention recommended that the members meet every Sunday and at least read the Bible, "if they have no other gift among them." Committees were appointed by the Convention to visit the associations.[40] Thus we find mention by the Convention in 1800 of the Eastern Association and those "at the southward." Eastern probably refers to the District of Maine; southward possibly to southeastern Massachusetts. These associations were advised to send "messengers" next year and to select them on the first Sunday in June, thus taking one step to introduce order into church business. A Northern Association for parts of New Hampshire, Vermont, and New York appears in 1804. A Western Association for the New York counties of Otsego, Chenango, and Oneida was approved in 1805. The Convention's attempt to send visitors to all associations imposed an increasing burden, an assignment said to have been faithfully executed at the representatives' own expense. The Eastern, Northern, Southern, and Western associations apparently soon became stable groups. A Providence Association was added in 1827; a New Hampshire Association (later Merrimac River Association) and a Rockingham Association in 1824; a Boston Association in 1829; a Connecticut River Association in 1833. Many others were formed, not only in New England but in the newer states to the west.[41]

Further growth led to the grouping of associations into state conventions: New York, 1826; North Carolina, 1827; Maine, 1828; South Carolina, 1830; Connecticut, New Hampshire, and Pennsylvania, 1832. In 1826 there was organized the General

Convention of the Western States, which included parts of Indiana, Ohio, and Kentucky, and which was later divided into separate state conventions. These dates are approximate.

At its second session in 1794 the General Convention adopted the platform of the Philadelphia Convention. But nothing in this platform provided for the inner structure of a convention. Thus each session of a convention could start anew with its set of rules. An example of such a rule is the appointment of two monitors in 1802 "to preserve silence and maintain order." At the same session a committee was instructed "to form a plan of fellowship in faith and practice, for the edifying of the body and building it up together." The recommendations of this committee were adopted unanimously in the following year. The story of its work and its Profession of Faith will be reported in Chapter Six. Here the plan of government will be briefly summarized.

The circular letter of 1802 carried the Profession and Plan to the several societies. It was introduced with the following explanation: "Whereas the diversities of capacity and opportunity for obtaining information, together with many attendant circumstances, have occasioned among the sincere professors of the Abrahamic faith, some diversities of opinion concerning some points of doctrine and modes of practice; we therefore think it expedient, in order to prevent confusion and misunderstanding, and to promote the edifying and building up of the church together in love, to record and publish that profession of belief, which we agree in, as essential; and that plan of ecclesiastical fellowship, and general subordination, which we, as a christian association, conceive we ought to maintain."

The Plan itself provides for an annual session, to which each society is entitled to send delegates. The number is not stated, but they are to "hold our general profession of belief and support a sober moral character." Ordained and licensed ministers in fellowship are considered Convention members. Others may be admitted by majority vote. Each member has one vote, except when it is decided that each state shall have one vote. Each session is to select a presiding elder, clerk, and any other necessary officers. The Convention is to examine the "state of particular Societies, Churches, and Associations, and to give or withhold, continue or withdraw their fellowship." Similar care is to be exercised over ministers, and the qualifications of applicants are to be examined. No penalty is to be imposed other than the withdrawal of fellowship. It is also the task of the Convention to promote "general order, instruction, and edification," and to approve ordinations.

Conspicuous by our standards is the lack of any mention of a treasurer. However, a treasurer had been appointed in 1801, after which the office was filled by different clergymen until 1825. Then for forty years the office was vacant. Also lacking was any provision for Convention business between sessions. This was partly remedied in 1811 by the appointment of a standing clerk. During the remainder of the life of the Convention this function continued to be provided for, under this or some other name.

This constitution proving inadequate, a new document was adopted in 1824, but still problems were arising out of the increasing numbers of societies and ministers. Examinations of applicants for fellowship and disposal of cases of discipline were becoming too burdensome for a single body meeting once a year. Moreover, as new associations were being formed and as some of these were being grouped into state conventions, the boundaries, powers, and functions of these bodies and their relations to one another were uncertain. Consequently, in 1827 Paul Dean, Warren Skinner, and Job Potter were asked to propose a remedy. Under Dean's leadership they acted with surprising promptness, reporting at the same session.

The report opens with this paragraph: "Each Society, organized and united in the faith of the final salvation of all mankind by the mediation of Jesus Christ, shall be considered as having in itself all the rights and privileges given by Christ our Lord to his disciples, and so long as they may choose, be perfectly independent of all other societies or bodies of believers, in the exercise of those rights. They shall judge for themselves in matters of faith and practice—choose their own modes, forms, and times of worship—call, settle, and dismiss their own ministers. These independent societies may, if they choose, unite themselves into Associations for the purpose of extending their fellowship and influence, and adopt such rules and regulations as they judge best for their mutual government and benefit; and each, when they please, may withdraw from said Association; and again these Associations may form themselves into Conventions, for the greater extension of the same benefit."

The report then urges the formation of such associations, to meet at least once a year for worship, the Lord's Supper, exchange of information, and the giving of advice. Somewhat inconsistently with the stated powers of societies, these associations are also to adopt regulations for "the government of its Societies." The state conventions are also to meet once a year for similar purposes, and for "the licensing of men to preach, and the ordination of preachers as evangelists." Delegates from societies to associations may be both clerical and lay, but ministers only are to serve as delegates to the state conventions. These conventions are then to choose delegates to the General Convention. All four types of organizations "shall adopt and retain unaltered the Articles of Faith now professed by the General Convention." This provision contains an implied contradiction with the earlier statement that individual societies are to "judge for themselves in matters of faith and practice."

The report was unanimously adopted, ordered sent to the societies, and recommitted to Hosea Ballou, Paul Dean, and Thomas Whittemore for a final draft at next year's session. At that time, partly because of the limitation to the clergy of the privilege of serving as delegates to the state conventions, it was voted inexpedient to adopt the new plan. But discussion continued. Assigned to report on the original problem—the relationship of the General Convention to the state conventions and associations—were Thomas Farrington King, Sebastian Streeter, Thomas Whittemore, and J. E. Palmer. They recommended that state conventions be formed in all the New England states in which none then existed, and that all state conventions be invited to send representatives to the next General Convention. At that same session Streeter and Hosea Ballou 2nd of Massachusetts, King and John Moore of New Hampshire, Warren Skinner and Winslow W. Wright of Vermont, after meeting with delegates from Maine and New York, reported that it was now expedient that the General Convention be composed of clerical and lay delegates from each state convention. The General Convention was not to exercise authority, nor govern, nor impose discipline.

The recommendations outlined above became the basis for the constitution of 1833. Now for the first time Universalists had, at least on paper, the outline of an ecclesiastical order, but the neat plan never did function smoothly. Nevertheless, it contributed to the morale of the denomination and marked the emergence of its activities out of the cocoon of rural New England into the larger world which the United States had now become.

OTHER INTERESTS OF THE CONVENTION

Interest in hymnals had manifested itself even before any organization had occurred. Since words of orthodox hymns were incompatible with the new doctrine, Murray had published (1796) an American edition of an English hymnal compiled by James Relly and his brother. Winchester produced two hymn books. The Philadelphia Convention and the New York City Society had made their contributions. The General Convention authorized Ballou, Kneeland, and Turner to prepare "a collection of not less than 400 hymns to sell at not more than 75¢," which shall contain "a just delineation of . . . the true character of God as manifested in Jesus Christ, and which shall be divested of anything contrary to reason and sound doctrine." In 1808 the committee published a collection at their own financial risk. In 1829 the use of Streeter's new hymnal was recommended.

Early Sunday schools were concerned with secular subjects; their function in religion was recognized slowly. In this sense they were still regarded as new in 1832. Even so, religious education of the young attracted some early attention. A committee to prepare simplified instruction was appointed in 1794. The Letter to the Ephesians was declared better than a catechism. A circular letter (1810) urged churches to teach pure principles of the gospel to little children. Young men were advised (1828) to form societies to purchase books, and when a preacher could not be obtained to meet together on the Sabbath, to read, sing, and pray. The minutes do not report to what extent these admonitions were heeded, but such an adolescent group was eagerly attended at Portsmouth.[41] Sunday schools were opened in Philadelphia (1816), Boston (1817), and Gloucester (1820). Although other denominations had developed their Sunday schools sufficiently to form the American Sunday School Union in 1824, a comparable movement did not develop among Universalists until later.[42]

A nascent missionary urge manifested itself from the beginning. Delegates were often called messengers. In 1794 Michael Coffin and Joab Young were sent out "in a circuitous manner" to preach "the everlasting gospel." The society at Cooperstown, New York, asked advice, which Miles Wooley was sent to provide. It was discovered that such enterprises required financial expense, as did other activities undertaken. In 1801 a fund was voted "to supply the wants of the Brethren sent forth to preach, to aid in the printing of any useful works, and to answer all such charitable purposes as the Convention may justly propose." Each church was asked to take an annual collection for the fund; to receive this money David Ballou was appointed treasurer. Ministers were asked to seek donations from those "blessed with the means and blessed with the will." The circular letter emphasized that many ministers and many churches were poor, hence the need for a fund. The circular letter of the following year regretted the suspicions aroused by the previous appeal—suspicions of an intent to provide "ecclesiastical revenue," and to entrust money to banks! Both accusations were denied. This second appeal brought in a total of $13.03½ from thirteen societies. Somewhat more encouraging was a collection on the spot of thirty-two dollars for a stone to mark the grave of Elhanan Winchester. Twenty years later it was still being urged that a charity fund be provided to aid widows and orphans of deceased ministers. But no appeal for general funds was notably successful until 1870.

Young people from Universalist families who desired an education were often limited in their choice of schools to those controlled by other denominations, in which Universalists were given unhappy treatment. Hence Universalists began to think of establishing their own. The issue was crystallized in 1814 by outlining the possibility of a seminary "embracing the united interests of Religion and Literature," which was to be both "directed and patronized by the General Convention." Later it was referred to as a Seminary of Science, for which the Convention ought to raise five thousand dollars and use the interest only. In 1819 the Convention received under its patronage the newly established Nichols Academy at Dudley, Massachusetts, on the condition that the trustees are "members of this Convention." Ballou, Dean, and Turner comprised the committee which had successfully fathered the project, and Amasa Nichols of Dudley was the donor. The destruction of the original building by fire and inadequate financing delayed development. Eventually Universalists permitted the academy to pass from their control. There was some talk of another academy at Woburn. Meanwhile, quite independently of the General Convention, Universalists in New York were able to open the Clinton Liberal Institute in 1831. Plans for Westbrook Seminary in Maine were initiated, but this and other educational projects did not receive much attention until after 1833.

A similar statement applies to theological education. The Convention had been in existence for nearly a quarter of a century before any record appears of thought being given to an educated ministry, although it had been in the minds of those who backed Nichols Academy. In 1827 Edward Turner, Hosea Ballou 2nd, and Stephen R. Smith were asked to devise a plan for a theological school, but nothing came of this until eight years later. There was objection to the idea, even among those who desired better-educated ministers; they asserted that with the Bible available for every man to consult for himself there was no need to teach creeds and theologies, and that the proposed free course of study would attract insincere young men.

PUBLICATIONS

For the forty years beginning in 1793 Eddy lists eight or ten times as many Universalist books appearing as in the previous forty years. He includes 695 titles, but many of these were merely pamphlets of but a few pages. He includes also anti-Universalist writings. Sixty-seven titles appear to designate actual books on the Universalist side. Of these ten are hymnals, four are histories, two deal with Sunday schools, twenty-five seem to be interpretations of Christianity, and twenty-six seem to be collections of sermons, letters, lectures, or essays. The histories aspired to be scholarly: the life of Murray edited by his wife, a general history of the doctrine of universal salvation by Thomas Brown, an ancient history of Universalism by Hosea Ballou 2nd, and a modern history by Thomas Whittemore. The most important interpretative book was Ballou's *A Treatise on Atonement* (1805). Also significant were Priestley's references to Universalism in his works on revealed religion and on Unitarianism. In 1824 Walter Balfour brought out the first of his several studies on the correct meanings of biblical terms usually interpreted as implying endless punishment. In 1833 Lucius R. Paige published a work, praised by the Convention, in which he examined the opinions of eminent commentators of the Bible. Among the authors or editors of collections are Murray, Ballou, Winchester, Kneeland, Dean, and (representing the younger men) Dolphus Skinner and Russell Streeter.

About fifty Universalist periodicals were launched during this period. The earliest, in 1793, was a quarterly, the *Free Universal Magazine,* edited by Abel Sargent, only one volume of which appeared. Many of the others were also short-lived. A few survived beyond 1833. Our present denominational journal, *Now,* is the successor to the *Unitarian Universalist Register Leader;* this was a merger of the *Unitarian Register* and the *Universalist Leader.*

The *Leader* has a long ancestry through earlier mergers; there are at least forty names in its family history. Among those which first appeared in the period now being studied are the *Universal Magazine* (Boston, 1819), the *Christian Repository* (Woodstock, Vermont, 1821), the *Religious Inquirer* (Hartford, 1821), the *Gospel Advocate* (Buffalo, 1823), and the *Christian Telescope* (Providence, 1824). The *Universalist Herald,* a small sheet still published in Georgia, has a similar ancient lineage. The *Trumpet and Universalist Magazine* (1828–1864) absorbed other journals to become very influential in denominational affairs. These and other magazines varied in frequency of issue from weekly to bimonthly. Content also varied: sermons, essays, personal and denominational news, announcements of future meetings, events among other religious groups at home and in Europe, and general news reports. Thus the printed word contributed greatly to giving Universalists a sense of being a part of an important movement and to informing them of the convictions of their leaders and the actions of their conventions.

THE WESTERN MOVEMENT[44]

At the beginning of this chapter there was reference to the seeds of Universalism being blown inland. As a transition to the next, something more will now be said of this westward tendency. Within the original coastal settlements an expanding population produced internal pressures. Already in the early eighteenth century a long period of speculation in land had begun. But there were discouraging barriers: foothills and mountains, resisting Indians, French territorial claims, and the diplomacy of the British government which was designed to prevent Indian uprisings. These difficulties did not keep out a dribbling of hunters and explorers. In New England the first large movement of settlers began about 1750, moving westward in Massachusetts and northward into Maine, New Hampshire, and Vermont. When the war with England began there were many new towns in these regions which had already been transformed into peaceful farming regions. There was a similar pressure and discontent in the central and southern colonies.

In 1763 one obstacle was removed, as the British took over French territory, obtaining jurisdiction as far west as the Mississippi. But their diplomatic policy, not completely successful, continued its attempt to pacify the Indian tribes by keeping the colonists out. During the Revolution military roads penetrated much of what had been beyond the frontier. With peace in 1783 British restrictions were removed and the new United States government was at first too disunited to provide similar legislation. There remained the hostility of the Indians, the legal possessors of the land. Then a new difficulty arose as several of the states, on the basis of old colonial charters, made rival claims to possession of the same areas. But Congress and other groups exerted pressure. New treaties were signed. The states ceded their claims for western land to the federal government, with an occasional reserve, for example Connecticut's Western Reserve in Ohio. Land companies, honest and dishonest, bought large areas, selling them off to settlers. Much of the contention was quieted by federal legislation, especially the Ordinance of 1787. The Louisiana Purchase of 1803 eased negotiations with the tribes.

By 1800 there had been a great movement into the Ohio Valley over several roads: from Boston and Hartford, from Philadelphia and Baltimore, from Richmond, and from New Bern. The completion of the Erie Canal in 1825 stimulated other constructions. Ohio developed an important canal network, including the Cleveland-Portsmouth Canal. When states to the south of New York found canals over the mountains impossible, they became more successful with railroads. The Baltimore and Ohio made it in 1842. Rapidly rails of other companies were laid. Soon several points on the Mississippi were reached. Among the travelers to the west by stage, canal boat, and railroad were Universalist clergymen and laymen, who often wrote accounts of their travels for eastern journals.

It will be seen that the spread of Universalism beyond Murray's original preaching stations along the coast was facilitated by these western migrations. Maturin Ballou's removal to southern New Hampshire was a part of it. Walter Ferriss' removal to northwestern Vermont was a part of it. The work of Barns in Maine and Stacy in central New York was a part of it. So also was the movement of laymen and preachers into the St. Lawrence country, into the Mohawk Valley, and into the Western Reserve and points beyond. Cincinnati became a great center for the denomination, from which circuit riders fanned out in all directions and from which publishers also sent out books and journals. Westward the tide moved into Indiana, Illinois, Iowa, and northward into Michigan, Wisconsin, and Minnesota. Up and down the Ohio Valley settlers from New England rubbed elbows with neighbors who had come over the mountains from more southerly states by way of Pittsburgh or Kentucky. Many varieties of religion there were, none with fixed abode or local history. Controversy, in the form of rude accusations or orderly debate, was the fashion. Religion was the major topic of public interest

The whole story cannot be told here, but a few illustrative details from the Ohio country may convey something of the spirit of those days.[45] An early event was the settlement of Marietta in April, 1788, by families from Massachusetts and Connecticut. There may have been Universalists in this party, although there is no record of a society there before 1817. On February 2, 1832, the legislature passed an act to incorporate "The First Universalian Religious Library Association of Marietta." Its purpose was to build up a large library; its funds were invested in books rather than in preaching. About three thousand volumes were collected, only to be destroyed in the flood of 1860. A church building was erected on Second Street in 1842.

Down the river at Belpre a society was formed in 1823; others at Coolville and Gallipolis in 1829. Many sprang up in the region formerly belonging to the Ohio Land Company. The first minister in this neighborhood was Abel Sargent. Quaker support may have been given to early societies in Ohio and beyond.

Among early Universalist pioneers was General James Mitchell Varnum from Greenwich, Rhode Island, a friend of John Murray. He became judge of Ohio Territory. There was also Captain William Sargent of Gloucester, secretary to the Ohio Company and adjutant to the first governor. Others prominent at this time were Colonel Joseph Barker and Aaron Waldo Putnam. In the Western Reserve, Gages Smith, coming from Preston, Connecticut, settled in Mesopotamia in 1805. To Bronson County about 1817 came Stewart Southgate and his son Robert. The father had been one of the earliest supporters of Universalism in Oxford and in Barnard and was an intimate friend of Ballou. The first minister in northern Ohio was Timothy Bigelow, who in 1814 came from Winchester to Palmyra. The many laymen who settled in the Cincinnati area were visited by traveling preachers from the East. A society was organized in 1827. It erected a building but had difficulty in securing a settled pastor.

Similar events can be recounted for Indiana, Illinois, Wisconsin, and Michigan as they became fields for Universalist planting. Organization followed much the same pattern as in the East. First came societies; then, probably in 1826, a General Convention of the Western States.[46] It entered into correspondence with "brethren of like precious faith residing in different parts of the United States," and with the London (England) Unitarian Society.

Projecting our story beyond the terminal date of this chapter, we can see the movement carried along in diminished concentration by population movement into Minnesota, Iowa, Nebraska, Missouri, Kansas, Arkansas, and Texas. Then it passed over intervening territories to the Pacific Coast.

But to return to 1833. With their General Convention plan now modernized, with at least their share of believers among the throngs of the western migration, with several state conventions established, with associations rapidly increasing in number, with new societies springing up everywhere, Universalists were now ready to enter upon a period of expansion.

CHAPTER 4

Urban and Westward Expansion
Brings New Concerns (1834-1864)

The period we are about to survey was one of continuing western migration. By the time it began Universalism had been preached in Nova Scotia, New Brunswick, and Quebec, in all the New England states, in the coastal states as far south as the Carolinas, and in Kentucky, Ohio, Indiana, and Michigan. At some points the movement had become thoroughly established. In areas beyond the Hudson or the Appalachians it varied considerably in numbers and stability. During these years its boundaries expanded and its older concentrations were strengthened. During the thirties its pioneers pushed northward into Ontario, southward into Georgia, and westward into Illinois, Iowa, and Missouri. In the forties West Virginia, Tennessee, Wisconsin, and Mississippi heard its gospel from adventurous preachers; in the fifties Minnesota, Kansas, Texas, Florida, and the Pacific Coast. Since early records are fragmentary, these dates are only approximate, but they correctly suggest the steady push, interrupted only by the Civil War.[1]

Ohio may be cited as an example of what was happening.[2] In the preceding chapter it was seen as a field for settlement. But by 1834 the wave of immigration was passing beyond its borders. By 1840 all vacant land had been occupied. Gradually the itinerant method and style of preaching was replaced by the more urbane approach of the settled pastor. But both laity and clergy were slow to understand this, continuing to imagine that education would separate minister from people. Itinerant work continued, but with more frequent arrangements for neighboring churches

to join in workable circuits. Some societies formed earlier had
deteriorated; some persisted. New groups appeared. There were
perhaps 16 by 1830, 89 by 1840, 163 by 1850, with a drop, very
likely due in part to more accurate counting, to 135 in 1860.

Brief references to a few individual churches will illuminate
the uncertain nature of western beginnings. At *North Olmstead* a
society was organized in 1834. Thirteen years later a brick building was constructed on Butternut Ridge, in a neighborhood settled
by New Englanders, many of whom were Universalists. In *Columbus* after earlier visits from itinerant preachers services were held
in the courthouse about 1836. In a decade the group was ready
to purchase a church home from another denomination. Many laymen settled in *Cincinnati,* where they were often visited by eastern
ministers. The first organization, although it acquired a building,
was not permanent. Under George Rogers' leadership a society
purchased the Merchanics Institute. In the same city a German
Universalist society enjoyed a brief existence. In 1842 there were
four societies there. On the other hand, the movement in *Cleveland* did not prosper at this time. Altogether, Universalism has
been represented in at least 313 Ohio communities.

Orthodox opponents, perhaps with occasional justification
but certainly with much prejudice, misrepresented our movement.
Our people were called "backsliders" (rather than "come-outers")
from some "Christian" church. It was asserted that in the absence
of a fear of endless torment they had no incentive for right living
and that their belief in universal salvation "irrespective of moral
conduct" could only increase the population of hell. If a Universalist woman were found within an orthodox family, she might
draw some such description as this: "She was a thin-faced, Ro-
man-nosed loquacious Yankee, glib on the tongue. . . . I had
a hard race to keep up with her, though I found it a good school,
for it set me to reading my Bible."[3]

A unique figure was Jonathan Kidwell. Born in 1779 in
Kentucky, he became a Methodist preacher. Soon he discovered
that a study of the Bible brought him to Universalism. He began
preaching in Ohio about 1820, moving to Indiana in 1826. In a

circuit including sixteen counties he reports increasing his constituency from two hundred to two thousand, building churches
and recruiting assistants.

In 1833 Kidwell laid out the town of Philomath (near the
present Liberty, Indiana), which was to be a Universalist community. With the aid of others, Western Union Seminary was
established. It was ready for students in 1836, free of religious
instruction, concentrating on arts, sciences, gardening, mechanical branches, and needlework. Henry Houseworth was its principal. A magazine was issued, the *Philomath Encyclopedia and
Circle of the Sciences.* It contained articles on the Pentateuch,
other essays, and a serial novel.

Kidwell, unlike most Universalists of that day, rejected miracles
and was much more of a rationalist than his colleagues. This led
to an unfortunate controversy, and this in turn contributed to the
failure of the projects at Philomath. He was active in the General
Convention of the Western States. It met yearly from 1826 or
1827 (records are extant only through 1834). Sessions were held
in Ohio, except for one at Philomath. In 1841 it became the Ohio
Universalist Convention. For a few years there were rival Ohio
conventions, one supporting Kidwell—many called him Father
Kidwell—the other his chief opponent, Manford.

Brief sampling of other ministers who worked in Ohio for
shorter or longer periods will illustrate the varied backgrounds
of the clergy of those days. Thomas Dolloff moved from Freewill
Baptists to Universalism and from Maine to Cuyahoga County,
where he both preached and farmed. George Rogers, born in
London, moved from Episcopalianism through Methodism to
Philadelphia Universalism. His Cincinnati home was the center
for a wide circuit. M. A. Chappelle, son of a charter member of
the Belpre church, was educated largely through the church library. John A. Gurley came west in 1838 and edited the *Star in
the West* for several years. He served two terms as congressman
and later was appointed governor of Arizona. A. W. Bruere, a
Vermonter and a Chillicothe physician, was ordained in 1843.
William B. Linnell of England became a blacksmith in Wood-

stock; ordained, he served as chaplain in an Illinois regiment. Simon Peter Carlton, a native Ohioan, was a famous debater, with a record of forty-seven public debates, usually running from three to six days each. Josiah Upton, a Yale graduate, was pastor at Cincinnati and Dayton. Paul R. Kendall of Massachusetts was a Universalist educator, connected at one time or another with various schools: Western Liberal Institute, Clinton Liberal Institute, Smithson College, Lombard College, and others. J. C. Pitrat, a physician and editor of a revolutionary paper in France, forsook the Roman Catholics of Cincinnati for the Universalists. Robinson Bruere, a resident of southern Ohio, was a Wesleyan preacher from the Shetland Islands, with pastorates in Edinburgh and Manchester. In Halifax he had dedicated the first Universalist church in Canada. These pioneer awakeners in Ohio were of diverse birth, background, and talent. Western Universalism is depicted by Erasmus Manford in his *Twenty-five Years in the West*.[4]

Although many sermons were delivered against revival methods, there was some imitation of the orthodox.[5] There are tales of Universalist mass meetings which drew from one to three thousand people. At a service in Woodstock, Ohio, in 1844 the church was filled; the overflow congregation stood in the rain outside the open windows with umbrellas for protection. In general, early Universalism in the West was a propaganda rather than an organization. George Rogers described the situation in 1834, as he recalled it. The number of ministers devoting full time to religious work did not exceed half a dozen. There were but three church buildings in the West owned exclusively by Universalists, all in Ohio. Worse than lack of organization, in his judgment, was the reluctance to enter into any ecclesiastical order. Often the early itinerants denounced creeds, organizations, and a paid ministry. As in early New England days, many societies or preaching stations rarely had services more often than once a month. Continuity was sometimes maintained with lay services or Sunday schools. In rural areas under favorable conditions a minister might present himself twice a month. In some of the cities weekly services were possible.

Iowa may be taken as another example of denominational expansion. Here the situation was much the same as in Ohio. Universalists were among the early settlers. Among them their doctrine was first preached in 1837. Their early societies were small, sometimes with less than a dozen adherents. Money was scarce. Financing was difficult. Appeals were often made to friends in the East. Phineas T. Barnum and Horace Greeley responded by contributing to a building for Iowa City. Public debates attracted large audiences. In Springfield, Illinois, Lincoln once attended such a debate which continued for four days and evenings.

A minister early active in California was A. C. Edmunds, who published a journal and organized societies, associations, and a state convention. When he moved to Oregon, these projects languished. In 1849 came Alpheus Bull. A native of Bullville, New York, he preached in Ohio at Cincinnati and Dayton, and in Indiana at Lafayette. Then he rode or walked across Mexico to Mazatlan, took a ship to Monterey, and walked to San Francisco. In California he became a prosperous businessman and eventually a warm friend of Starr King.

The California Universalist Convention met at least once: at Benicia on June 16 and 17, 1860. Delegates were present from Sacramento and from the counties of Sonoma, Contra Costa, Solano, Alameda, Calaveras, and Tuolumne. Approval of the Winchester Profession was voted and a large committee was appointed to report on the state of the denomination. It was agreed to meet in Sacramento in September. Earlier, in 1853, and later, in 1873, efforts were made to establish a society in San Francisco. But these organizations were not permanent.[6]

Whatever the situation on the denominational frontier, back east the leaders of the movement in 1834 felt that they were off to a new start, provided as they were with a new constitution, a broadened vision associated with the expansion of their movement west of the Hudson, and a strengthening and maturing in its original habitat. The period began with a confident optimism, which in spite of occasional disappointments and disillusionments continued to energize their organized religious life. The years ahead brought to the whole nation unforeseen situations which the church had to face and to which it had to adjust.

THE GENERAL CONVENTION TAKES FORM[7]

The new spirit was manifest in the selection of meeting places for the General Convention. Previously these had been for the most part rural communities; now the trend was to the cities. The first four sessions in this new period were in large communities where the Convention had never met before: Albany, Hartford, New York City, and Philadelphia. Subsequently it met again in Hartford and Philadelphia, twice in Providence, twice in Portland, and four times each in Boston and New York City. In 1843 it ventured into Ohio at Akron; in 1857 into Illinois at Chicago. Other western meeting places included Rochester, Buffalo, Erie, Columbus, and Cincinnati.

In many of the Convention cities Universalists had buildings of their own, often accommodating sizable congregations. Some are mentioned specifically: in New York City, Orchard Street, Bleecker Street, Ely Street, and the buildings in Brooklyn and Williamsburgh; in Philadelphia, Lombard Street, Callowhill Street; in Boston, School Street. Sometimes public buildings were used for Convention sessions: the Hall of the House of Representatives in Hartford, the new City Hall, Portland; Eagle Hall, Concord, New Hampshire. For supplementary meetings or simultaneous preaching services offers were accepted from other churches for the use of their buildings: Unitarian, Baptist, Lutheran, Methodist, and German Evangelical are mentioned in the minutes.

The custom established earlier was continued whereby overnight accommodations and perhaps meals were provided by the host church for attendants from out of town. When this became burdensome, members of other denominations sometimes offered hospitality. Advance planning was difficult because secretaries of state conventions often neglected the request that they furnish certified lists of delegates. Actual numbers of delegates at business sessions, or of audiences at preaching sessions, are difficult to estimate. In the 1830's the number of official delegates was about 40 to 45, representing the six New England states, New York, and Pennsylvania. In 1838 and for a few years afterward South Carolina was represented. Virginia supplied delegates in 1840 and 1841. Gradually members from New Jersey, Ohio, Michigan, Illinois, Indiana, and Kentucky appeared. In 1838, when the meetings were "thronged," over 120 ministers were present, but usually their number was probably from 70 to 100. Eight hundred persons were once present for a communion service. But the effects of the Civil War are indicated by the notation in 1863 that twenty-five appointed delegates failed to appear.

Expansion of railroad systems facilitated travel, but not always with comfort. En route to the Buffalo convention the engine broke down at Attica, whereupon the engineer went to bed and refused to be seen. Sometime the next morning the railroad president happened along, bound for Albany, and hunted up another locomotive for the party.

Railroads began to cater to conventions by offering excursion rates, provided that a specified number of tickets were sold. A railroad agent would open an office during sessions, validating return tickets. It became the custom at each session to receive invitations for next year's meeting place. Hartford, New York, and Philadelphia offered hospitality for 1835. In 1858 there were five competing invitations. But the war changed this; in 1862, there were none.

Originally the chief attraction which drew people to a Convention was its role as a feast of sermons to be enjoyed. Even in 1841 there were fourteen sermons preached during three days. But the desire grew for greater emphasis upon practical purposes. Increasing demands for more time for consideration of denominational business led to a change in the character of the meetings. This new emphasis was definitely noticeable by 1859. The minutes frequently use such phrases as "perfect harmony," "no bitterness," and "no bickering" to describe the proceedings. But there were some differences of opinion. Delegates were once admonished that when business sessions and either preaching sessions or social gatherings were set for the same hour, they should attend to business. At another session they were forbidden to absent themselves from these deliberations.

The reference to social meetings is ambiguous, for *social* was sometimes used with a different connotation from ours. Elbridge Brooks described such a meeting in New Hampshire in 1837. "Went into the meeting house to attend the social meeting. And oh! what a glorious time we did have there! It was the happiest season of my life. Never before did I feel so much of heaven within me— never before, in all the meetings I have attended, did I ever feel so thrilled with joy and gladness. My soul was full of bliss. Remarks were made by brothers Whittemore and Thayer, Father Ballou, and Brothers Spear and Adams. Brothers Cilley and Thompson led in prayer. We sang—all sang and rejoiced, and wept for joy. It was a glorious, rapturous, gladsome season. Long may I remember it, and feel its influences."[8]

Whittemore, banker, businessman, and preacher, advocated and led such meetings. Accepting the accusation of "Methodism," he wrote, "Let us always have such enthusiasm. It is a prelibation of heaven, and foretaste of the glories of the eternal world. I was obliged at times to repress my feelings; I did not wish to set the example of being too highly transported."[9] Sawyer objected to such emotional displays, but Whittemore dreaded "frost more than fire." Every week since the days of Murray, he reported, such a "conference" had been held by the First Society of Boston. Others, he thought, should follow this example.

As projects increased in number and range, some convention hours came to be set aside for discussion of Sunday schools or missions or women's work. Reports from delegates in writing concerning their state conventions were repeatedly asked for, but even when obtained might be passed over under the pressure of other matters. Through it all optimism prevailed. Such expressions as "we were never so prosperous" were common. Yearly circular letters continued to report actions and to offer impressions about the sessions, but in less biblical language than formerly. They became less necessary as denominational papers entered the field and as the Convention began to issue printed reports of the minutes. In 1853 was recorded the first mention of secular newspapers, to which thanks were extended.

THE CONVENTION MANIFESTS CONCERN

One of the principal specialized interests was "missions," better described today as church extension. Several plans were proposed, among them a committee on supplying vacant pulpits, and a general itinerant ministry. In 1852 a resolution was adopted for the formation of a General Missionary Union with a responsible board of directors and with yearly membership dues of one dollar. The union was to appoint an agent, with ample salary and traveling expenses, who should awaken the missionary spirit, solicit funds, recommend appropriations, and supply pastorless churches. The committee appointed to execute this plan began their report in the following year by saying that they would "not willingly utter a word that should tend in the least degree to discourage persevering efforts." They then uttered two hundred such words or more, concluding that "the time is not yet," since there were not enough ministers to staff the existing churches, let alone new projects. Upon their recommendation it was voted to encourage missionary groups in the several state conventions. A few years later a committee on religious "tracts" was appointed. Eventually many pamphlets, usually containing a doctrinal Universalist sermon, were issued by various denominational bodies. Again in 1858 a Board of Missions was appointed, only to report a year later that it had held no meetings and done no business. It was therefore discharged.

Another concern during these years was the fostering of Sunday schools. A resolution of 1840 urged the formation of such schools and the organization of Bible classes for the young. Although these were to be found already in many Universalist churches, there was no provision for any denominational facility for the study of what is now known as religious education. Growing interest led to the appointment of a yearly committee on a Sunday School Union. This idea, still regarded as "inexpedient" in 1845, was revived in 1852, but without any immediate result. A stronger resolution in 1858 not only called attention to the need for Sunday schools staffed by competent instructors but also proposed a national meeting to which teachers would be asked to attend.

An even greater concern during this period was general education at college and secondary levels. Public high schools were then not available. In keeping with the rising social status of Universalist families and to protect their children from adverse criticism by narrowly orthodox teachers while providing them with a proper education, it seemed extremely important to Universalist leaders that the denomination sponsor its own institutions. From time to time the Convention passed recommendations affirming the importance of education, or when denominational schools had begun to function, commending them. An educational meeting in New York in May, 1846, made its influence felt two years later in a resolution asserting that human learning can improve the mind and character as well as promote the success of the Christian faith and of our denomination. After condemning the typical college for proselytizing, the importance of establishing our own colleges was reasserted. The same session which favored a General Missionary Union also proposed a General Educational Union. The custom developed of appointing each year a committee on education to report a year later. In 1864 each state convention was urged to establish a first-class academy within its borders.

The general temper of the times, plus an interplay of influences no longer clearly recognizable, led to a growing sophisticated dissatisfaction with sermons from an uneducated ministry. The type of minister successful under pioneer conditions and on the frontiers of the westward wave was found inadequate to meet demands upon settled pastors in the cities or even in the growing small towns. Warm feeling for the establishment of a theological school was expressed in 1835 and 1836. Yet there was determined opposition. Although some theological instruction was being offered ten years later at Clinton Liberal Institute, for which additional funds were then being solicited, realization of the goal came slowly. In 1855 establishment of a theological school was still being urged, this time more successfully.

To the session of 1858 Thomas J. Sawyer, referring both to general and theological education, reported, "We are beginning . . . to feel a just and lively interest in Education. We are coming to see, as we did not a few years ago, what an influence it exerts over our prosperity." Both our growth, he said, and our great mission were demanding increased devotion to it. "We hear on every side the call for an educated ministry." Our people, sharing the higher intellectual culture, were no longer satisfied with meager or ordinary attainments. Ten years before, he said, we had had only two struggling academies; now there were six, plus a theological school, a college, and a university. A similar note was sounded in 1859. Our established schools were praised as first-class. Each was reported to have funds of from ten to thirty thousand dollars, building, "cabinets, apparatus," able teachers, and large classes.

SOME THINGS ARE ACCOMPLISHED

Thus we see that not all energy was dissipated in resolutions. Thirty or more secondary schools were established by Universalists prior to 1863. Before the need for them was negated by the development of public high schools, three others were added in the period 1866 to 1873. Most of these early institutions were fostered by people in their own and neighboring communities. Due to unexpected building costs, general financial conditions in the nation, poor management, deaths of expected donors, and doubtless other causes, many of these schools were short-lived. Because of conflicting reports it is difficult to assess the amount of loyal Universalist support, or the lack of it. A few managed to survive. Westbrook Seminary in Portland became a junior college, as did

Dean Academy (1866) at Franklin, Massachusetts.[10] Illinois
Liberal Institute at Galesburg became Lombard College. Green
Mountain Institute, originally at South Woodstock, Vermont, is
now Goddard College.

Clinton Liberal Institute was the most immediately successful
venture. Plans were formulated and the first appeal for funds was
issued in April, 1831. With the endorsement of the New York
State Convention, and under the leadership of Stephen R. Smith,
sufficient funds were subscribed by November to warrant opening
the school at Clinton, New York. From the beginning it was under
the control of Universalists, and after May, 1845, specifically under
the New York State Convention. In 1879 the school was moved
to Fort Plain. In the early years several young men, including
many later active in the ministry in the Midwest, obtained their
education here.

Three colleges and two theological schools were launched
during the period covered by this chapter, but since most of the
development occurred in the following period, their story will be
postponed until Chapter Five.

Sawyer and Smith, already mentioned, were devoted leaders
in educational enterprises. Another was William S. Balch. But the
outstanding advocate and organizer was Hosea Ballou 2nd (1796–
1861),[11] grandson of Hosea Ballou's elder brother. A Universalist
from birth, he studied with his uncle, preached extensively in Massachusetts and Connecticut, and became pastor at Roxbury in
1821. Here he soon opened a private school and began a long and
successful career as writer and editor. The *Universalist Quarterly*
was largely his creation. For several years he was a member of the
Massachusetts Board of Education and of the Board of Over-
seers of Harvard University. Harvard conferred upon him the
degree of Master of Arts and Doctor of Divinity. He was the first
Universalist to receive the latter degree. (Thomas J. Sawyer was
the second.) On vacations he frequented the White Mountains,
encouraging his onetime pupil and lifelong friend Thomas Starr
King to write about them. His talents were not merely academic,
for he was active in denominational enterprises of all kinds. For

fifteen years he was the standing clerk of the General Convention, continuing long after that to be prod, counselor, and peacemaker. His biographer calls him "the scholar and critic of our denomination."

Sunday schools and Sunday-school associations rapidly increased in number during the pre-Civil War period. The custom of holding special church services once a year for the dedication of children, inaugurated by Murray about 1780, was revived in 1856 by Charles H. Leonard of Chelsea, who instituted Children's Sunday as a day of religious significance for the young. The Universalist Historical Society was formed in 1834. It soon had correspondents in twenty states, three provinces, England, Ireland, and Scotland. Of this event Thomas Whittemore wrote to Thomas Farrington King: "I have the strongest confidence, Brother King, that this society is the beginning of one of the most valuable institutions connected with our denomination." This society both reflected and stimulated the researches of Eddy, Whittemore, and others. It now maintains a valuable historical library at Tufts University.[12]

Meanwhile Universalists were continuing and developing the use of the printed word. In comparison with the 772 titles for the forty years ending in 1833, Eddy cites 990 for the period ending in 1864. As before, many refer only to brief pamphlets. Some works are by opponents who argued for endless punishment. There are 238 which seem to be of book length and to advocate Universalism. Among these are 19 reports of debates. About half of the remainder may be roughly classified as works on theology, both popular and scholarly, interpretations of Universalism, or collections of sermons or lectures or controversial exchanges of letters. But marking a change from earlier emphases, over 50 concern public or private worship. There are 18 hymnals for adults, 23 books for Sunday schools (catechisms, manuals, hymnals), and 11 books of comfort, meditations, liturgies, and manuals for ministers or laymen. The historical interest appears in 32 memoirs or biographies of deceased or elderly ministers, and 6 serious historical works. Aids to ministers were supplied by 11 books on the Bible, including several commentaries by Lucius R. Paige, an edition of the New Testament by Sylvanus Cobb, and the *Universalist Book of Reference* (1844) by E. E. Guild. The last, reproduced in several editions, discussed every biblical passage which supported Universalism, as well as every passage asserted by partialists to prove the contradictory view.

The published sermons of this period show a change in the organization of material. The older style of preaching made use of many biblical texts to prove God's loving nature, His plan for mankind, the saving work of Christ, and (with little attempt at specific details) the general character of life after death. The new style, not always sharply distinct from the old, was the sermon essay, with a text used as a point of departure. A notable and skillful employer of the new style was Edwin H. Chapin, who after pastorates in Richmond, Charlestown, and Boston, was for many years a popular orator-preacher in New York City. Several volumes of his sermons were published. Although some of their titles pointed to biblical discourses (*The Beatitudes, Evangelical Discourses*) and some bridged the gap between the old and the new (*Characters in the Bible Illustrating Characters at the Present Day*), others are modern (*Humanity in the City, Moral Aspects of City Life, Philosophy of Reform*). These were titles of collections. Some of the individual sermon topics were "The Dominion of Fashion," "The Circle of Amusement," "Humanity in the City," "Man and Machinery," "The Children of the Poor." Contrast in sermon topics and structure may be seen also by comparing those of Thomas Farrington King with those of his son, Thomas Starr King.

In addition to journals surviving from an earlier day, other periodicals, nearly a hundred of them, continued to appear. Some were mergers of previously existing magazines; some were new. Among them were new types. A more scholarly approach already had been developed in the *Expositor and Universalist Review* (Boston, 1833), owned by Whittemore and Ballou 2nd, which was a continuation of the earlier *Universalist Expositor,* sponsored by the two Ballous. In 1844 this was replaced by the *Universalist*

Quarterly and General Review, which continued to appear through 1891.[13] Its essays were often products of serious and able study, expressing the more thoughtful reactions of Universalists to then vital issues, such as biblical criticism and the theory of evolution. One notes, for example, the careful study by Thomas Starr King to show that Plato was something of a Universalist. Other journals endeavored to provide a magazine for the whole family or emphasized regional concerns or stressed church expansion or promoted reform movements. Now also appeared expressions of the growing interest in Sunday schools: the *Sabbath School Contributor* (Lynn, Boston, 1839), *Child's Gospel Guide* (Boston, 1847), the *Myrtle* (Boston, 1851), and the *Christian Teacher* (Boston, 1860). Of these the *Myrtle* survived into recent years; it was familiar to me in my youth. An important innovation was the *Universalist Register and Almanac* (Utica, 1836), containing yearly statistics of the denomination; it is an ancestor of our present *Unitarian Universalist Association Directory.* A purely literary journalism, and the opening of denominational activities to women, is illustrated by the *Rose of Sharon* (Boston, 1840–1857), an annual edited by Sarah Edgarton and later by Caroline Sawyer.

These and earlier publishing ventures had been undertaken by various individuals, both clerical and lay, or by organizations committed to the spreading of Universalism.[14] But a desire grew for a corporation under control of Universalists which would be able to inject wiser planning and more consistent continuity into editorial policy. In 1862 such a corporation was formed in Boston which will be referred to in Chapter Five.

New Problems Arise

While throughout the denomination rather satisfactory progress was being made in several lines of endeavor, by far the greater portion of General Convention time and energy was occupied with perennial problems of internal organization. In 1833, as we have noted, a new constitution had been adopted, supposedly to clarify procedures that had been troublesome. For about ten years it seems to have worked reasonably well. But with the increase of societies, associations, and state conventions, their several inter-relationships became increasingly perplexing. The system was with some pride labeled Republican. Looking back upon it seventy-five years later, Isaac M. Atwood described it as modeled upon the Presbyterian plan.

Sawyer could report in 1844 that now our system was complete. But, he added, it was largely a mere form. Determination of the respective powers of the several bodies was entirely lacking. The General Convention could not enforce its decisions; in fact, it had less power than any of the others—namely, none at all. It was limited to offering advice. In 1834, he went on, we feared vested ecclesiastical powers. But now powers should be granted.

In the West there was vigorous opposition to this reorganization, leading to regional feuds. In Indiana Kidwell and Manford became bitter opponents. Kidwell's motion at the Indiana Convention that "we do not surrender the right to legislate for ourselves, but reserve to ourselves the right of making our own laws and regulations" was "thrown under the table." But his position was sustained at the 1841 session of the Miami Association, which voted that "the Universalists of Indiana are of age and consider themselves capable of self-government, and therefore cannot submit to any dictation or control, either on the part of our brethren in the east or elsewhere, and that our delegates to the United States Convention be so instructed."[15]

Such regionalism continued, but in a less factional spirit. In 1855 it was proposed to form a new western convention to include Indiana, Michigan, Wisconsin, and Iowa. The plan was not adopted, but ten years later, out of dissatisfaction with the inactivity of the General Convention, a Northwestern Conference was set up, largely to promote Lombard College.

Frequent complaints were directed at state conventions for failures to submit statistical reports, to supply accurate lists of ministers in fellowship, or to accept advice. Occasionally there was a word of commendation, as in 1859, when the Massachusetts

Convention was cited for having been legally incorporated, thus becoming eligible to receive and hold funds. Its action was held up as an example to other bodies and to the General Convention itself. When the Confederate States had seceded from the Union, questions were asked by New Jersey Universalists. May a local society or church withdraw from one association to join another? Yes, said the Convention. Somewhat earlier, when the problem of finances was arousing discussion, it had been recommended that each society voluntarily offer 3 or 4 per cent of its income to its association, which should then "equitably" divide these monies between its state convention and the General Convention. It was understood that time would be required to establish this custom; presumably little immediate support was obtained. Also discussed was the suggestion that a better representation would be secured if a part of the delegate's expenses were to be paid by his society.

At the session of 1841 there was a call for reorganization which would give the General Convention real authority. Such a plan, upon the urging of Sawyer, was adopted in 1844. It seems to have had small effect, since in 1853 there was another committee to revise the constitution, whose proposals were adopted two years later. This made the General Convention, at least on paper, a court of general appeal, with power to adopt rules of fellowship and discipline. Yet dissatisfaction continued. Still other changes were approved and gradually ratified by the requisite number of state conventions.[16]

Closely related to the irritating matter of relationships with the state conventions was the task of enacting and enforcing rules for the fellowship and discipline of ministers, undertaken during a period of increasing emphasis upon an educated leadership. At first there were makeshift proposals. Ministerial candidates, it was asserted in 1834, should qualify themselves in gospel doctrine and in the duties of their profession. State conventions were advised not to ordain a man until he had been in active fellowship for a year, unless such action was requested by his society and then only after an examination by a council. The General Convention tried to persuade the state conventions to adopt specific rules for ordination and discipline. These precautions were proposed after some instances of ministers who had reportedly neglected their duties or even brought reproach upon their calling. So far as the minutes of the Convention deal with this problem, they say little about specific cases.

When the state conventions failed to heed advice, the General Convention began to look to its own need for rules and to seek some method of dealing fairly with men under accusation, other than by public charges and hearings. The session of 1843 adopted a set of such rules, which had been proposed a year earlier. The next step was gradually to work out and propose a similar plan for adoption by state conventions. A plan proposed in 1863 failed to receive enough ratifications.

APPLYING UNIVERSALISM TO NATIONAL PROBLEMS

Post-Revolutionary social and political changes, described in Chapter Three, continued in various forms during the years now being discussed. Although western life was often drab, in the eastern cities conditions were quite otherwise. These were the times of the telegraph, better heating and lighting, better kitchen and dining utensils, carpets, varied home architecture, occasional bathrooms, water systems. Attention was being turned to attractiveness in church architecture. New professions were beginning to open: writing, lecturing, science, journalism. Universalist Horace Greeley founded the *New York Tribune*. Universalist Phineas Barnum opened his first museum and promoted a tour by Jenny Lind. More and more people read, danced the polka, played cards. Masculine dominance of church life was gradually challenged by female activity. Such changes brought new variations in political and social problems, from which no ethical religious body could turn away.

It is not surprising that in addition to strictly denominational matters, the Convention discussed and sometimes expressed opinions on public issues. Resolutions of this type were an early form of social action. It was recognized in 1835 that although the General

Convention and the churches of which it was ultimately composed
were ecclesiastical bodies, the Convention might properly advise
the denomination on a subject affecting public morals and that it
should "labor assiduously for a more thorough development of the
moral power of our denomination." Eleven years later these principles were reaffirmed by supporting the propriety of ministerial
advocacy of liberty, peace, temperance, and all the moral and
religious interests of man. The session of 1856 proclaimed that
all institutions which opposed the advance of a divine order should
be examined, exposed, and condemned, and that ministers should
receive cooperative sympathy as they exercised their essential
freedom. Economic conditions moved Sawyer to state in his 1858
report that "the sharp-sighted wisdom of the keenest and shrewdest
devotees of Mammon was turned to naught, and many an airbuilt
castle tottered to its fall."

Interest in reform, in "practical Christianity," broadened in
scope and spread among the grass roots. Through the influence of
the Massachusetts State Convention in 1846 a Universalist General Reform Association was organized.[17] Its first meeting was held
at Boston in May, 1847, concluding with an eight-o'clock breakfast
attended by two hundred persons. The purpose was to unite in
one organization the several protests against slavery, war, intemperance, capital punishment, and neglect of the poor. It collected
information on the progress of Christianity and the best methods
of promoting and applying it. It urged Universalists to assume
their proper place in society by actions demonstrating the implications of their religious sentiments. It countered opposition,
initiated projects, and gave courage to clergy and laity. Many
churches had local reform clubs, presenting lectures and debates
and engaging in local reform movements.

The association held sessions in various cities, but the May
Breakfast or Festival in Boston, sometimes in Faneuil Hall, was
an annual affair until 1859. It was the custom of many denominations to hold "anniversary week" meetings in Boston at that season.
Opposition to the Fugitive Slave Law was the dominant theme
in the year that Colonel Suttle of Virginia, protected by martial law

and by military forces with guns loaded and bayonets fixed, was present in Boston to reclaim his Negro slave.

The *Christian Freeman* (1839–1862) and other periodicals were anti-slavery and featured articles on Lowell mill workers. There was much opposition to the war with Mexico. Such concerns, always implicit in Universalist preaching, moved Emerson Hugh Lalone later to assert in his *And Thy Neighbor as Thyself* that early Universalism was "an ethical movement and a revolt against spiritual oligarchy." Its gospel led out into the affairs of the world.

Probably the most frequently discussed and resolved-about problem was drinking and the advocacy of temperance. It was noted in 1835 that temperance, long approved by Universalists, ought to be promoted by our state conventions. Sometimes the opinions expressed were vaguely general, but in 1842 it was voted that it was not proper for any person engaged in manufacturing, vending, or using intoxicating liquors to represent the religious interests of our denomination. Objections to this statement, raised the following year by delegates from Pennsylvania, led to substituting a resolution expressing sympathy with the cause of total abstinence but disapproval of any test of fellowship or of seating delegates other than that founded on Christian faith and character. In the 1850's prohibition as defined in the "Maine Law" was approved. Indeed, at one time prohibition was declared sanctified by divine authority as truly as the condemnation of any other sin. Thus it is evident that there was no universal and abiding agreement on the details of the crusade against alcohol.

Opposition to capital punishment was another subject on which opinion was strong. The question was obviously related to beliefs about God's punishments, which Universalists regarded as remedial. The Convention of 1835, mentioned in connection with several of the above topics, was confronted with a resolution declaring that capital punishment was contrary to the spirit of the gospel. Society might punish an offender for his own good, it claimed, but not by death, for there is possibility of injustice through human fallibility or false testimony. Moreover, to execute a man devalued respect for life, violated the social compact, and failed to restrain. After "protracted debate," this resolution was tabled, but genuine concern had been aroused. The next session voted that "capital punishment is a relic of a barbarous age and decidely anti-Christian; it engenders a spirit of cruelty and is highly dangerous, and that therefore, although we deem an interference with the legislatures of our states . . . by ecclesiastical bodies improper, yet we recommend to Universalists throughout the United States to use their exertions for its abolition, by the adoption of such measures as in their deliberate judgment may appear proper for forming and directing public opinion on this subject."

As the Civil War loomed, concern for our Indian population was rising. Work being done for the Rhode Island remnant of Indians was noted with approval, with the hope that a national convention might be called to stimulate action by the federal government. On the other hand, there soon followed news of distress among the white population of Minnesota resulting from Indian raids.

The developing conflict between the North and the South gave rise to conflicting opinions. At one time in Massachusetts, for example, it was felt that consideration of the subject would "peril the peace and prosperity of the denomination." But in 1843 a resolution of the General Convention, passed with one dissenting vote, asserted that slavery of members of the African race was contrary to the gospel and "pernicious alike to the enslaved and the enslaver." Sympathy and affection for the oppressed was voiced, along with the duty to labor for restoration of the rights of freedom. "While we regard the holding in bondage of our brethren for whom Christ died, or the treatment of any human being with obloquy, harshness, or any indignity on account of his color or race, as contrary to righteousness, inconsistent with Christianity, and especially with the doctrine of Universal Grace and Love which we cherish as the most important revealed truth, we are well aware that many worthy and upright Christians have sustained the relation of slave-holder in ignorance of its true character, or from inability to relieve themselves therefrom, and

while we earnestly entreat all Christian and especially all Universalist slave-owners to consider prayerfully the nature and tendencies of the relation they sustain, we recognize or countenance
no measure of indiscriminate denunciation or proscription, but,
appealing to the gospel, to humanity, and to their own consciences,
we await in implicit confidence the perfect working of the principles of Divine and Universal Love."

At the session of 1845 in Boston, with two hundred ministers
present, there was authorized the preparation of "a solemn, earnest,
and plain Protest Against American Slavery." This was submitted
to every Universalist clergyman in the United States for his
signature, with the request for an explanation if he did not sign.
The protest was signed by 304 ministers. Some forty reasons for
not signing, both provocative and superficial, were supplied by
the non-signers.[18]

In 1854 disapproval was voiced at congressional repeal of the
Missouri Compromise. As the political crises intensified, slavery
was frequently attacked by resolution. In 1861 came the denunciation of the "atrocious rebellion against government constitutionally
chosen." Sympathy was proclaimed for our rulers, our country-
men in arms, our ministers in camps. The Convention pledged
means and prayers for the success of federal arms and for an
honorable peace. The same session heard an address advocating
deportation of Negroes and their colonization in Africa, whereupon approval was voted. A subsequent proposal for approval
of arming the Negroes was tabled. A proposed resolution declared that the war was a "national infidelity to republican principles" and offered "our hearty support" to the President. After
nine speeches for and seven against (arguments not recorded),
all in "a spirit of great kindness," it was rewritten and a copy
sent to the President.

As the end of the war approached, a long resolution on the
state of the nation declared that the conflict had been a punishment
for arrogance and oppression, that fraternal chains must be riveted
anew, that although bloodshed was to be deplored, yet an unsettled
end would be dastardly, that praise was due not only to Grant,

Sherman, Farragut, Stringham, and Pater but also to the common soldier and sailor. Occasionally resolutions were offered on the morality of war in general, but after consideration these were often tabled.

During the years other topics had been considered: juvenile delinquency and exposure, enlargement of the sphere of employment for women, prison discipline, poverty, and education.

These were some of the details of the growth of the movement prior to the end of the Civil War. There was geographical expansion, a steady shift from itinerancy to settled pastorates, increased stability of organizational life in churches, associations, and conventions. Leaders and constituents were rising in standards of living and of education. Clergymen were beginning to play down theological debates and to seek techniques for promoting an ethical religious life. Universalists were becoming "respectable." Universalism was learning to direct its energies to social reform. All this was rudely interrupted by the war. Yet the Convention had sufficient vitality to continue its sessions during those years of armed conflict, holding itself ready for its era of reconstruction after violent hostilities had ceased.

CHAPTER 5

Reconstruction Develops a National Church (1865-1925)

This period begins with a date supplied by our nation's history. It ends arbitrarily in 1925. The years covered are from the end of the Civil War to a point between the two world wars. Or, personally, approximately from my parents' birth to my leaving the active parish ministry. The White House was occupied by a line of presidents from Lincoln to Coolidge. My parents grew up in a rural area using candles and kerosene; I, in cities with gas and then electric lighting. Together we used to dash to the front of the house every time the first automobile in Portland chugged up our little hill. By 1925 I hardly bothered to look at even a passing plane. My parents commonly walked or used railroads, streetcars, or horse and buggy. I had acquired a Model T.

During this period the General Convention might choose any city east of the Mississippi for its sessions. In 1915 it traveled to Los Angeles in two special trains, with a few hours of sightseeing in Salt Lake City, a reception at the Riverside church, and post-convention ceremonies at the San Francisco World's Fair. During this period occurred the Spanish-American War and World War I. New veterans' organizations replaced the Grand Army of the Republic. Families moved to the cities to participate in the spectacular developments of the industrial revolution, paying little heed to labor disputes with violence on both sides, to business conducted with little regard for ethics, and to corruption in government. Nevertheless, churches were increasingly involved in a growing moral reaction against these conditions and in the beginnings of a reconstruction of society. In these years the educational goal of the common youth rose from the hope to complete grade school to the hope to go to college. In these years the old-line "respect-able" denominations mellowed. Polite religious toleration replaced the old rough and ready challenge and counter challenge.[1]

At the close of the Civil War, denominations, like the nation, found themselves torn asunder and faced with the necessity of a new start. Methodists, Baptists, and Presbyterians had been split by the regional conflict. As for Universalists, their southern churches were like the lost tribes of the house of Israel. Three per cent or less of their societies had been in Confederate territory, and now contact with them for several years had been broken. In 1790 some Maryland Universalists had been slaveowners; how many there were in 1860 is not determined. Northern societies could hardly have done otherwise than to regard themselves as having been on the right side, proud that in 1843 over three hundred of their ministers had signed a protest against slavery, proud of the war record of their ministers as chaplains and officers and soldiers, proud of their laymen who had served in the armed forces and of their women who had acted as nurses.[2]

In the Convention session of 1865 the state of the nation was discussed. Warmly expressed was gratitude to God for the end of civil strife and the realization of a special duty to minister to the needs of the South. The best they could do for southern churches was to vaguely affirm something about these societies' being points of identity between the flag and the cross. Speakers found it pos-sible to understand why God had won the war for them but not why He had permitted Lincoln to be killed. Lincoln's compas-sionate nature endeared him to Universalists. Although he joined no church, there is evidence that he was influenced by, and believed in, the promise of universal salvation. His words and his actions imply a faith in a forgiving God rather than in the God of Jona-than Edwards.[3]

Reconstruction in the denomination, little of it well planned in advance, took various forms: reconstruction in internal organiza-tion, in plans for extension, and in thought and outlook. Worship, work, and instruction were all up for discussion. Much remained conventional and rurally based.[4] It is appropriate to call this a period of reconstruction, however, even though the denomination has been undergoing reconstruction throughout its history.

Notwithstanding chronic reports of ministerial shortages and financial adversities, the general mood, if one may judge from the records, was one of growing strength and prosperity and success, with optimistic glances toward the future. Our task, it was said in 1867, was to restore the Christian church to its original purity and to supply the present spiritual needs of the world. Or in other language, as Lalone later interpreted the situation, the emphasis was on moral training leading to moral practice.[5] In 1917, after another war, it was asserted that "after the guns are stacked, if the philosophy of Universalism shall not prevail, there shall be no permanent peace." To carry on the spiritual enterprise which Jesus had begun twenty centuries before and to promote Christian unity through community of ideals and Christian culture was the high goal.

RECONSTRUCTION IN ORGANIZATION

The General Convention soon resumed its habitual interest in rewriting its constitution. Plans of 1844 and earlier had been adopted and repudiated; the plan of 1863 failed to receive approval from state conventions. Amendments of 1864 were ratified, however. The Convention was incorporated in 1866, with revisions in the charter in 1881. But the tinkering continued. Minor alterations were proposed to secure a uniform system of denominational organization. The constitution of 1870, employing the name Universalist General Convention, was properly ratified. Even though amendments were later adopted, a revision was proposed in 1880. But at this point agitation for changes became less frequent. Beginning again about 1907, amendments, simplifications, or complete revisions were under discussion, but not always voted. In 1921–1923 a new constitution was adopted. Accompanying these changes were related modifications in rules for ministerial fellowship.[6]

Rights, privileges, and duties of delegates were often consid-

ered. How many should be selected from each state? Who should
be delegates *ex officio?* Should state conventions pay delegates'
expenses? Among prominent persons received as delegates were
many successful businessmen: Greeley the journalist,[7] Augusta
Chapin the lecturer, and A. G. Throop of Chicago and Pasadena.
Gradually the base was widened from which delegates were received: West Virginia, Maryland, Georgia (1872), Oregon
(1876), Dakotah [*sic*] (1879), Ontario (1881). The basis of
representation was changed from state conventions to churches.

Quite early excursions were introduced. At Minneapolis delegates visited the University of Minnesota. In 1866 two hundred
attendants were guests of the Chicago, Burlington, and Quincy
Railroad for a trip from Galesburg to Burlington and return.
Some railroads issued passes to selected clergymen. There were
usually special rates for travel to the annual meetings. But in
1925 it was noted that increasing use of automobiles, by dim-
inishing rail travel, was working against this arrangement.

Various plans were adopted to select and pay a full-time executive officer who should carry out Convention plans and act
as traveling missionary and trouble shooter. Lack of adequate
financing, general unwillingness by societies to accept such national leadership, and frequent shifts in Convention policy interfered with continuity and with constructive advance. To the
first appeal for support for a general agent, only 67 societies
out of 440 responded, and they with only $579. Societies were
more ready to appeal for aid than to give it. Nevertheless, plans
went ahead to appoint an agent of the board who should super-
vise denominational work, perfect the organization, visit state
conventions and societies, consider appeals, nominate regional
sub-agents, and plan preaching circuits. By a special committee
of one from each state this proposal was approved. E. G. Brooks
became the first general agent on October 1, 1867, at a salary
of $3,200 (increased to $3,600) and expenses. He was also
standing clerk. Previously the only official of the Convention with
duties between the annual sessions had been the standing clerk.
During the years 1811 through 1823 this position had been held

for short terms by Samuel S. Loveland, Hosea Ballou, Jacob Wood, and Richard Carrique. In 1824 Hosea Ballou 2nd took over for a term of fifteen years. He was followed by John M. Austin for a twenty-year period. Richard Eddy had an eight-year term.

In his report for 1868 Brooks reported on his travels, correspondence, and addresses. He had appointed several state agents, but there was no activity in Virginia or west of the Rocky Mountains. Unfortunately his term of services was cut short by illness and resignation.[8] His successor, James M. Pullman, could spare so little time for the office that it was practically vacant and so continued for several years.

In 1883 the Convention voted to appoint two agents, one each for West and East. But the board, having no success in finding even one agent, did not try to appoint two, especially since there were already several state agents appointed by state conventions. Such actual or potential agents were coming to be called missionaries or mission secretaries. Finally, twelve years later Quillen H. Shinn was appointed general missionary, beginning a period of vigorous, somewhat free-lance service, largely concentrated in the South, that ended with his death in 1907.[9]

In 1898 the board revived the original idea of a general agent with the title of General Superintendent of the Universalist Church, with the assignment to encourage, revive, and extend centers of Universalist activity and to promote unity and continuity. Isaac M. Atwood was choosen for the position.[10] During the period in which there had been no general agent some functions had again devolved upon the standing clerk, in the person of G. L. Demerest. There are references to Demerest's visiting state conventions. Atwood's personality and his efficient activity and extensive traveling, combined with the increase in the number of state superintendents, led to better cooperation and eventually to a National Council of Superintendents. In fact, Atwood was so successful that some even wished to call him bishop. (He looked the part.) But the idea was rejected.

In 1903 the Convention voted to add a field secretary, who was to try to augment funds at the rate of twenty-five thousand dollars a year, but the board combined this position with that of general superintendent. The conviction grew that the superintendency policy was "paying off." With readjustments in duties, Atwood became part-time superintendent and part-time secretary, and C. Ellwood Nash became field agent. In 1907 Nash had gone to California, and William H. McLaughlin became general superintendent, with Atwood still secretary.

Meanwhile the office of Moderator or President took on an enlarged character. From 1794 to the 1850's it was usually filled by clergymen. From then on prominent laymen were often chosen. About 1917 more responsibility was placed upon the president for guidance between sessions.

The general impression one receives is that this was a time of overcoming friction between the General Convention and state conventions. The superintendency system undoubtedly eased the situation. At the national level the system also gave a continuity to the movement which earlier it had lacked. Increased financial support through drives for special funds enabled new projects to be undertaken. The permanent fund for the benefit of retired ministers grew from about $8,000 to about $866,000.

After 1889 the Convention sessions were held biennially instead of annually. (This had been suggested in 1874.) In the alternate years during the 1890's one or more conferences each year were held in various cities: Portland, Lowell, Roxbury, Syracuse, Rochester, Buffalo, Akron, Chicago, Oak Park, New York, Baltimore, Chattanooga, and Atlanta. In these conferences purely denominational topics were increasingly outnumbered by discussions of general problems. Here are a few of them: Ideals, Agnosticism, Socialism and Anarchy, Evolution, Biblical Criticism, The Study of History, Crimes and Criminals, Organized Charity, Ethical Factors in Social Unrest, The Institutional Church, and The Church and the Laboring Man.

CONVENTION FINANCES

One of the many concerns during the entire period was to secure financial support for running expenses of the Convention and for permanent funds. For this purpose state conventions and associations were often bypassed and the appeal was made directly to the societies and to individuals. Societies were assessed, but it was always difficult to predict how much of the amount requested, if any, would be paid. Assessments, or as they were sometimes called, quotas, were levied at different times by different methods: 10 per cent of the minister's salary, 2 per cent of the yearly expenses, a "fair share" of $15,000, 2 per cent plus $1 per member, an every-member canvass. Pledges from individuals were sometimes asked for at convention sessions. Sometimes the goal was, say, twenty pledges of one thousand dollars each. Bequests in wills were suggested. For the less well-off there were family missionary boxes, and later pledges of a cent a day. At first response was halting, but they soon improved. Yet there was always a problem in collecting. Individuals did better than societies, it was once reported, in meeting their pledges.

Intensive drives for funds were facilitated under special names: the Gunn Fund for the benefit of retired clergymen, the Murray Fund, the Twentieth Century Fund, the Million Dollar Drive, etcetera. Beginning in the 1870's a simple three-way budget was employed, appropriating specific sums for missions, for scholarships, and for executive and office expense. More recently a detailed budget plan was developed.

SUBORDINATE NATIONAL ORGANIZATIONS

Concerns of the denomination were gradually differentiated by the formation of organizations of national scope, yet regarded as subordinate to the Convention itself. The Historical Society, organized in 1834, has already been noted. In the 1880's and 1890's its importance was recognized by setting aside a time for its program at the annual meeting and by taking a collection for its benefit.

Next to be formed was the Universalist Publishing House, incorporated in Boston in 1862, which immediately went into business by purchasing a journal, *Trumpet and Freeman*, and a bookstore. Other properties were soon added. Until merger with the Unitarians it published many Universalist books and issued the denominational journal. It served and cooperated with the Convention. Occasional minor misunderstandings were met by steps towards a more organic relationship.[11]

Next in chronological order was a women's movement. Women delegates began to present themselves at the Convention, whereupon it was voted that they were welcome as delegates and that they should not be excluded from serving as officers or committee members. Although subsequently several women became ministers and although women served as delegates and trustees and on committees, I find no record of a woman holding one of the chief offices or preaching the occasional sermon, except that Esther Richardson was secretary from 1943 to 1961.

A women's organization first appeared in 1868 as a state movement in Illinois, with the prime purpose of providing a building for Lombard College. Soon it expanded into the national Women's Centenary Aid Association. The claim has been made that this was the first national organization for women in the United States. It was originally set up for the sole purpose of raising $35,000 out of a total centenary fund (1870) of $200,000. In welcoming the new ally the Convention was careful to emphasize that it was a subordinate organization, from which annual reports were to be received.

Their assignment having been successfully accomplished, the association met in 1871 to wind up its affairs. Instead it was decided to continue in order to promote the interests of the denomination, but to spend under its own direction any money raised. In spite of some initial male objection the work prospered. As with the Historical Society, time was set aside at Convention sessions for its business and program.[12]

In 1905 a new name was adopted, the Women's National Missionary Society of the Universalist Church. Subsequently this was simplified to the Association of Universalist Women. Financial support has been given to many projects: to individual churches, to workers in western and southern mission fields, to the Japan Mission, to professorships and other aid at colleges, to Murray Grove, to a church building loan fund, and to interdenominational projects. Like the Convention, the Association has been active in social action and welfare, and in the promotion of study groups in churches and summer institutes. The Clara Barton birthplace was purchased and maintained as a historic shrine. Here remedial camps for children are operated.[13]

In 1884, acting on the information that there were already several young people's societies operating in our churches, the Convention announced a campaign to set up a Young People's Missionary Association in every church. Twenty-three were functioning a year later. In 1887 the youth society at our church in Rochester, New York, was admitted into the interdenominational Young People's Society of Christian Endeavor. Challenged three years later, it was retained.[14] There were similar member societies at Victor, Troy and elsewhere. But apparently the Christian Endeavor approach was too orthodox for our youth, for a Young People's Christian Union was formed at the Bay City, Michigan, church. Soon a national denominational group emerged: the Young People's Christian Union (YPCU) of the Universalist Church. There were those who urged that the new organization, like the women's group, should meet at the same time as the autumn sessions of the Convention, a time most inconvenient for students. The early summer was therefore chosen. The first session was held at Lynn in 1889 with 140 delegates from fifty societies.[15] From its inception this organization promoted church extension, supporting churches in Harriman, Little Rock, and elsewhere.

Neither in its local, state, or national groups was the YPCU strictly a youth organization. That is, although it included youths of high-school and college ages, and even children as members of a junior YPCU, there was no upper age limit. National officers were often young persons, but nevertheless mature. Many of those who regularly attended and spoke at the YPCU in Rochester in my own high-school days were men and women in late middle life. Members of my own age were few, yet I do not recall that objection was ever raised to this arrangement. Its national organization, however, expressed something of a mild revolt by young adults against their elders.

As early as 1840 a general Sunday-school association was recommended. But it was not until 1913 that such an organization was formed. Meanwhile, as will be noted below, there were many Sunday-school unions comprising the schools of several neighboring churches.

Last of all to appear were men's organizations, relatively short-lived and under various names. In 1907 it was the Laymen's League, in 1915 the Order of Universal Brotherhood, in 1917 the Loyalty Fellowship, in 1921 the Order of Universalist Comrades. Usually chapters were formed in local churches. Somewhat later when Harold Latham was president he created the National Association of Universalist Men. Like the women's organizations these all sought to promote devotion and gifts to the cause.

THE MINISTRY

Objections to giving financial aid to theological students were silenced in 1866, when such aid was voted. There was some initial discussion of selectivity, on the basis of need or circumstances, but it was decided to leave this matter to the schools themselves, which were then requested to furnish to a committee regular reports on the progress of individual students. In 1880, however, it was voted to give no aid to users of tobacco. This rule was still being enforced in my student days. It was thought by many students to be paternalistic and unfair. At that very time some ministers were advising young ministers to smoke, as a means of establishing rapport with the men of the church.

A system of lending $180 each year to students was followed for thirty-one years. During this total period $210,000 was lent, of which $86,000 was repaid. Many who did not pay were financially unable to do so. In 1898 this plan was discontinued in favor of gift scholarships of $125 a year. During my three years of preparation for the ministry I received scholarships totaling $375 from the Convention, even though half of this time was spent at a non-Universalist school, Union Theological Seminary. In addition I received a $50 scholarship from Tufts College and $160 from Union.

As the country became settled, as means of travel and communication improved, and as the denomination settled down under a systematized plan, accusations and charges against ministers diminished—at least in the Convention minutes. Securing an adequate supply of educated clergymen became the great concern. In 1880, although never again, it was claimed that we had an oversupply—620 ministers available for 488 churches. Pastorates were brief, most commonly for only one year. The mean duration was two years and four months. The average age at death of our ministers in 1881 was sixty-six. Very soon the conviction grew that something had to be done to recruit replacements. An address by Charles Conklin on "The Attractions of the Ministry" (1886) led to the appointment of a committee, more or less continuing, on ministerial increase. At first it was believed that its activity was producing desired results, but by 1910 there were laments about an "ebb tide" and withdrawals of men to other denominations. Speculation as to whether this was due to the salary situation, to advancing age, or to personal discouragement gave no certain answer. In 1917 a new principle of dual fellowship permitted the granting of Universalist fellowship to a minister of any denomination which would agree to take reciprocal action.

GENERAL AND THEOLOGICAL EDUCATION

At the close of the Civil War, Universalists were optimistic about their educational projects. Even while the war was being fought they had obtained gifts to endow their colleges. It was regarded as our duty to do our share of the Christian education of the Republic by sustaining institutions of sound learning. In addition to schools founded prior to the war three academies were established after its close: Dean Academy at Franklin, Massachusetts, organized earlier but opened in 1866; Jefferson Liberal Institute at Jefferson, Wisconsin (1868); and Mitchell Seminary at Mitchelville, Iowa (1873). Jefferson and Mitchell became high schools and Dean a junior college.

Usually at Convention sessions during the sixties and seventies reports were presented outlining the condition of each school, including the colleges described below. In comparison with registrations of today these courageous efforts seem puny. The total enrollment of a dozen or more schools was once estimated at about 1,450. The conviction was widely held that somehow, without stressing theological doctrines, these schools would be able to manifest a distinctive character, radiating the Universalist attitude.

As to colleges, Universalists have had six successes and two failures. Of the successes, Goddard has attained college status so recently that for historical purposes it may be classified as an academy, to be omitted here. Four of the others, successfully established by Universalist promoton, aid, persistence, and sacrifice, are each memorialized in printed form. *Light on the Hill* (1966), by Russell E. Miller, tells the story of Tufts. *Candle in the Wilderness* (1957), edited by Louis H. Pink and Rutherford E. Delmage, deals with St. Lawrence. *Fifty Years of Buchtel* (1922), edited by A. I. Spanton, directs our attention to what is now the University of Akron. "A History of Lombard College" (1955), by James A. Swanson, is apparently a mimeographed student thesis, Western Illinois State College. Also, "Annals of

Lombard College" appears on pp. 452 f. of *Knox Directory,
1837-1963* (Knox College, 1963). All give credit to Universalism
for origin and support.[16] The history of the California Institute of
Technology has not yet been written.

The best of these accounts is Miller's, since there is but a
single author and he is a historian. Lalone's chapter in *Candle,*
dealing with the theological school, is relevant to the Universalist
tale. Spanton's own chapters in *Buchtel* are of special interest,
since he was a graduate of Buchtel in 1899 and joined its faculty
in 1905. He was thus personally acquainted with many of those
who were identified with the early days of his institution. Swanson's study includes bits of information on Universalism in Illinois.

It is universally acknowledged that not only the establishment
of the colleges but also their nurture to maturity were due
chiefly to Universalist support. This often took the form of
money gifts, frequently in sums of less than a hundred dollars.
Few indeed were those who could give ten times that amount.
Other supporters who should be remembered are the promoters,
usually clergymen. They were the men who kept the projects
alive, who even prior to railroads traveled widely, who spoke and
wrote on the importance of liberal colleges, who solicited funds,
who lent a hand in unexpected emergencies. And there were the
small bands of faculty members, who taught long hours without
adequate, or even any, library or text books or the rudimentary
science equipment of that day. Sometimes they taught for a time
in buildings which had neither heat nor light. When college income was low, they accepted cuts in salary. Such conditions
would be intolerable to American teachers today, but they were
then accepted as a part of the Universalist contribution to higher
learning.

The goal was visualized as a choice: college or theological
school. Some advocated the one, some the other, some both. The
chief obstacle was lack of capital. The chief motivation for a
college was to make available to Universalists an opportunity to
send their youth to an institution free from orthodox theology

and ecclesiasticism. The chief motive for a theological school was to provide for the growing denomination a ministry adequately educated to meet increasingly sophisticated demands. Already John G. Adams was lecturing on Universalism in Literature. But recognition of the need for such training emerged slowly. The opposition was led by no other than self-made but venerable Hosea Ballou himself. He and others, unappreciative of advancing biblical scholarship and insensitive to the extent of cultural changes, held that no capable, convinced, and consecrated man needed other preparation than careful study of the Bible and Christian history under a brief apprenticeship to a knowledgeable preacher.

But the promoters, seeing the situation more clearly, set about convincing others. In 1819 some had hoped that Nichols Academy might train ministers. Later Sawyer at Clinton Liberal Institute, although independently of it, attempted to offer private instruction. Persuaded by him and others, the Convention (1826) set up modest requirements for ministerial status, these to be enforced by a committee. Gradually the Convention gave more respectful attention to arguments for a school, referring the disputed question in 1835 to state conventions and associations for their advice. Four choices were available: continue the apprentice system, already a burden to the more popular teachers; send students to orthodox theological schools; add a professor of theology to some existing school; establish a new school. There was no general enthusiasm for any plan except the last.

In 1839 and 1840 the Massachusetts Convention was ready to sponsor a theological school in that state and to elect trustees representative of both New England and New York for what was to be known as the Walnut Hill Evangelical Seminary. Walnut Hill was the name of a bit of high land on which Tufts College was later located. But a campaign for funds was unsuccessful. Five years later the General Convention voted to support Thomas J. Sawyer's plan to make Clinton Liberal Institute a college and to endow an adjacent but separate theological school. But this dream also evaporated.

Meanwhile there had been sufficient interest to encourage
Sawyer to call an educational convention in New York City for
May, 1847. Its proposals, soon approved by the Convention, called
for a college in the Hudson or Mohawk Valley and a theological
school in New England. But Massachusetts Universalists wanted
a college and proceeded to get one. After three years of canvass-
ing, Otis A. Skinner secured pledges of $100,000, including
some from New York State. Trustees, elected in 1852, faced
rivalries concerning location, the outstanding contenders being
Oliver Dean of Franklin and Charles Tufts, owner of Walnut
Hill, both of whom offered land. The decision, over the opposition of Ballou 2nd, was in favor of the Hill. A cornerstone ceremony in 1853 attracted a throng of happy Universalists. By
1855 the college was ready for opening, under the presidency of
Ballou, with "one building, four professors, and seven students."

Still there was no provision for a theological school. New
Yorkers did not like this, nor the location chosen for the college.
The New York Convention appointed another committee. By the
time that Tufts opened, pledges of $26,000 for a theological
school had been received and the committee was ready to select
a site. Again there were rivalries, but over objections that northern
New York State bounded on the north by Lapland and too remote,
Canton won. St. Lawrence County had been largely settled by
Vermonters and other New Englanders, among whom were many
Universalist families. Even in 1830 there were already several
successful churches. One objection to the Tufts location had been
its nearness to a large city, a type of objection common among
rural people. No such accusation could be made against Canton.
Even in my time there a student, returned from a convention at
Syracuse where he had met an attractive girl, informed the Lord
in public prayer that "we are 139 miles from the nearest large
city."

Outside the Canton area there was no desire for another
eastern college, but Universalists of the north country so strongly
demanded an "academic department" that the legislative charter
obtained authorized both a college and a theological school. When

the cornerstone was laid in 1856 the local resources were already exhausted and the dual task was achieved only with great difficulty. The theological school opened in 1858 under Ebenezer Fisher of Massachusetts, with two students. The academic department was under way in the following autumn, directed by John Stebbins Lee.

In Illinois efforts of the Spoon River Association led to the formation of a joint-stock company which obtained a charter to open a school at Galesburg. This small community had been settled by emigrants from the Mohawk Valley, among whom were enough Universalists to organize a society in 1846. The Illinois Liberal Institute, a coeducational academy, opened in 1852, but it was rechartered as a college, soon renamed Lombard. An early historic occasion, the fifth Lincoln-Douglas debate, was staged in the college building. It was perhaps the only college that Lincoln claimed to have "gone through." He entered by a door and left by a rear window.

Forty-five colleges in Ohio (1850) presented to Universalists the same objectionable features found elsewhere. The Universalist Collegiate Association of Ohio and Indiana met at Oxford in 1857, chose trustees, and selected Oxford as the site of another college. But again sectional and local rivalries blocked these plans. So for several years generous support from Ohio went to Lombard. But in those days Galesburg was a long way from Ohio. In 1869 the Ohio Convention authorized a financial campaign, which became a part of the denominational centenary appeal. The site problem was settled in advance by directing that the decision go to the city which promised the most money. Through the gifts of John R. Buchtel, a convinced but previously inactive Universalist, Akron won. There was some other initial local support, but much came from Universalists throughout the state.

Five thousand out-of-town visitors swelled the city-wide ceremonies in 1871, when Universalist Horace Greeley delivered the cornerstone address on "Human Conceptions of God as They Affect the Moral Education of our Race." Under this topic he was able to hope for future graduates in engineering and science. A year later, with Sullivan H. McCollester as president, the college opened with a curriculum "comparable to that of Yale."

The problems which each of the four colleges had to face were similar, not only to those of the other three but to those of all private colleges. None of them even had the money needed to operate effectively. In the early years financial problems, ever acute, were met by denominational drives and resulting gifts, each likely to be small in amount but cumulatively enabling the young institutions to keep going. There were a few Universalist benefactors better able to give larger sums: at Tufts, Thomas and Mary Goddard, Sylvanus Packard, Phineas T. Barnum; at St. Lawrence, Silas Herring and John Craig; at Buchtel, Mr. Buchtel himself; at Lombard, Benjamin Lombard, Amos Throop, and William Ryder.

The General Convention, various state conventions, and the national women's organization supplied much assistance. After the colleges produced graduates who became wealthy, new sources of income were opened. Noteworthy in this category was Universalist Owen D. Young at St. Lawrence.

In conformity to the custom of those days the presidents of the colleges were for many years Universalist clergymen. At Tufts there was Hosea Ballou 2nd, Alonzo A. Miner, Elmer H. Capen, and Frederick W. Hamilton, plus layman John A. Cousens. At St. Lawrence, John S. Lee, Absalom G. Gaines, Alpheus B. Hervey, Almon Gunnison, Richard E. Sykes, and one or more laymen. At Buchtel, Sullivan H. McCollester, Everett L. Rexford, Orello Cone, Ira A. Priest, Augustus B. Church. At Lombard, Paul R. Kendall, Otis A. Skinner, James P. Weston, Nehemiah White, C. Ellwood Nash, and Lewis B. Fisher.

All the colleges eventually gathered for their faculties men and women of excellent reputation in their fields. All except Tufts were coeducational from the beginning, a policy consistent with what most Universalists had long advocated. Tufts finally admitted women in 1892, but the unhappy situation which followed led to a segregation policy—equal but separate education in Jackson College.

Turning now from college to theological school, the number of institutions is reduced to three, since Buchtel supporters never succeeded in establishing theirs. The school at Canton opened, as stated above, in 1858; that at Tufts in 1869 with four students and two teachers; that at Lombard in 1881 with three students. Enrollment always tended to remain low—sixty-odd one year at Tufts was perhaps the maximum. During the 109 years of its activity the Canton school graduates each year have ranged in number from zero to twelve—the median number three, the mean four.[17] At Lombard the numbers were probably smaller.

Financially the story is the familiar lament: there was never enough money to do the task with satisfying efficiency. Sometimes the schools were better off than the colleges. In the early days St. Lawrence College kept open only by borrowing money from theological funds. For two emergencies the Crane School at Tufts lent its buildings to the college.

Heads of the Crane school, usually called deans, have been Charles H. Leonard, Lee S. McCollester, son of the former president of Buchtel, Clarence Skinner, John M. Ratcliff, and Benjamin Hersey. At Canton the office of president or dean has been held by Ebenezer Fisher, Isaac M. Atwood, Henry P. Forbes, John M. Atwood (son of I.M.A.), Angus H. MacLean, and Max A. Kapp. Available Lombard records are somewhat unclear, but apparently the president of the college was usually dean of the school. Among those so serving were Nehemiah White, John C. Lee, C. Ellwood Nash, and Lewis B. Fisher. All those mentioned in this paragraph were Universalist clergymen.

The faculties of the three schools included many who were highly competent in their fields and some who were professionally acclaimed outside the denomination, of whom Orello Cone, Morton S. Enslin, and perhaps Henry Forbes would be outstanding examples.

The Lombard School was named Ryder Divinity School, in

honor of another minister, William H. Ryder, its chief donor. In 1912 it was moved to the University of Chicago, Fisher going along as dean. After the Unitarian school moved from Meadville to the same university, it united with Ryder, and the boards of the two schools were amalgamated. It is now known as Meadville Theological School of Lombard College.

A common problem was the relationship of the schools to their colleges and to the denomination. Independence from the colleges was maintained in theory and on paper, but in practice the ties were close, although often strained. The denomination has generally continued to feel responsible for its schools, even for its colleges. Growing out of conditions long prior to the merger, but augmented by it, there has been a weakening of these ties. Within the schools a sense of kinship with the denomination diminished, whereas the colleges came to think of the schools as their property.

Early in the present century, with the advent of the great foundations, denominational control over the colleges was relinquished, except that Lombard continued to elect Universalist trustees. In 1913 Buchtel became the University of Akron. Lombard and Knox colleges, both in Galesburg, discussed merger in 1911. Nothing was done; rumored explanations do not agree. A quarter of a century earlier Lombard had refused a generous offer from Lydia Bradley of Peoria conditional on moving the college to that city and renaming it. Under the vigorous presidency of Joseph M. Tilden[18] from 1916 to 1928 the college drew more registrations, secured additional endowment, and erected new buildings. After his death, however, loss of endowment income from unwise use of funds and deficit spending, coupled with the stock-market crash, led to an arrangement whereby Unitarians were to give financial aid and assume control. Unitarian Curtis Reese became president. Nevertheless, within two years Lombard was absorbed by Knox, under an arrangement which preserves Lombard's past status, records, and traditions. Its charter remains with Meadville Theological School of Lombard College at Chicago.

In 1880 a zealous layman, Amos G. Throop, moved to Los Angeles and six years later to Pasadena. A native of New York State, he became a successful businessman in Chicago, where he was a member of the Church of the Redeemer and where he served in responsible positions in city, county, and state governments. He had given financial support to Lombard. In California he sponsored the Universalist cause. In Pasadena the church is named the Throop Memorial.

In a letter of January 24, 1889, Throop urged Quillen Shinn to come to California to promote the cause there, concluding with these words: "I am about changing my will and donating fifty thousand dollars to Universalism in the State of California, thirty thousand to endow a theological professorship and twenty thousand for missionary and church extension work."[19] Stanford University offered a spot on its campus for the proposed school. But to Throop's disappointment, Shinn decided to go to Rutland, Vermont, instead.

In 1891 Throop established a college in Pasadena. It seems certain that he first intended this as a Universalist college, with James Pullman as president.[20] But Pasadena Universalists have no such tradition, believing his motive to have been the welfare of his city and its growing population. At first known as Throop University, two years later it became Throop Polytechnic Institute. In 1914, long after the donor's death, it became Throop College of Technology, and finally in 1920 California Institute of Technology (Caltech). Its growth was promoted by gifts from another Universalist layman, Norman Bridge. Caltech differs from other Universalist-sponsored institutions in that, although established and once strongly supported by Universalists, it was not created or officially endorsed by the denomination.

Less ambitious undertakings were small mission and school combinations in the South. Joseph Jordan, a Negro ordained at Philadelphia in 1889, began a work in Norfolk, Virginia, which spread to Suffolk. The Southern Industrial College was another such project, at Camp Hill, Alabama.

Partly offsetting successes were two failures. One was the

premature effort of Kidwell to set up a school, perhaps a college, at Philomath, Indiana. The second was Smithson College at Logansport. Even while funds were desperately needed for Lombard and Buchtel, Indiana Universalists had found money enough to open the doors of Smithson in 1872. It was in trouble from the beginning. Low registrations, internal dissension, and unpaid pledges led to lawsuits and a court judgment. It closed in 1878.[21]

EDUCATION IN THE SUNDAY SCHOOL

The General Sunday School Association was organized in 1913 and continued to function until it was absorbed into the Convention as a department of education. Let us go back to 1865 to note some of the events which preceded it. With respect to what we now call religious education, the period opened with complaints, general statements of achievement, and unofficial expressions of goals. The complaints were varied, voicing the difficulties which societies had in obtaining teachers, objecting that too many teachers were not church members, pointing to the failure to maintain adult Bible classes and to lack of proper control of the schools.[22] Dates for the opening of some of the earliest schools were proudly recalled: Stoughton (1819), Gloucester (1820), Providence (1821). Although the importance of Sunday schools had been stressed at Philadelphia in 1790, after that there had not been much discussion about them at General Convention meetings. But now interest was growing. In some regions the need for some kind of teacher training was met by Sunday-school unions, organizations which brought together teachers from more than one society for study, lectures, or discussions. This type of program persisted in some cities, for in my student days the union of the greater Boston churches held monthly meetings in several communities, attended by perhaps two hundred people, for dinner and lecture.

Goals recommended at Convention sessions by committees or individuals, even if general, were forward-looking. We should "work according to some well-considered plan of religious instruction," including something about the Universalist Church and its rites. Each church should provide a "summer among orthodox icebergs." The school should meet in rooms convenient, light, airy, comfortably furnished, and with fountains, flowers, and pictures. We should develop better methods and better lesson materials. (All these date from 1867 to 1872.) Later we find suggestions for a salaried worker for larger schools, teacher training, and normal courses in theological schools.

The question of the most desirable type of lessons was frequently debated. At first uniform lessons were favored, as prepared by an interdenominational commission. Each Sunday every pupil in every school was expected to study, or at least to be taught, the same Bible passages, but the interpretive material was graded by age groups. This was favored because it permitted the minister to have a weekly teachers' meeting to consider how the next lesson should be taught. Materials were relatively inexpensive. These lessons were still being used at the Columbus Avenue church of Boston in 1909, when Stephen Roblin taught our college-age class. After a perfunctory reading aloud of the Bible verses for the day, he would toss the leaflet aside to launch us into a Socratic discussion of some ethical topic. In the Convention session of 1889 substitution of graded lessons was proposed. Some graded lessons were available in 1901, but general use was retarded by publishing-house commitments to the uniform system. An interesting suggestion in 1872 was the planning of courses in biblical geography, archeology, history, and biography. But the concept of a completely graded course emerged slowly.

A project assigned to a Convention committee in 1883 was to persuade Sunday schools to provide a library for their children and youth. A list of six hundred recommended books was compiled. Such a library was maintained during my childhood by the Congress Square Church in Portland. Supplied with a printed pamphlet catalogue, we were asked to indicate several books we would like to take home. The boys in our class poured over this catalogue. In my case the books so obtained were a weekly source of still remembered pleasure, stimulating my love for reading and giving me the courage to use the public library as well, which did not then cater to children. In addition to recreational books for children there were books being issued by the publishing house and other bookmen for direct use in the schools or by teachers. Eddy's list of Universalist publications, which ends in 1886, contains a few of this type, including half a dozen hymnals and three catechisms.[23] Other books for Sunday schools, not listed by Eddy, are to be found in the library of the Universalist Historical Society.

CHURCH EXTENSION

Propaganda for the spread of Universalism took the forms of aid to individual churches and regional or general missionary work, although these were not always clearly distinguished. Missionary work in some of its forms was later called evangelism. The first selections of churches to receive aid were made without reference to any over-all plan. Several are mentioned only once or twice in the minutes, either as possibilities or as actually receiving financial assistance. Portland (Maine), Lincoln (Nebraska), Indianapolis, Omaha, St. Paul, Denver, Oakland, and Riverside (California) are definitely referred to as being aided. The most consistently aided church was at Washington, D.C. The first proposal for a representative Universalist structure in the national capital came in 1867. With some initial skepticism the Convention began a program which turned out to be successful. But in 1907 there was a new desire for a more adequate "Cathedral Church." The resulting program made possible the present structure on Sixteenth Street, N.W. The national organizations of women and youth also aided specific churches: Harriman (Tennessee), Atlanta, Little Rock.

Early efforts at general missionary work had been feebly supported. But a memorial from the Indiana Convention in 1865 stimulated new measures to collect a fund to aid weak churches and to establish new permanent congregations, especially in the West, Northwest, and South. As for the South, it was at first thought that northern ministers would not be accepted there. The most dynamic, vigorous, and persistent worker for church extension was Quillen Shinn, whom it was my privilege to know at Ferry Beach in 1904.[24] When the Convention or other agency employed him, he accepted the assignment and the pay. When there was no salary in sight, he worked on his own. Mary Goddard, benefactress of Tufts, was one of his supporters. He roved the entire United States but concentrated on the southern states. He had memorized so much of the Bible that he recited, rather than read, the Scripture lesson. By no means un-educated, he preferred people to books and a ministry of personal helpfulness to one of scholarly discourse. He liked sawing wood or hoeing a garden for an incapacitated neighbor. The small groups he organized often resembled the fellowships of today, but since there were no headquarters techniques for serving them, many were short-lived. Others became successful churches, both rural and urban.

In the cities mass meetings were held to develop interest in missions, and the subject was discussed by the Convention again and again; yet in 1894 both C. Ellwood Nash and R. A. White lamented that little had been accomplished.[25] Over 90 per cent of our societies were east of the Mississippi. The denomination was urged to follow popular trends by moving to cities of the West. At the Convention of 1905 a cumulative report of mission points aided or subsidized furnished this information:

	Total	*Alive*	*Dormant or Occasional*	*Dead*
Single grants	91	45	17	29
Plural grants (2 to 5)	43	24	4	15
Subsidized	21	13	0	8

It is difficult to supply explanations of the failure to carry through on a mission program. As I recall the situation in my youth, there was a healthy interest in the subject and mission-study classes enjoyed a period of popularity.

Contacts with Scotland led to the discussion of foreign missions in general. Presently the focus was on Japan. After some delays work was begun there on the whole more successfully than mission work at home. The first workers to be sent, in April, 1890, were George I. Perin, I. Wallace Cate, and Margaret C. Schouler. They purchased a lot in Tokyo, found a home, and started learning the language. They held religious services, taught English, and lectured. Clarence Rice joined them in 1892. From time to time there were other changes, some persons returning to this country, others replacing them.

These workers were sent out by a board of the Convention, with the object of extending liberal Christian thought, establishing Japanese churches of a liberal type, building up their congregations, and encouraging them to become self-supporting. To this end the training of native ministers was undertaken. In other cities than Tokyo preaching stations were set up, staffed when possible by Japanese. Some of these developed into Japanese churches with buildings of their own. The momentum of early enthusiasm carried through for over forty years, making this a period of steady expansion.

The Women's National Missionary Association sent out its own women missionaries to Japan and financed its own work. Its object was the welfare of girls and young children. It set out to train women as leaders and homemakers. To this end it established the Blackmer Home, whose purpose was to take in promising girls who were orphaned, impoverished, and potential school dropouts and destined for the sweatshop or geisha house. At the home they were housed and fed, sent to outside schools, trained in household and child care and in music, and introduced to liberal Christianity. Upon graduation they spent a year or two of service in Universalist kindergartens, in church schools, and in the home itself. Altogether probably 250 girls were thus educated.

There were two kindergartens, designed like kindgartens everywhere to give small children a helpful start in life and preparation for public school. Well managed, these kindergartens were sufficiently popular to have capacity enrollments with waiting lists. Many hundreds of children, and their parents, felt the influence of these institutions.

The two types of missionaries sponsored other activies—a playground, work for young men, a reading room, and Bible classes. The whole project was thus a combination of social service and religious enlightenment. It captured the imagination of the denomination to the extent that it was supported fairly adequately and with fair unanimity. Our national organizations of women, men, and youth in America all cooperated. It reached its peak in 1933, with five churches in Japan and one in Korea. The Women's Association also had three buildings in Tokyo—the Blackmer Home and two kindergartens.[26]

OTHER ACTIVITIES

Plans were begun two years in advance for celebrating the one hundredth anniversary of Murray's first New Jersey preaching. In part this took the form of raising $200,000 as a Murray Centenary Fund for the aid of theological students and for church publications and extension. More fundamentally "all our people" were urged to give special attention "to the perfecting of their own religious life and the spiritual growth of their respective churches." All our societies were asked to pay their debts.

During the spring of 1870 large mass meetings were held in several cities. On the first Sunday in June appropriate services were held in the churches. And in September the Convention itself met in Gloucester, Murray's first home in America. Sessions were well attended. Horace Greeley and other outstanding laymen were there. Enthusiastic plans were adopted. The women perfected their national organization. Greeley tried unsuccessfully to persuade the Convention to abandon its policy of aiding colleges, which he said was of little benefit to the denomination, and to substitute increased endowment for a publishing house.

The committee permitted itself to indulge in prophecy. This

quote will convey something of the spirit of that era: "The new century on which we are to enter is to witness an advance of the Nation in all that is highest and noblest in political achievement,— a result never before possible to American civilization, because cursed with the barbarism of human slavery. It will also, so the signs of the times clearly indicate, witness, as its religious characteristic, the supremacy of the church whose doctrines give the most unmistakable support to its advanced civilization. All harsh and partial theologies will surely be outgrown and repudiated; and whatever puts contempt on human nature here, or intimates its hopeless ruin hereafter, will be spurned with righteous indignation. The American Church of the future, based on the divinity of Jesus Christ and his religion, firm in its conviction of the truth of the fatherhood of God and the brotherhood of man, and accepting all the logical results of these for its theory of retribution and of destiny, must, whatever name it may choose to be called by, rely, for its organized effort, on those who are already faithful in these Christian doctrines."[27]

Fifty years later the anniversary was again celebrated, not only at Gloucester but at Murray Grove in New Jersey. A John Murray lectureship was set up and a denominational campaign initiated for relief of war victims in Armenia.

During the period of expansion into frontier regions, Universalists had often held open-air meetings. Sometimes these had taken on some characteristics of the camp meeting, to the emotional features of which Universalists had been opposed. In New England grove meetings were inaugurated in Maine in 1878. In 1882 Quillen Shinn began similar meetings at The Weirs, New Hampshire. In 1898 the sessions were moved to Saratoga Springs, New York, and in 1901 they became permanent at Ferry Beach, Maine.[28] Some summer institutes continued in session for a week or longer. Programs varied. It was at The Weirs that a Japanese mission was first proposed. Teacher training was often on the program. Presently summer meetings at other locations became popular: at Murray Grove beside the old Potter Meeting House, at Chattanooga, at Camp Hill, and elsewhere.

The early Weirs meetings were a "part of the great intellectual movement of the period," in which schools, colleges, libraries, museums, art galleries, theaters, concert halls, and opera houses were springing up. They provided cultural group opportunities similar to those provided for somewhat more sophisticated and educated groups by other institutions. St. Louis had its Philosophical Society, Massachusetts had its Concord School of Philosophy, Emerson delivered five lectures in San Francisco, Harvard was developing "the first well rounded department of philosophy," Johns Hopkins was pioneering in graduate education. Quillen Shinn at one end of the beach, James and Royce and Santayana at the other, were riding the same tide.[29]

PROGRAMS FOR THE CHURCHES

From time to time the Convention turned its attention to problems of, and programs for, individual churches. Most recurrent of the topics was ritual and worship. Among the suggestions were conferences, prayer meetings, the importance of baptism, the dedication of children, and the communion service, or, as they usually spoke of it, the Lord's Supper.[30] But there was the reservation that each minister be free to choose his own rituals. In 1880 a plea was voiced to compile a uniform order of service, but this was then deemed inexpedient, for such details were to be determined by congregational preferences. Nevertheless, the topic was reintroduced in 1899, to find outlet in the service book, *Gloria Patri.* Lenten services were urged in 1886; many churches habitually made some observance of this season, even if nothing more than a series of midweek meetings and sermons.

Little attention had been given to church architecture. "No more box-like buildings" was a slogan in 1866, accompanying a demand for better architectural design. In 1870 an essay on "The Vestry and its Uses" by J. G. Adams advocated the multi-purpose use of the lower story or basement of the church building.[31] This space was frequently called the vestry, although sometimes the vestry seems to have been a separate building. The essay suggested that a vestry may be used for several types of gatherings: business meetings, social affairs for promoting acquaintance among members of the society, meetings of the church (as distinguished from the society?), prayer and conference sessions, and sessions of the Sunday school.

What actually went on in individual churches week by week and year by year is not easily determined. The record in Iowa offers some clues. Our churches occupied an important place in the social life of their communities. There were hay rides, suppers and ice-cream socials, dances and group singing in private homes, square dances, charades, readings, expeditions to the circus or the theater, day excursions by boat or train, travel lectures, plays, and festivals and fairs, in all of which participants were likely to include non-Universalists. Such activities made for warm fellowship. There was concern that children have good times, that youth have advantages and education. When feasible there were young people's societies, with their own social functions. Sunday schools were maintained, even when preaching could not be provided. In the face of discrimination and intolerance by other denominations, their buildings were often "equally open to all denominations." The ideal was a "liberal religion socially applied and practiced." There was interest in women's rights, temperance, and peace. The membership roll might include a banker, a school superintendent, an editor, a lawyer, a physician, the postmaster, teachers, and prominent members of the Masonic order. Some were sufficiently affluent to make generous gifts to schools and colleges or to give a park or a library to the city. Yet the raising of church funds was always a difficult task.

The subject of architecture was revived in 1915, when a Commission on Church Architecture was authorized. Its recommendations were much needed. That it was not created earlier is a misfortune, if my own experience was typical. During my student ministry the building at Ellisburg burned. I received no guidance on how to proceed and had no idea to whom I should turn. Upon request the board of the New York State Convention voted a contribution to the building fund but with no provision for any control over the architecture. My proposal for a building which might also serve as a community center was rejected by the Ellisburg committee. The final product I have always regretted.[32]

As population shifts rendered some societies dormant, concern developed for the disposal of abandoned church property. This led to the policy of urging all societies to deed their property in trust to the General Convention or to one of the state conventions. Consideration was given to the possibility of improving civil codes to ensure a legal basis for denominational control in such situations. It is surprising to find so little reference to the needs of rural churches, since the denomination was composed of so many of them.[33] Church financial methods were discussed. The pioneer plan of having pews owned by individuals was supplanted by a system of pew rentals. This in turn was at first supplemented, and then replaced, by weekly pledges and envelope systems.

ASPIRATIONS AND GOALS

The character of Universalism during this period is partially reflected in resolutions adopted or rejected. Many were general in content. Attention was called to humanitarian problems: to the poor and unfortunate and fallen, to cases of cruelty to animals and children, to greed. The brotherhood of man, it was declared, should be incarnate in all public life. Agencies for good health, sane thinking, and clean living were upheld, and on occasion a co-operative system of life.

By far the most frequent subject of resolution was temperance —on an average of about one resolution every other year for the entire period. The scope varied from general approbation of moderation in the use of alcoholic beverages to support of specific measures. Benjamin Rush was recalled as a pioneer in this field. The dram shop was condemned. Temperance lessons for Sunday schools were called for. Disapproval of the use of wine in the communion service was voiced in 1868 and repeated later. Suppression of the liquor traffic, usually by state and national prohibition laws, was acclaimed in 1873, 1884, 1886, and 1895.

After the Eighteenth Amendment was passed, Universalists were urged to support it and to assist in carrying out its provisions. One gets the impression that temperance resolutions originated in a period when public opinion on this question was based on emotional reactions to obvious evils and that they were continued as a matter of course until the need was seen for a thoughtful study. The demand for absolute prohibition was replaced by a call for "all reasonable efforts" to suppress the traffic. The legitimacy of using alcohol for mechanical, medicinal, and scientific purposes was recognized.

A commission, working with the General Sunday School Association, deepened the work by compiling reliable information on the effects of drinking and broadened it by including in their studies the effects of nicotine, the use of cigarettes by women, and "Kola beverages." Accordingly it became the Commission on Temperance and Public Morals (or Public Welfare). Harry Adams Hersey compiled valuable data based on careful research in these fields. Prior to this commission little action had been taken about tobacco.

Marriage and divorce were often made the subject of resolution from 1883 on. In that year disapproving notice was taken of the increase in divorce and of the need for better legal safeguards for home and the family. More complete statistics on this subject were requested of Congress. Hasty marriages were condemned, and caution was urged in the remarriage of divorced persons. The campaign for uniform divorce laws was supported in 1905 and subsequently. In that same year approval of woman suffrage was proposed, but notwithstanding frequent attempts, no strong resolution supporting suffrage was accepted until 1911, and then by a vote of 61 to 59.

Capital punishment was a recurrent theme. Abolition of the death penalty was urged in 1882 and at several subsequent sessions. A long report by Quillen Shinn on penology, advocating a committee for further study and the setting aside of Prison Sunday, was not acted upon when received, but eventually support was given to scientific penology, "combining love and skill."

The attention of the Convention was called to labor relations by G. M. Harmon in 1879.[34] For some years the idea had prevailed that all that was needed to solve labor problems was the application to them of the teachings of Jesus, plus attendance at church by laboring men. In the *Universalist Quarterly* Harmon wrote on "Social Reform and the Churches," advocating preventive measures against social strife, rather than merely remedial action. He argued that various social evils were interconnected and that there was thus need for a cooperative organization to avoid duplication of current efforts. All this he thought the task of the church. A few years later E. A. Perry discussed "Workingmen's Rights." These rights include the right to recognition that they have rights, to act untrammeled in accordance with their own political views, to have their complaints fully investigated, to receive an equitable share of the proceeds of industry, and to earn more than is actually needed for their comfort. Soon after appeared R. O. Williams' essay on "Monopoly, Labor Combinations, Strikes, Boycotting."[35]

By 1915 these more informed approaches were in evidence. The Convention then favored government publication of the work of the United States Commission on Industrial Relations, but not without opposition. In one of my few appearances before the Convention I summoned courage to speak in favor of publication. In rebuttal I was told that we should trust the kind men who run our government to take care of such matters. Study of actual strike conditions was later recommended.

During World War I a Cincinnati Universalist, Arthur Nash, started a surprisingly successful business, manufacturing clothing for men, conducting the enterprise on the basis of the golden rule and apparently winning the sympathetic cooperation of his many employees. It aroused much interest among Universalists, both for the enterprise itself and for its bearing upon labor relations in general.[36]

War and peace could not escape attention. In 1893 the board cooperated with other groups in a public conference and in sending a petition to thirty-one governments favoring arbitration of international disputes. Beginning at a much earlier date anti-war and pro-peace and pro-arbitration resolutions were frequently voted. The League of Nations, an international conference on reduction of armaments, search for the causes of war, and the World Court were all approved. Observation of a mobilization day was opposed. In 1917, in urging the military chaplaincy upon ministers, the Convention also requested the Secretary of War to accept men over forty years of age in this service. In 1925 it was voted, 80 to 53, that the Convention "recognizes as being in accord with our fundamental principles, the right of members of this church to refuse on conscientious grounds to participate in any warfare." Four years earlier, upon recommendation of a meeting of ministers, the Convention considered the need to restore American ideals of freedom of speech and the press and to release Eugene Debs and other conscientious objectors from prison. Commitment to postwar relief work produced more than resolutions. It was supported, especially under the leadership of George Huntley, for victims in Armenia. Interest in these subjects culminated in commissions on International Relief and on Foreign Affairs and World Peace, in cooperation with the Federal Council of Churches.

To some degree Universalists shared the concern of the more orthodox against the encroachments of the Continental Sabbath and for the preservation of traditional Sunday observance, provided the interests of all persons concerned were properly considered. Public Sunday amusements were frowned upon in 1887; this seems to have been the general attitude through 1911, after which there is official silence on this subject.

An obligation of churches and societies to serve their communities was recognized in 1880. An incomplete list of projects of this nature being carried out in 1909 was presented: Bethany Union (Boston), Fresh Air Farm and Chapin Home for the Aged (New York), Messiah Home (Philadelphia), Thompson Memorial Home (Indiana), Everyday Church (Chicago), and Unity House (Minneapolis). In Boston under the leadership of Harold Marshall, in San Diego under the guidance of Howard Bard, and in other cities, open forums were successfully maintained.

Resolutions urging justice for minority groups were frequent. Work for and among American Indians, better treatment of Chinese on the Pacific Coast, homes for the aged and infirm, laws against cruelty to animals, opposition to child labor and favoring playgrounds, and work among the Swedes of Minneapolis were all up for consideration at one time or another. The group most often mentioned was the Negro. His education and his rights were seen as problems. Positive action was taken in financial support of the Southern Industrial Institute at Camp Hill, Alabama, and the Suffolk Normal Training School in Virginia. Other social service projects are described in Scott's *The Universalist Church in America*.[37] A 1917 Declaration of Social Principles may be found in an Appendix in Lalone's *And Thy Neighbor as Thyself*. At Convention sessions different speakers at different times expressed their varied convictions and aspirations.

Later sessions gave less time than earlier to preaching and more to business or mass meetings for discussion of themes of current interest. But there was always a Convention sermon. Reference to these gives insight into the varied emphases and points of view. The typical "occasional sermon" was traditionally a biblical exposition of Universalist doctrine, later giving way to more philosophical arguments joined with self-congratulations that we had found the truth. But other notes were struck, less biblical, less traditional, with respect being paid to the sciences. Sullivan McCollester quoted Plato, Lucretius, and other classical scholars. Everett Rexford praised the British Association for the Promotion of Science as having more faith in its acquired knowledge than the Westminster Assembly of Divines ever had in God's thought. Henry Rugg countered by affirming that science and philosophy do not answer the great questions; Christ and Christianity remain the prior source. Edwin Sweetser pointed out that at least man's apprehension of revelation changes. We must hold to the truths of the past, yet be ready to revise our opinions and to change our beliefs. Charles Eaton referred to scholars who were recognized authorities in the field of biblical scholarship, and denied that the Bible was literally infallible. Its miracles were to be denied not a priori but on the basis of probability. We had to choose between agnosticism or even atheism and human interpretations of God's nature as seen in man and revealed through psychology and philosophy. Isaac Atwood acceptingly acknowledged the proponents of biblical criticism and social reform, but argued for the need for an underlying personal religion. Thomas Sawyer, however, condemned what he called the New Universalism, with its undue reliance on theories from the critics and the scientists. Joseph Mason called for a religion of deeds, a working church from whose pulpits social questions should be discussed. A. J. Canfield presented three contemporary "passions": for expansion, for fraternity, and for philanthropy. John Coleman Adams turned back; in a thoughtful analysis he paid tribute to Hosea Ballou as a pioneer of thought. Lee McCollester presented the "Greater Universalism"—a faith in the universal reign of law and in continuous revelation. Frank Hall indicted current ills: child labor, overworked women, sweatshops, standing armies, predatory wealth, abject poverty, charity without justice, and government for the benefit of the few. Similar themes were selected by Marion Shutter and Frederick Perkins. In 1915 Hall denounced the world war. But Henry Rose confessed that that war had converted him from his former pacifism. He now believed that God had been with certain armies and in decisive battles and that He was now with Kerensky, Liebknecht, Lloyd George, and Woodrow Wilson. Thus the leaders groped their way towards formulating the changing character of their denomination.

This account of events in the reconstruction period of our church life may serve as a basis for understanding how the later merger came about. But before reviewing this story let us return to the beginning to discuss two topics so far mentioned only casually: (1) formulation and development of Universalist belief, and (2) early relationships with Unitarians.

CHAPTER 6

Changing Universalist Beliefs (1778-1935)

Up to this point little about Universalist doctrine has been presented. It has been sufficient to define Universalism as a denial of endless punishment for any and as an affirmation of salvation for all. These teachings are corollaries of a more fundamental belief: God loves all men and is to be worshiped as the Father of all. These doctrines, as we have seen, developed independently among many individuals, some of whom rather quietly held the faith, whereas others formed a new denomination to which they sought converts. All early active Universalists agreed in accepting these tenets, in thinking of their movement as representing uncorrupted primitive Christian gospel, and in looking to Jesus as the agent of that universal salvation which they joyously proclaimed.

But within the Universalist circle there were differences of opinion. Controversy, usually friendly, erupted over several questions: Will punishment for sin be imposed solely on earth? Or solely after death? Or in both situations? Just how does the office of Saviour operate to save men? How should certain passages of the Bible be interpreted? Is the trinitarian or the unitarian position correct?

At the beginning these early Universalists accepted in some respects the common faith of American society—the Americanism of that day which then as now went under the name of Christianity. Stressing his divinity rather than his deity, that is, that he is like God but not God himself, they strongly affirmed that Jesus is the Christ, assigned by God to a central position in the scheme of salvation. They based their theology on the Bible, regarding it as a divine revelation. In denying the everlastingness of punishment, they were increasingly careful to insist that all would be justly punished for their sins. Their confidence in divine benevolence was shared with all churches, most of which were able to reconcile belief in a benevolent Deity with the prospect of an endless hell. This common faith had been generated by the European Enlightenment. Religious liberalism of New England was inspired by Platonism, introduced by Protestant reformers to combat the Aristotelian Christianity of the Catholics. It became the basis of New England political thought. The democratic faith included the Platonic concept of a moral law created by a just and benevolent God.[1] Platonism, or more precisely Neo-Platonism, had also guided the thought of the second-century Universalist Origen of Alexandria.

STATEMENTS OF BELIEF

The earliest formal statement of Universalist belief seems to have been written in 1778 by Caleb Rich for his congregations. Other early statements for local use were prepared by Murray for his society in Boston (1791), by Sargent for societies in New Jersey (1792), by Richards for the Portsmouth society (1796), and by Mitchell for his group in New York City (1796). Murray's Gloucester congregation had seen no need for a creed. They did not "associate for belief in any particular tenets or peculiar doctrines, because we conceived that all convictions must rise from evidence rationally applied to the understanding, and we did not suppose that the same evidence would strike every mind in the society with the same force."[2]

The first creed known to have been accepted for wider use was the Articles of Faith of the 1790 Philadelphia Convention.[3] The views expressed show evidence of compromise. Although many members of the Convention had brought from their former Baptist connections a belief in baptism, yet out of deference to Murray and others, this subject was not mentioned. Although the language was compatible with a trinitarian belief, there was no clear-cut reference to that doctrine. In fact, objection was raised to it in Boston on the ground that it was not sufficiently trinitarian. But the society there did adopt it. Apparently a few other New England societies accepted it also, but it had no wide usage.

In order to compare it with the statement adopted at Winchester, New Hampshire, in 1803, let us set down the two statements side by side. The New Hampshire profession is often referred to as the Winchester Profession. Elhanan Winchester played no part in its formulation; he had died a few years earlier.

Two Statements of Belief Compared

Articles of Faith *Philadelphia* *1790*	*Profession of Faith* *Winchester* *1803*
We believe the scriptures of the old and new testament to contain a revelation of the perfections and will of God, and the rule of faith and practice.	We believe that the holy scriptures of the old and new testament contain a revelation of the character of God and of the duty, interest, and final destination of mankind.
We believe in one God, infinite in all his perfections, and that these perfections are all modifications of infinite, adorable, incomprehensible, and unchangeable love.	We believe that there is one God, whose nature is love, revealed in one Lord Jesus Christ, by one Holy Spirit of grace, who will finally restore the whole family of mankind to holiness and happiness.
We believe that there is one Mediator between God and men, the man Christ Jesus, in whom dwelleth all the fullness of the Godhead bodily, who by giving himself a ransom for all, hath redeemed them to God by his blood; and who, by the merit of his death, and the efficacy of his spirit, will finally restore the whole human race to happiness.	

We believe in the Holy Ghost, whose office it is to make known to sinners the truth of this salvation, through the medium of the holy scriptures, and to reconcile the hearts of the children of men to God, and thereby to dispose them to genuine holiness.

We believe in the obligation of the moral law as the rule of life; and we hold, that the love of God manifested to man in a redeemer, is the best means of producing obedience to that law, and promoting a holy, active and useful life.

We believe that holiness and true happiness are inseparably connected, and that believers ought to be careful to maintain order and practice good works, for these things are good and profitable unto men.

One should note also a sentence from Richard's Portsmouth creed of 1796: "They who believe in God should be careful to maintain good works, for these things are good and profitable unto men."[4]

THE WINCHESTER PROFESSION (1803)

Unlike the Philadelphia Articles the Winchester Profession played an influential role in the Universalist drama. Let us then go back to the beginning to relate its story. Chapter Two contained a brief account of the life of Walter Ferriss.[5] In May, 1799, after he had gathered a congregation about him, he realized that he and his associates were but little informed "respecting the general State of the Universalists of New England. . . . We knew not what mode of discipline had been adopted where there were regular churches. We were unacquainted with most particulars concerning our brethren in different parts, which we conceived might be for our edification to know." Jumping on his horse, he rode the forty miles or more to spend a few days with Farwell at Barre and another twenty to visit Joab Young at Strafford. After talks with them he returned home, bringing a copy of the Philadelphia Articles.

That same year Ferriss attended his first General Convention session at Woodstock, where he was chosen clerk and writer of the circular letter. At the Orange session in 1800 he unsuccessfully proposed that "a platform should be adopted and published by the general association, setting forth the more essential points of doctrine in which those whom we consider as universalists were agreed, and the outlines of the regulations followed in the association." At Strafford in 1802 he again introduced the subject, explaining the reasons for his position. "I considered some measure of this kind as necessary to prevent confusion, dispel ignorance, and remove the charge which other denominations laid against us of being wholly divided among ourselves and agreeing in nothing essential, but to vilify other sects and oppose all ecclesiastical order. The diversities of opinion in circumstantial points among us, some holding to the system of Winchester, some to that of Relly, some to that of Huntington,[6] and some to others, seemed to justify in part this charge, as long as we had no regular public approved testimony of those essentials in which we did agree."

There were still those who objected. "Some brethren were afraid that if we entered on this business we should find our opinions so different as to cause our association to fall to pieces. The greater part of the elders seemed so terrified at the idea of creeds and platforms that they were at first for rejecting my motion. But after some small discussion of the subject they consented to appoint a committee to draft a general profession and plan to be laid before the next convention when it might be adopted or rejected as might appear best." The minutes state that a committee was appointed, charged "to form a plan of fellowship in faith and practice, for the edifying of the body, and building it up together."

Members of the committee, together with their approximate ages, were Hosea Ballou, at 32 the youngest member, Ferriss (35), George Richards (48), Zephaniah Lathe (50), and Zebulon Streeter ("venerable"). Ballou was barely on his way to his later Ultra Universalism. Lathe, a follower of Winchester, held to a future, but not endless, punishment in hell-fire. Streeter probably held similar views. Richards, a follower of Murray, was a trinitarian and accepted the vicarious atonement. Ferriss rejected the Trinity.[7] Thus the committee represented a sampling of Universalist divergences and was sufficiently weighted on the side of age to overcome any possible objection that its report might represent wild ideas of the younger members.

During the intervening year between the Strafford and Winchester conventions the committee did not meet. Ferriss prepared a statement, using the Philadelphia Articles as a point of departure, but shortening them and simplifying the language. It went as far as he "had reason to hope the brethren of the Convention at large would agree to accept" and was so drawn "as to leave liberty to the several churches . . . to adopt any more full or particular plan as they should see best, provided it was not contrary to the general plan." At Winchester nearly every recognized Universalist minister was present.[8]

"When I proposed this plan which I had drawn," Ferriss records, "to the rest of the committee, they agreed to it with very little amendment, and laid it before the Convention, which was the most numerous I had ever attended. When it was laid before the Convention I had the pleasure of seeing it instantly assented to by the brethren who had opposed me the year before at Strafford. They saw nothing in it of the tendency to divide the association, which they had been afraid of, but were convinced that it would rather tend to strengthen our union. But the Rev. Noah Murray, from the north part of Pennsylvania, who had never before attended one of our Conventions, though he had long been a preacher of our order, objected in a new and singular manner against having any written form at all. He said much on the subject, and enlivened his pleas by quaint similitudes, drawn from calves, bulls, half bushels, etc., in which I thought he displayed more wit than solid sense, and more pathos than sound reasoning. But as he was a venerable old preacher, a man of real natural abilities, and possessed in some degree of a winning address, he was followed immediately by a number of other brethren who had not attended at Strafford the year before, amongst whom was the Rev. Mr. Glover, of Newtown in Connecticut. These brethren all seemed to approve of the plan which we had produced, as to its substance both with regard to doctrine and external regulations, but argued that it would be of no utility, if not of dangerous tendency, to commit that, or any other form, to writing as an act of the association. I have seen good honest men, before this, who, because they could not write themselves, thought that writing was but of little use in the world.

"On the other side it was powerfully argued by brothers Richards, Young, H. Ballou and others, that not only the reputation of the Universalists already suffered much for want of an evidence to the world that they were, as a Christian people, actually agreed in something essential both as to faith and practice, but that also individuals suffered considerably for want of some document to evince that they belonged to a denomination of Christians distinct from the standing order of congregationalists. Amongst other cases, that of brother C. Erskine was dwelt upon, and with propriety, as the convention had already made some public efforts for his relief, without the desired effect. He had been obliged to pay heavy taxes to the support of a congregational minister, and large costs of suit for want of being able to prove that the universalists were not the same denomination as the congregationalists.

"The discussion was carried on with decency and with great ingenuity on both sides. At length the opposition rather seemed to flag. Brothers Murray and Glover with their companion Deacon Peck of Newtown expressed a desire to withdraw, as the time grew late, and they had far to go. They assured us that they did not withdraw for reasons of disgust or coldness towards us, and took their leave very affectionately. After they had retired the discussion still went on. Several brethren of the opposition made a handsome retraction confessing themselves convinced, and when the question was put for adopting the platform all the brethren present voted in the affirmative."

A list of clergy and laymen so voting, together with a list of the societies which they represented, is given by Eddy.[9] The accounts by Eddy and Ferriss differ slightly.[10] Eddy says that the Convention voted changes in the Profession, whereas Ferriss says changes were made by the committee prior to presentation. However this may be, the evidence just quoted corroborates the traditional opinion that Ferriss was the author.

In accordance with Ferriss' original report, the Convention declared, "We leave it to the several churches and societies . . . to continue or adopt within themselves such more particular articles of faith . . . as may appear to them best . . . provided they do not disagree with our general profession or plan." It also asserted, "We consider that every Church possesses within itself all the powers of self-government."

ANALYSIS AND EVALUATION OF THE PROFESSION

Eddy devotes considerable discussion to the motives which led to the adoption of this document, arguing that Ferriss was trying to establish his legal right to perform marriage ceremonies and that the Erskine case played no part. But Ferriss reports that this case was mentioned in the debate. The right to marry was not mentioned in his account, although it may have been a factor. At a later date Brooks suggested that the need for a strong united front before the courts might have been an underlying motive. I see no reason for not accepting as the prime motive Ferriss' original dissatisfaction over the lack of any authoritative summary of Universalism, plus the statement of the Convention itself. This mentions the difficulty of "obtaining information" about the denomination, the need "to prevent confusion and misunderstanding," and the claim that these articles established Universalism as "a distinct denomination," entitled to receive "the external privileges which, according to the free Constitution of our country, every denomination was entitled to enjoy."

A strange sentence concludes the minutes for 1803: "There is *no alteration* of any part of the three articles that contain the *profession* of our *belief* ever to be made at any future period." Ferriss does not allude to it. One can only speculate. It reads like a motion impulsively made at the close of a long discussion and adopted because the delegates did not wish to take time to think about it. Whatever the case, nobody seems to have paid any attention to it. Only forty miles in space and seventeen years in time from Winchester the society at Springfield, Vermont, adopted a statement similar in spirit, whose language offers no hint that the authorized document was even known.[11] In 1823 a society was organized at Belpre, Ohio, which adopted a profession patterned on the Winchester statement but with modifications. Perhaps someone had tried to reproduce it from memory. In 1829 the Maine State Convention adopted a Declaration of Faith obviously not the Winchester version.[12] In 1840 Whittemore proposed his idea of a profession in four articles.[13] In 1850 and 1855 Williamson made his suggestion for a statement to be adopted by societies.[14] It had five articles with little resemblance to Winchester. An essay in the *Quarterly* in 1864 ignored it. In 1869 there was a proposed Roxbury Confession which also diverged.[15] In general one may say that for several decades not much attention was paid to the official pronouncement. One may surmise that it had little liturgical use.

Neither was there much fault found with it until 1867 and later. Some have inferred an implied criticism of the Profession from Hosea Ballou's silence about it. It is asserted that he mentioned it only once. But from the above account it is clear that he did argue for its adoption. His silence was but a part of the general silence.

One bit of evidence of its perfection of composition is that when attempts were made to amend it, as we shall presently see, no one was able to come up with an acceptable modification, and it was finally left unchanged as a venerated historical landmark.

What had come to give dissatisfaction was the word *restore*. For Ferriss and his contemporaries this was a synonym for *save*. Formerly I was inclined to infer that the author was influenced by neo-Platonic Christianity, for example, Origen and his successors, but I find no evidence that Ferriss either was, or was not, a student of philosophy and of ancient Universalism.

At the Winchester Centennial in 1903 J. S. Cantwell called attention to certain words and phrases.[16] The following comments are partly his, partly mine. *We believe* connotes brotherhood and emphasizes the idea that this is a statement of principles about which there is common brotherly agreement. The whole tenor is inclusiveness. It is not a creed to shut people out. *Contains* avoids any argument as to whether every word in the Bible is divinely inspired. *Finally,* leaving open the question of future punishment, seems to say to Elhanan Winchester and his followers, "All right, Brother Winchester, maybe God will punish men 50,000 years, but *finally*. . . ." The closing phrases are distinctly utilitarian; order and good works are praised because they are profitable aids to true happiness. *True happiness* is in implied opposition to worldly happiness. *Order* probably refers to the need in a new denomination for order in conventions, Sunday services, and ecclesiastical rules but also may reflect something of the then national concern in a post-revolutionary period for a well-ordered society. *Interest* was a popular word in political oratory but here refers to objective or goal for human life. That holiness and true happiness are *inseparably* connected is ambiguous; perhaps this means only that holiness is a necessary condition for happiness.

It is a document, I am convinced, that stands up solidly under criticism. Certainly it was far superior as a symbol around which Universalists could be invited to rally than the cumbersome theological language of the Philadelphia Articles. That a committee representing such diverse views could accept it promptly and that a Convention perhaps even more diverse could adopt it is proof of the skill with which it was written. It proclaimed neither the views of Lathe and Streeter nor the position towards which Ballou was moving, yet was compatible with both. With the exception of the reference to a final restoration almost any liberal Christian of that day could have accepted it, yet it was neither unitarian nor trinitarian. Significant indeed is what it omits. There is no mention of the doctrines of original sin, virgin birth, or vicarious atonement.

According to John Coleman Adams this Profession was the first explicit statement of liberal Christianity in the form of a creed to be adopted by any Christian denomination. He calls it "the Magna Charta and the Declaration of Independence of the Broad Church in America."[17]

Ferriss possessed a poetic trait which gave this Profession a deeply moving poetic quality. This has seldom been commented on. Frederick Perkins does mention it in three lines of a pamphlet.[18] And an unknown writer calls attention to its "words fitly chosen, like apples of gold in pictures of silver."[19] It would be easy for a modern reader to ridicule this claim, asserting that its concepts are meaningless today. But to me, with memories of its weekly repetition by a large room full of children and adults, it remains the most impressive congregational ritual in which I have ever participated. Not that as a child I was fully aware of this. But in repeating it today by myself it rises to the sublime, expressing something of the reverential awe with which our forefathers looked out upon life.

THE RESTORATIONIST CONTROVERSY

As indicated earlier, there are several names by which Universalists chose to refer to themselves. Restorationist and Universalist were both in common use, sometimes interchangeably. Elhanan Winchester had called himself a Universal Restorationist. But through an unfortunate series of events these terms came to label opposing groups in an unhappy division of the denomination, or more accurately in that part of it located in southeastern New England. Some ministers, from a perusal of the Bible and from inferences which they drew from it, concluded that (*a*) at the time that sin occurs punishment for it is automatically imposed in the sense of an alienation from God and the righteous life; (*b*) sin results from physical bodily temptations; (*c*) when the soul by death is separated from the body, temptation and therefore sin will cease; and (*d*) therefore there will be no punishment whatever after death. This form of Universalism may be called either (respectfully) Ultra Universalism or (disrespectfully) Death-and-Glory Universalism. Those who held this position were usually called merely Universalists. On the other hand, those who were convinced that after death punishment for sin would continue for a limited period called themselves Restorationists. Both opinions were to be found in the 1790's but for a long time caused no ill feeling. Since both were represented in the committee which formulated the Winchester Profession, it is unfortunate that that document could not have mediated for a peaceful tolerance.

The controversy started in the Providence-Attleboro-Medway vicinity and never penetrated very far from that center. In 1817, long before the differences were crystallized, Jacob Wood represented to Hosea Ballou that Edward Turner wished to enter into a public discussion of the subject. Whether Turner did is not clear. But Ballou accepted the information as true, writing Turner that such an inquiry might be of value and giving him the choice of positions to defend. Turner replied that he would find the discussion informative; that he had no firm conviction but inclined towards believing in future punishment and would therefore uphold that view. The ensuing exchange of polite controversial letters appeared in the *Gospel Visitant*. It uncovered some facts about the past, including the information that Sargent had favored Ultra Universalism, whereas Restorationism had been the faith of Murray.

After the exchange ended Ballou seems to have been inclined to drop the subject. But others would not permit this. It was carried on for several years, waxing warmer. Wood himself entered the controversy as a Restorationist, using some harsh invective against the opposition. The editor of a Unitarian journal, the *Kaleidoscope,* attacked Ballou's form of Universalism. Presently many letters on one side or the other were appearing in the *Universalist Magazine.* In spite of himself Ballou was drawn back into the fray, although he sought to calm it.

Paul Dean joined Turner in his opposition to Ballou. When in 1822 Sylvanus Cobb first met Turner and Dean, he found Turner "a pleasant combination of dignity and geniality," and Dean "a man of much social affability." But his pleasure in their conversation was abridged by their discussion of their proposed withdrawal to establish a new denomination, to which they expected to attract "the most polished and literary" clergymen.[20]

At Wood's home in Shirley there was a meeting of Restorationist sympathizers. At the Convention in Charlton he tried unsuccessfully to persuade some ministers to withdraw to form a rival Restorationist convention. As the debate continued it had less and less to do with theology and more and more with attacks on personal integrity. At the Convention in Clinton formal charges were made against both Dean and Ballou. Both were exonerated. But Dean withdrew his fellowship. (Later he arranged to be reinstated.) The Southern Association of New England in 1823 and 1824 effected a temporary reconciliation. Ballou, preacher on that occasion, invited Dean and Wood to participate with him in the worship service.[21]

"To all appearances harmony was restored." Nevertheless, the prevailing opinion at that time among Universalists was on the side of no future punishment, a situation which made the Restorationists sensitive and uncomfortable. In 1827 a new association was formed, the Providence Association, to include societies in parts of Rhode Island, Connecticut, and Massachusetts, and composed largely of Restorationists. It was in this area that Elhanan Winchester had preached his Restorationism thirty years earlier. With real or fancied justification the minority nursed their grievances until August 31, 1831, when eight ministers and several laymen formed the Massachusetts Association of Universal Restorationists. Others joined them to make a total of thirty-one ministers, almost exclusively from Massachusetts and Rhode Island.

The association adopted a Profession of Faith which included the first two articles of the Winchester Profession. The third article read: "We believe in a retribution beyond death, and the necessity of faith and repentance; and that believers ought to be careful to maintain order and practice good works, for these things are good and profitable unto men."[22] Many who held Restorationist views did not join the new association. During the ten years of its existence attacks from Ultra Universalists diminished, exchanges of pulpits opened up, and a new passion for social reform was displacing theological controversy.

In retrospect the affair appears largely as a series of personal clashes and quarrels. Already at the Convention of 1803 the close friendship between Ballou and Turner had suffered from a misunderstanding fanned by overzealous partisans. Moreover, Turner was shocked because in the debate he thought that Ballou had insincerely changed his interpretation of a text.[23] Dean was ever jealous of Ballou as his rival in Boston. And Wood seems to have been a busybody.

A quite different account is offered by the historian, Bates, who asserts that Adin Ballou, by now second only to Hosea Ballou as a denominational leader, had come to believe than an unyielding Universalist orthodoxy had developed "a respectable, complacent staticism which used the once liberating doctrine of universal salvation as a cloak to cover existing social evils."[24]

An account of the schism as seen by Adin Ballou himself does not so much dispute the details as alter the emphasis.[25] According to him, he and Thomas Whittemore were the chief antagonists. A native of Rhode Island, Ballou became a preacher of the Christian Connection, a small denomination founded in 1793, among whose doctrines was the annihilation of the wicked, or "Destructionism." Study of the Bible led him to Universalist belief and fellowship. There was some hesitation, as he was a Restorationist rather than an Ultra Universalist, but Hosea Ballou 2nd, a distant younger cousin of "Father" Ballou, assured him that within the denomination there was room for those of both opinions.

At first he was made so at ease by friendly hospitality from Hosea Ballou the elder and others that he suppressed his opposition to the overwhelmingly prevailing view. Yet he became convinced that Restorationists were welcome only if they did not proclaim their convictions. Moreover, circumstances connected with a call to Hosea Ballou, Sr., to become his successor in New York City, and Hosea's treatment of David Pickering at a session of the General Convention, disillusioned Adin Ballou to the point of unhappiness.

There were three Ballous representing three opinions. Hosea stood for Ultra; Adin for Restoration; Hosea 2nd as peacemaker for a denomination which could welcome both. (The situation suggests the later confrontation of Humanist, Theist, and Inclusivist.) Adin, later an ardent pacifist, might have joined forces with Hosea 2nd to work for harmony. This seems never to have occurred to him. Instead his pride in being intellectually honest and logically consistent led him to accept battle.

The proximate cause was a Restorationist sermon which Adin innocently delivered in April, 1830, at Medway. The congregation requested that it be printed, whereupon Adin sent it to Whittemore for publication in the *Trumpet.* Instead of using it, Whittemore abused it with a hostile editorial attack on the preacher and his position. Adin now felt justified in fighting back with his pen and by secession.[26] This he formalized by joining the Providence Association, already outlawed by the General Convention. Soon after, in August, 1831, he fathered the Massachusetts Association of Universal Restorationists. In his autobiography he makes no reference to the Winchester Profession.

The new association was apparently composed of individuals, mostly ministers, rather than of churches. Annual and frequently quarterly sessions were held; these were devoted chiefly to preaching. A journal, the *Independent Messenger,* was published for several years, usually under Ballou's editorship. The association died because of a situation much like that which developed among the transcendentalists of the Unitarian fold. Both groups polarized into two segments. One segment became increasingly interested in reform; the other clung to its intellectual concerns—philosophical or theological.

It was Adin Ballou's passion for logical consistency that killed the Restorationist movement which he took credit for establishing. Becoming successively a zealous convert to new crusades—temperance, anti-slavery, peace—he wanted his association to support these reforms. To him they were logical implications of his theology. When many of his friends and associates declined, he lost interest in maintaining a separate Restorationist organization. Although a meeting was called for in 1841 in Millville, it was not convened. The final session was in 1840.

To my readers, many of whom may have no expectation of any future life whatsoever, it will seem queer that intelligent and self-consecrated men should have behaved in such an uncooperative and unbrotherly manner. But it must be remembered that all those involved were concerned with ethical ideals and that for them a sound ethics must be based on a sound theology. Adin Ballou thought Ultra Universalism to be as productive of immorality as endless punishment. An orthodox critic, Samuel C. Bartlett (1856), asserted that if all misery ceases at death, persons who so believe ought to kill themselves.

Adams has called attention to the ironical aftermath. "In a few short years," there occurred "the swing of practically the whole denomination back to the original position of the founders of the Association" of Restorationists. The majority of Universalists came to believe that "not only do we get our punishment as we go along," as advocates of Ultra Universalism had claimed, but with the Restorationists that "it may go a long way with us into the future."[27] In 1878 this view was acceptably formulated by a group of Boston ministers, who repudiated "death and glory" to assert that "punishment and repentance are possible after death."

CANONIZATION OF THE PROFESSION

The controversy and its aftermath revealed a hitherto dormant tendency to interpret Universalism as a new orthodoxy. In 1847 the Convention approved a resolution proposed by Hosea Ballou, affirming that "this Convention expresses its solemn conviction that in order for one to be regarded as a Christian minister with respect to Faith, he must believe in the Biblical account of the life, teachings, miracles, death and resurrection of the Lord Jesus Christ."

Ballou, now fifty-one years of age, with his only slightly younger protégé, Whittemore, was beginning to be challenged by some of the younger generation, but with no great success. Perhaps this Universalist orthodoxy may account for the restlessness of Starr King and Chapin, who represented a broadening of the denominational horizon and may well have felt uncomfortable under conservative restraints and criticism.

In 1841 Chapin had written: "While I do most truly consider the doctrine of Universal Restoration as the most consistent with the best results of reason, with all our conceptions of the Divine Character, and with the Spirit of the Scripture, I do not see it so clearly revealed in the Bible, as that I should feel justified in pronouncing it a plain unequivocal Doctrine of the Gospel. Understand me. I believe it can be deduced from scripture by collateral arguments and by irresistible inferences; but the texts that are relied upon as unequivocally teaching it are to me not so satisfactory as I wish they were."[28] Chapin escaped by leaving Boston for a Universalist pulpit in New York City; King remained in Boston but escaped to the Unitarians.

The reference to Whittemore scarcely does him justice. True, he was critical of King and of Unitarian Transcendentalism. Emerson's "Divinity School Address" he found "tainted with atheism." But so did many Unitarians. Yet Whittemore made the *Trumpet* one of our great journals and a source of profit to himself. In *And Thy Neighbor as Thyself* Lalone credits him with being concerned with a practical expression of the gospel in better conditions "for men here and now on this earth." Boston-born in 1800, educated in the schools of Charlestown and by apprenticeship in several trades, he was introduced to Universalism as a member of the choir. Ballou persuaded him to play bass viol in his church, took him on as a student and guided him into the ministry, into an editorial career, and into the writing of a modern history of Universalism. A resident of Cambridge, he was a selectman, an alderman, president of Cambridge Bank, president of the Massachusetts and Vermont Railway, and for five years a representative in the state legislature, where he was a proponent of the law of 1833 disestablishing the church in Massachusetts.

At the session of 1867 a committee proposed "that in order for one to become a Christian minister, or a member of a Universalist Church, he or she shall believe in the Bible account of the life, teachings, miracles, death, and resurrection of our Lord Jesus Christ, and any interpretation of the Winchester Confession of Faith that makes it compatible with the denial of that account is a false one." This proposal was rejected, but a substitute was adopted, 49 to 1. "In framing the Winchester Confession, it was the evident intention of our denominational fathers to affirm the Divine Authority of the Scriptures and the Lordship of Jesus Christ; and in the judgment of this Convention, only those comply with the prescribed conditions of fellowship who accept the Confession with this interpretation." Prior to the vote the character of the discussion and maneuvers aroused such a "pandemonium" that Quillen H. Shinn, a young man of twenty-two, violated parliamentary rules by arising to say that he was on his way to enter the theological school at Canton but after witnessing this exhibition, was considering a return to his West Virginia mountains.

By this action the original "freedom clause" was ignored. Although this decision aroused opposition, three years later it became a part of the law of the denomination. But like many

other decisions of the Convention, efforts to enforce this interpretation were seldom successful. Gradually such efforts ceased.
Canonization was officially repealed in 1899. At the Indiana
Convention of the following year, T. E. Ballard, a respected but
by then conservative minister, introduced the Ballou resolution
of 1847. It was defeated 51 to 10.

Types of Universalist Theology

Several early expounders of Universalist theology distinguished
between types of Universalism. Eddy quotes Murray at some
length on this. Frank H. Foster offers one of the more scholarly
analyses,[29] as follows:

1) Calvinist James Relly. There is "union" of *all* men with
Adam (as the partialists taught), but also with Christ (as they
did not). Faith consists in believing that the gospels are true.
But there is no need for repentance or conversion, since all men
are saved because they are men; that is, because as men they enjoy
union with Christ. John Murray's doctrine was essentially the
same. The elect are those who have faith, in Relly's sense; at
death they go to heaven. Unbelievers will suffer after death until
the truth enlightens them.

2) Calvinist Joseph Huntington. A partialist minister, whose
posthumous book disclosed his Universalism. All men are elected
to salvation. Human guilt, like property, can be transferred and
is transferred to Christ. There is endless punishment, but it will
be borne by Christ. Hence God is both just and merciful.

3) Arminian Elhanan Winchester. God, the creator of all, is
universally benevolent. He has given all things to Christ, who died
for all; nothing is to be lost. Men, now dwelling in ruined condition, need repentance. But all men will repent, either before
death or after. Thus some will need punishment in the future life.
But punishment, which at first enrages the recipient, is adjusted
to a man's abilities and opportunities to live righteously. Eventually it softens and humbles.

4) Unitarian Hosea Ballou. Human sin is a part of God's plan; it is finite and not, as the partialists taught, infinite. Sin injures only man, not God. If any man is miserable, all are miserable. The human will is not free but determined. Thus man acts in accordance with the strongest stimulus. What he needs is to recognize the strongest of all. He needs an atonement, an at-one-ment, a reconciliation to God. Contrary to partialist teachings, God does not need to be reconciled to man. He is at least as good as the best which good and great men have hoped for. It is this goodness, rather than any scheme of bargains about punishment, which ensures universal salvation.

Foster's analysis does not take us beyond this point. Since Universalist thought shifted from God's role to man's, since sociological and ethical considerations came to the fore, no comparable analysis has appeared.

Moreover, the above classification is concerned chiefly with ideas about the future life. It ignores two questions: (*a*) By what process does a man arrive at the conviction of universal salvation? (*b*) How does he seek to establish the truth of his conviction?

With respect to the first question this account has pictured individuals who, accepting the then common assumption of the divine inspiration of the Bible, studied it book by book, chapter by chapter, verse by verse, and then submitted their findings to their own best powers of interpretation. But powers and styles of interpretation vary. Before the acceptance of the principles of modern literary criticism, interpretation was usually fanciful and allegorical. Metaphysical meanings were given to words and texts. For example, when one read of Adam and of Jesus, these names did not call to mind human individuals on this earth; they were read as theological symbols of metaphysical forces affecting mankind.

This type of interpretation was habitual with many scholars within the more extreme early Protestant groups in Europe. In her recent thesis "Pietist Origins of American Universalism," Charlotte Irwin has traced in considerable detail the development of Universalist belief among several of these groups on the Continent and in England. She contends that there is a demonstrable connection between them and the positions taken by De Benneville, Relly, Murray, and Winchester. On the other hand, Ballou, influenced by the deism of Allen and by other rationalists, initiated a shift in the thought of American Universalists towards the ideas of the European Enlightenment. Reliance was still placed upon biblical texts, but these were given a more common-sense meaning. As biblical scholarship gradually became more widely understood, this approach was increasingly accepted.

Still another possibility may be suggested. Universalists were repelled by transcendentalism, especially by Parker's. But, although their conclusions might differ from his, some of them were probably transcendentalists in method, without knowing it. That is, they grasped, or believed themselves to grasp, the truth of Universalism intuitively. Theoretically there was no need to prove this truth by experience or logic, although like Parker they were impelled to try. In my youth I heard a minister tell his congregation that none of us need doubt for a moment the assurance of salvation for all, for he knew it to be unquestionably true.

What of the second question: How does one establish the truth of such a doctrine? Again in the early days the appeal was to the Bible. But as illustrated by Chapin and King, other methods supplemented this. For example, if one makes the traditional assumptions that God is both all-loving and all-powerful, it is easy to construct a logical argument for final righteousness for all.[30]

As our own intellectual climate began to admit widening skepticism concerning any future life whatsoever, Universalist emphasis shifted from the future life to universal brotherhood on earth. What appeal to the Bible remained was an appeal to its spiritual insights. Belief in universal brotherhood was either a fact to be supported by scientific evidence or a transcendental truth, or an ideal goal for human endeavor.

The Effect of Hegelianism and Darwinism[31]

Reference was made at the beginning of this chapter to the basic tenets of American thought, shared by Universalists with other denominations. Just as after the Revolution the pattern was shaken by deism, so after the Civil War a new threat appeared. The common faith was disturbed by the injection into American life of two revolutionary ideas: Hegelianism and Darwinism. I have found no evidence that Hegelianism, transmitted chiefly by New England transcendentalists and St. Louis educators, created any great stir among Universalists. But one may assume that indirectly it reinforced the Universalist gospel and played its part in the later developments of Restorationism. Certainly Universalists must have found the Hegelian doctrines more than compatible: man and nature are all parts of a single world process; ours is an expanding universe, capable by a roundabout process of indefinite progress; nothing is isolated, for all are bound together in a spiritual wholeness. In fact, the Universalist vision of salvation may be cast into a dialectic pattern of which the three moments are creation, sin, and salvation.

The second disturbing factor, Darwinism, offered a more severe challenge to those who maintained the faith of the Winchester Profession, for in asserting that natural law applies to life and mind it brought implications of mechanism. With its claim that only the species counts, it subordinated the individual, eventually reducing the once eternal moral code to a series of evolving human inventions. When in the years following 1871 these implications were fully grasped, American religious leaders diverged into three different courses: total repudiation of Darwinism as atheistic and hostile to religion, compromise, or frank acceptance of it as capable of fusion with religious views. These were years of confused thinking during which the concepts of development, growth, and progress had to be clarified as preliminary to accurate understanding of evolution. Religious liberals had to learn that natural selection casts doubt on the theory that

God is the great designer and that evolution does not necessarily imply conservation of all good. From 1860 to 1880 the doctrine of evolution was on probation even among scientists. During the next twenty years it infiltrated into various scholarly fields to become popularized by educated clergymen.

All these shades of opinion found expression in essays scattered through the volumes of the *Universalist Quarterly* from 1845 to 1888. Prior to Darwin's *Origin of Species* in 1859 the findings of geologists were sympathetically summarized, accompanied by expressions of respect for geology, with warnings against hasty misinterpretations. The writers generally accepted the biblical account of creation, finding no contradiction between it and geologic theory. Indeed, they felt that the study of nature promoted religion.

There were no discussions of biological evolution in the *Quarterly* until after the publication of Darwin's *Descent of Man* in 1871. The numbers of essays against evolution and for it are about equal. Several of those who were opposed set forth arguments to show that it had not received scientific acceptance. There was also opposition to Spencer's application of Darwinism to ethics.

Essays favorable to evolution began to appear in 1879. T. S. Lathrop, expressing some reservations, nevertheless wrote, "That God works by evolution, there can be no doubt." Orello Cone applied evolutionary theory to stages of biblical development. James Eastwood quoted Le Conte: Evolution is the "law of the divine working in time, as gravitation is . . . in space." Elsewhere Charles Fluhrer expressed similar sentiments: "Evolution is the law of Christianity—the law of its origin and of its life. . . . Evolution and Christianity may be considered names for one great process." It is interesting to find, as early as 1851, a phrase similar to that later used widely among Unitarians: "Our progress is upward and onward forever." The Unitarian version, suggested by James Freeman Clarke in 1886, proclaimed "the progress of mankind onward and upward forever."

Essays dealing with the relationship between science and

religion were frequent during this period. A few were critical of
the trend towards science in education, asserting that while both
science and religion are necessary, the popular emphasis was
depriving the young of training in conscience and spiritual growth.
On the other hand, S. H. McCollester lamented that in 1865
the study of natural history was neglected, not being required
until the senior year of college. One writer was thankful that the
study of science led to a better knowledge of God. Another con-
ceded that by science "the antiquity of man has been set back
for many centuries, the flood proved to have been only a partial
overflow . . . and a thousand theological dogmas exploded; and
yet religion, the true Divinity, stands even more securely." "The
best worship springs from the broadest minds," wrote John Coleman Adams in 1876. "The interest of both science and religion
will be promoted by an attitude of intelligent understanding of
each other on the part of both," was Orello Cone's message in
1882. And again in 1885 we hear from Adams: "The dreaded foe
is a friend in disguise."

From this sketch it will be seen that development of Universalist thought during these critical years closely paralleled the
general trend. Minot J. Savage, Unitarian, is often given credit
for being the first American clergyman to try to harmonize evolution and religion; his *The Religion of Evolution* appeared in 1876.
The definite acceptance of evolution by Henry Ward Beecher in
1885 gave it respectability. Gradually the clergy followed his lead
and that of Lyman Abbott. Protestant thought, according to Stow
Persons, moved into an evolutionary theism, finding evidence of
a divine plan in the cosmic order. The universal experience of the
race took the place of the Bible as a religious textbook; interest
shifted from a future life to the problems of ethical living. Out
of the old Calvinist struggle in which few are chosen there emerged
a "more charitable universalist economy of abundance which
promises room at God's banquet table for all who would work
for the privilege."[32]

THE EFFECT OF BIBLICAL CRITICISM

The real problem confronting American Christians at this time, according to Robert Scoon, was: How are devout Christians going to deal with advances in knowledge? We have seen how Universalists dealt with evolutionary theory. It remains to consider their reception of the higher criticism of the Bible. Early American Universalists generally based their belief upon literal acceptance of the entire Bible, including the miracles. The Ohio Western Reserve Association voted in 1834 that the only heresy should be the "denial of the authenticity of the Scriptures of the Old and New Testaments." In 1853 the Ohio State Convention, although disclaiming all right to prescribe formulas of faith, recognized the Holy Scriptures as a revelation and as a directory of faith and practice. The Boston Association, disturbed in 1847 by the rationalism of Theodore Parker, adopted by a large majority the resolution against rationalism, prepared by Hosea Ballou and mentioned above. Several writers in the *Quarterly* defended in whole or in part the authenticity of the Bible, or even the special responsibility of Universalists to act as defenders of this view.

But very early opposing views began to appear, so much so that Universalists, accused of being infidels, felt obliged to reject the friendly overtures of the freethinkers. As early as 1849 a writer in the *Quarterly* admitted that there were discrepancies in the Bible. Presently a historical sketch of biblical criticism appeared, and gradually voices were heard in favor of a modest retreat from the old position.

In 1865 I. M. Atwood, taking a hint from the Winchester Profession, used the phrase, "The Bible *contains* a revelation." Others continued the theme: the Bible as a whole is not the perfect word of God, but there are divine elements in it. It must be read intelligently and understandingly. Instead of isolated texts one must consult the scope and drift of the whole. Thus one would "pass from the deadness of a letter . . . to the glowing power of its underlying spirit." A distinctly modern voice was heard when Henry Blanchard asserted that the Bible was literature and not the word of God, that it contained words of inspiration but was not inspired, and that its matchless writings were full of power to induce noble living. He spoke for liberal Universalism, ethical, humanitarian, rationalistic. Certainly the Universalist who made our greatest contribution to biblical scholarship and to our acceptance of it was Orello Cone of St. Lawrence University and Buchtel College. He was for many years a regular contributor to the *Quarterly* and to other journals, as well as the author of several reputable books on biblical criticism. Recently Schlesinger has repeated the appraisal of Cone by J. M. Atwood and others before him: Cone's *Gospel Criticism and Historical Christianity,* appearing in 1891, was then the "ablest work from an American pen" in this field.[33] Forbes' paper on biblical criticism aroused intense debate at the Convention session of that year.

Cone was born in Lincklaen, New York, in 1835.[34] At the close of the Civil War he became a Universalist minister, soon joining the theological faculty at St. Lawrence. Most of his life was devoted to teaching there and at Buchtel and to writing scholarly books and journal articles.[35]

RATIONALISM

In American church history rationalism frequently refers to the views of Unitarianism's great heretic, Theodore Parker. In general his positive influence among Universalists was slight. Nevertheless, the Boston resolution of 1847 was a manifesto of dissociation from him. To Alonzo Miner and Elbridge Brooks his gospel was nothing but a Christless deism. These men distinguished between Parker's rationalism and their own milder concessions necessary to accommodate the new biblical criticisms.

Another whipping boy for Universalists was Abner Kneeland, convicted in Boston of blasphemy. He had been an able Universalist clergyman and denominational official. Eventually he came to hold a position which marks him as a forerunner of later humanism, whereupon his former comrades abandoned him. In his first trial he asserted that he had written, "Universalists believe in a God which I do not," whereas the prosecutor insisted that what he had really meant was, "Universalists believe in a God, which I do not." The comma made the difference between a divergent concept of God and atheism.

The early incident in Indiana was in part a conflict between a rationalist and his opponents. Kidwell, the rationalist, rejected miracles, whereas Rogers and Manford insisted upon the conventional position. Indiana Universalists were so bitterly divided that no real solution was ever worked out, but with the death of Kidwell the controversy ended.

In the 1880's the rationalist position was strongly advocated by a group of ministers, including J. M. Pullman, E. L. Rexford, S. A. Gardner, and Henry Blanchard. They supported a monthly journal published in Newark by W. S. Crowe. Their opponents, led by A. A. Miner, insisted on superimposing upon the denomination what had previously been generally accepted: a more literal interpretation of the Bible, miracles, and the uniqueness of Jesus.[36] Candidates for ordination became victims of conflicting examiners, and George Perin was hampered in his effort to unite liberals in Japan.

ATTEMPTS TO CHANGE THE WINCHESTER PROFESSION

As the new knowledge from the natural sciences and from a critical study of the Bible permeated Universalist circles, it seems that the denomination was fairly successful in meeting these challenges and adjusting to them. But differences of opinion, illustrated by the *Quarterly* articles mentioned in the preceding section and by the sermon titles listed in Chapter Five, appeared in other forms. One such form was a growing criticism of the Winchester Profession. In 1893 the Pasadena Church "suspended" the creed, ridiculing the phrase "contains a revelation." Other churches interpreted the phrase to mean whatever they wished. In 1894 the Iowa Convention voted disapproval of the Profession. One writer commented, "We will work under the old creed with local option."[37]

Critics of the Profession objected to the hedonism of the third article. Even more the word *restore* gave trouble, not because it implied Restorationism but because it implied the truth of the Garden of Eden account and, later, the falsity of the theory of evolution. In 1878 a simple motion to change *restore* to *bring* was lost by a vote of 3 to 25. Opposition to change was partly based on sentimental affection for the seventy-five-year-old document, by many regarded as historic and sacred. But at every Convention session from 1878 through 1894 the subject came up in some manner. New forms of thought, social life, and industry were thought by many to call for a new statement of Universalist religion.[38] None of these efforts succeeded.

In the sessions of 1893 and 1895 a combination of committee recommendations and amendments by delegates led to what was seemingly going to be accepted. The proposal went to the session of 1897 for final ratification. It read approximately as follows: We believe in the universal Fatherhood of God and in the Brotherhood of man; that God, who hath spoken through all His holy prophets since the world began, hath spoken unto us by His Son Jesus Christ, our Example and Saviour; that salvation consists in spiritual oneness with God, who through Christ will finally gather in one the whole family of mankind. The proposal was adopted, 69 to 15, and went over to the next session for final ratification. But at the 1897 session it was defeated, 1 to 102. Something had been happening in the meantime.

In April, 1897, George T. Knight of Tufts College, who had been appointed chairman of a revision committee, addressed a letter to ministers, asking three questions: What creed is used in your parish? What creed is a condition of church membership? Does the use of the Winchester Profession deter people from joining the church? One should note that these questions tacitly admit that the creedal requirement imposed by the General Convention was not being enforced. Twenty-four replies are preserved in the Universalist Historical Society Library, but several of them failed to answer the questions asked. They indicated, however, that six parishes used the Winchester Profession; one used another statement; five used none. One minister stated that he did not know what creed was supposed to be used. As to the requirement for church membership, nine used the Winchester Profession; two used a modification of it; ten used some other creed; five used none. Of the other creeds used, no two were identical. Four ministers thought the Winchester Profession a deterrent to church membership; eight thought it not; three said they did not know; the remainder expressed no opinion. Among Sunday schools of the Boston area thirteen repeated the Profession every Sunday; one, three times a month; one, twice a month; three, occasionally; one, not at all. At Waltham the children were taught the Profession as the historical creed of Universalism, but as something which the majority of the church members did not believe.

Even from this small sampling it is evident that there was much variation in the use of the Winchester Profession. The correspondence with Professor Knight also showed confusion as to whether the documents discussed were to be taken historically, ritualistically, or dogmatically. Out of this and other discussions under Knight's leadership there was brought about in 1899 an agreement by which the Winchester Profession was retained without amendment as a historic statement; the provision making it a condition of fellowship was withdrawn, a new statement of five principles was adopted, and the Winchester Profession was commended as containing these principles.[39]

THE BOSTON PROFESSION OF FAITH (1899)

At the 1897 Convention the following statement was adopted, 94 to 30; it was ratified at Boston two years later, 130 to 10:

We believe in
  The Universal Fatherhood of God;
  The Spiritual Authority and Leadership of His Son, Jesus Christ;
  The Trustworthiness of the Bible as containing a Revelation from God;
  The certainty of Just Retribution for Sin;
  The final Harmony of all Souls with God.

The fourth clause, not included in the committee's original recommendation, was introduced as an amendment. The new Profession, widely used, often served as a basis for a series of sermons on what Universalists believe.

THE HUMANIST CONTROVERSY

The humanist controversy is usually thought of as a Unitarian affair, but it had its effect upon Universalists also. *Humanism* is a word with many connotations. There is Renaissance Humanism, humanism as a tool of literary criticism, humanism as a synonym for the pragmatism of William James, humanism as proclaimed in a series of books edited by Ruth Anshen, and a vague popular humanism confused with humanitarianism. What is here being considered is humanism as introduced into Unitarianism in the 1920's. It first came forcibly to my attention in the summer of 1921, when Curtis Reese was urging upon a group of ministers attending the University of Chicago the proposition that theism is philosophically possible but not religiously necessary. By this he meant that it is possible to be religious without believing in God and immortality.

Conservative Unitarians found this shocking. The battle was on. Theistic attacks pushed humanists to counterattack. Soon some were asserting that belief in God was mere superstition. A historically important document, the Humanist Manifesto, was issued in 1933 by a group of philosophers, clergymen, and others. It was signed by two Universalists: Clinton Lee Scott and Charles Potter. Potter was already leader of a humanist society, but specifically called attention to his continuing Universalist status.[40]

Many believed that the controversy would split the Unitarians, but this threat was averted. Nevertheless, the situation was aggravated as many non-religious people joined the humanists. Thus its opponents could contend that the movement was anti-religious. Ultimately a reaction to this tendency within the movement itself prompted a new Society of Religious Humanists.

This condensed statement must serve as a background for Universalist reactions. At first those opposed to cooperation with the Unitarians were able to say, "I told you so." But soon Universalist humanists began to be heard within the fold. By 1930 many favorable articles, especially from the younger men, were appearing in the *Leader*. The YPCU journal *Onward* deleted the phrase "For Christ and his Church" from its masthead. Theists and humanists battled for a hearing and for disapproval of opponents. Some, John Murray Atwood for example, urged tolerance.[41] The debate was often bitter and never decisive. Gibbon's Convention sermon of 1949 contended that Universalism was not a Christian denomination; it was a universal religion of Christian origin. In the legal charter what had been the Christian ministry became the Universalist ministry.[42] Gradually the debate, like earlier debates, lost its urgency if not its importance.

THE WASHINGTON PROFESSION (1935) AND ITS CRITICS

The Boston Profession was perhaps out of date from its very beginning. At the Winchester Centennial in 1903, for example, the use of *retribution* was challenged by Cantwell. The Boston Profession, adopted in the year when Dewey published *School and Society*, when Veblen brought out *The Theory of the Leisure Class,* and Starbuck his *Psychology of Religion,* when the first long-distance automobile trip was made—from Cleveland to New York—gives no indication of the changes then impending in American life and thought. About 1900 the ethics of American industrial and business methods were beginning to be challenged economically, morally, and socially. A great gulf had introduced itself between the churches and the underprivileged. The social gospel, now beginning to be heard, was accentuated in 1907 by Rauschenbusch in his *Christianity and the Social Crisis* and in the following year by the adoption of the Social Creed of the Churches. Universalists followed suit with a Declaration of Social Principles, adopted at Worcester in 1917. During these years an increasing number of Universalists became active in preaching and practicing the social gospel. Outstanding among them was Clarence Skinner of New York, the Boston area, and Tufts College.[43]

A Universalist social gospel was not new. A century earlier Universalism had come to mean a glorious way as well as a glorious goal. Sentiment for anti-slavery and for temperance had been strong. Abner Kneeland and Orestes Brownson were early advocates of social action. Morse, Pickering, and Fuller had opposed the efforts of Ezra Stiles Ely to organize an American theocracy. Adin Ballou had been an activist. Perin and others had developed institutional churches. Thus the adoption of a set of social principles was in harmony with tradition. The Washington Profession, eighteen years later, was the work of a committee, of which Frederick Perkins was chairman. Appointment of the committee had been authorized in 1931. With minor amendments and a decision to retain both the Winchester and the Washington professions, the committee's proposed statement was adopted unanimously by two successive General Convention sessions.

The Washington Profession, which supplemented rather than replaced the two earlier professions, read as follows:

> The bond of fellowship in this Convention shall be a common purpose to do the will of God as Jesus revealed it and to cooperate in establishing the Kingdom for which he lived and died.
>
> To that end we avow our faith in God as Eternal and All-Conquering Love, in the spiritual leadership of Jesus, in the supreme worth of every human personality, in the authority of truth known or to be known, and in the power of men of good will and sacrificial spirit to overcome all evil and progressively establish the kingdom of God. Neither this nor any other statement shall be imposed as a creedal test, provided that the faith thus indicated be professed.

Perkins thought that the statement of a common purpose would emphasize the primary business of the church, lessen regard for creed as an end in itself, and furnish a new motive for loyalty. He admitted that the phrases were not designed for ritualistic repetition.

Some did not like the new form. The *Leader* soon began to print its own profession: We believe in the Fatherhood of God, the Responsibility of Man, the Leadership of Jesus, the Victory of Good, and the Life Everlasting.[44] Neither this nor the Washington Profession pleased the humanists. A dozen years later critics were vocal with objections to the final clause, "provided that the faith thus indicated be professed." This they judged contradictory to the traditional assertion of liberty. For several years this debate went on.[45] In 1953 the clause was deleted.

COMPARISON OF THE THREE PROFESSIONS

It is convenient in this section to refer to the three documents by the names of the communities in which they were adopted: Winchester, Boston, and Washington.

As possible ritualistic elements to be included in a service of worship the three statements show a deterioration in poetic quality. Winchester is rhythmically recitable. Boston is marred by an awkward unevenness of line length. Washington was not intended by its author to be used in public worship. But it has been so used, perhaps rather widely, by congregations who seem to have difficulty in repeating it in unison.

The content of the three professions reflects something of our history. All three agree in asserting the continuing theistic emphasis on God as a God of love. The important corollary, universal salvation, is proclaimed in Winchester and Boston but is not explicit in Washington. The ethical note moves from individualism in Winchester to social ethics in Washington. Jesus, who is Lord in Winchester, is elevated to a place of authority and leadership in Boston but loses his authority in Washington. Authority is there to be found in truth. Washington shifts the basis of loyalty from belief to purpose. Boston introduces one new idea: the certainty of just punishment. In Washington there is reference neither to punishment nor to a future life.

Washington includes two new ideas not expressed earlier: "the supreme worth of every human personality" and "the power of men of good will and sacrificial spirit to overcome all evil and progressively establish the Kingdom of God." The first, somewhat awkwardly and illogically, may be intended to express the idea of universal salvation. The second reflects the influence of religious humanism. We learn that evil is to be abolished and the kingdom of God established, but not by God as our forefathers would have asserted: that men of right will and spirit are to accomplish this, or at least they have the power to do so. Men have the power to overcome not only moral evil but indeed all evil, which must include physical evil as well. What stronger statement could a humanist ask for? It is a long passage from Winchester to Washington, from the day when men merely had to maintain order and practice good works to the day when they are given the power to vanquish all evil.

HERESY

It has been claimed that the Universalist story has been marred by but a single heresy trial. This statement may be technically correct, but it is misleading. Both Brownson and Kneeland were dropped without hearings. Doubtless Brownson did not object, but Kneeland might have appreciated kindlier treatment. How many may have been given similar dismissal is not known. Others have chosen to withdraw from lack of support or from open opposition. Roland Conner was forced out on account of his activity in the Free Religious Association.[46] Everett Rexford, longtime denominational and educational leader but inclined towards rationalism, was accused by T. J. Sawyer of "infidelity." When I called on him fifty years ago in Columbus, Ohio, he was minister of an independent church.

The Brownson and Kneeland cases excited the denomination. So did the case of unstable Matthew Hale Smith. At the age of twenty, after three years as an orthodox preacher, he was ordained a Universalist at Hartford in 1830. Five years later he renounced Universalism, soon claiming that he was insane when he did so. Restored to fellowship, he served as minister at Quincy and at

Haverhill. By the Massachusetts Convention he was accused of deceptive letters and once forgiven and once censured. He then withdrew from the Convention, but continued to preach to Universalists at Salem. In 1840 he again renounced Universalism, again claimed that he had been insane, was reinstated, and then made his third renunciation. After these vacillations he preached in orthodox pulpits.

The one clear case of heresy concerns Herman Bisbee, minister of the St. Anthony Society. (St. Anthony is now within the city limits of Minneapolis.) His elder colleague in Minneapolis was J. H. Tuttle, an anti-evolutionist. Bisbee was gradually modifying his views under the impacts of Darwinism and rationalism. In presenting his new insights in sermons and lectures he criticized the position of Tuttle. Tuttle was offended. Another minister, William Haskell, recently from another state and a sympathizer with Bisbee, became involved. The controversy was fanned by the denominational press. The society supported its minister, but the Minnesota Convention refused to accept Haskell and by a vote of 47 to 23 withdrew fellowship from Bisbee, without any formal charges. Upon appeal the General Convention found him guilty of preaching heretical doctrines.[47]

A Concluding Question

Orthodox Christians once insisted that religious living is impossible without a belief in everlasting punishment; Restorationists, that it is impossible without a belief in limited future punishment; traditionalist Universalists, that is impossible without a belief in biblical revelation and miracles; theists, that it is impossible without a belief in God and immortality; humanists, that it is impossible without a belief in man and his capacities.

Is religious living promoted or hindered by official statements of religious belief?

CHAPTER 7

Relationships with Unitarians and Others (1778-1925)

"How about Universalism in England?" I am sometimes asked. An adequate answer requires much more data than is available to me. But as a partial response let us go back to "the beginning." The traditional story in America opens with Murray bringing the message from the mother country. Murray had heard it from a London preacher, James Relly (1722–1778). Under the influence of George Whitfield, Relly became a Methodist missionary, first in Wales, then in England.[1] By independent thinking he became a Universalist, spreading the doctrine as a traveling preacher until he settled in London about 1757. A century and a half later plans were drawn to remodel the "Cavendish Road property" as a James Relly memorial.[2]

ELHANAN WINCHESTER IN LONDON

Information about Winchester in American accounts of his life permit one easily to infer that his departure for England was a sudden impulse just a few days before sailing, that he arrived totally unacquainted, remained several years with no steady employment, and returned to America for no apparent reason. An English account of his life reveals that such inferences are incomplete and partly incorrect.[3]

The doctrine of universal salvation was proclaimed in England as early as the fourteenth century, but the group of believers with which we are concerned began to assemble perhaps as early as

1757.[4] Prior to Winchester's arrival it was meeting for weekday discussions in a private home in London. At its sessions some persons defended, some attacked, Restorationism. Also it met for worship on Sundays, first in a small room "in Moorfields," then at the home of the Clegg family. After a worship service anyone present was invited to inquire about or explain any theological question. When a copy of Winchester's sermon, "The Outcast Comforted," arrived, it was read with approval by members of the group, which apparently had no contact with Relly's followers.

Clegg's business required a journey to America. With him went his son. Eagerly making the acquaintance of Winchester, the older man developed a close friendship with him. Indeed, he died in the arms of his new friend, but not before he had told him of the Universalists in London. Winchester's earlier thought of going to England was strengthened by this account. Thus, although his arrangements for departure in July, 1787, were made within a few days, the decision to go was not a mere sudden impulse. Moreover, although he had neither acquaintance nor correspondent in England, he was armed with, or preceded by, a note from Clegg's son to an uncle. It was this note, rather than introductions furnished by Benjamin Rush, that gave him his entree.

The Universalists, although few in number, found opportunities for him to preach occasionally. Soon they provided for him the Chapel in Parliament Court, where he won a following. He was the first to state publicly the position of English Universalists of that period. As an assistant he recruited William Vidler.[5] This permitted him to find preaching appointments in other places. Support developed to the point where he discussed with Vidler the possibility of organizing a conference.[6]

In England Winchester acted as interpreter of American life. "An Oration on the Discovery of America" was delivered in October, 1792. "A Century Sermon" in November, 1788, commemorated three events. In 1588 the English defeated the Spanish Armada. In 1688 they brought William and Mary to the throne, securing liberty of property, personal security, trial by jury, freedom of the press, and liberty of conscience and of religion. These ideals were reinforced by the adoption of the American Constitution in 1788.

On the morning of May 1, 1794, Winchester disappeared. His London friends never saw him again. Eighteen days later he sailed for America. But like his eastward voyage, this was no mere whim. Before sailing, he wrote several letters to his friends, some of which are reproduced in Vidler's account. Immediately after receiving the first, a committee visited his home. Here they secured confirmation from his wife and a servant of the truth of his assertions.

Winchester was married five times, but this was no laughing matter. He believed that to avoid gossip and criticism, a minister ought to be married. Perhaps this was especially necessary for him. His own testimony is that he was deeply attached to his wives. The first four were brief but happy unions, all ended by death. At least two wives died in childbirth; one died of a very painful cancer. Although he had several children, none lived beyond infancy. Two of his marriages were in Philadelphia: to Mary Morgan in July, 1781, in Christ Church, and to Mary Knowles in October, 1784, in the Baptist church.

He thought his fifth mate suitable and attractive, but actually she was what we would call a mental case. There were then neither physicians nor hospitals for such as she. Divorce was not to be considered. Outwardly she was so normal that no one suspected her condition. At home she was subject to severe tantrums of rage and abuse. Not only this, but she repeatedly attacked her husband physicially with blows, acts of torture, and threats to kill him. It was after one such violent episode, on a background of ten years of similar episodes, that Winchester left home.

Winchester interpreted his parental and marital experiences as punishment from God for his pride. He even developed his theological ideas of punishment, I believe, out of his own suffering. His English friends made comfortable provision for his wife, but she insisted on following him to America.

LIBERAL CHURCHES IN GREAT BRITAIN

The Chapel in Parliament Court continued with diminished vitality under Vidler's leadership. He soon accepted Unitarianism, and was succeeded in 1817 by an interesting Unitarian, William Johnson Fox.[7] The relationship between Universalists and Unitarians in England differed from the relationship here. In this country Unitarians were at first members of the Establishment. In England they, as well as Universalists, were "come-outers." Perhaps this lack of distinct cleavage between the two sects explains why some of the early letters from American Universalists to England were addressed to Unitarians.

For example, in 1828 at Eaton, Ohio, the General Convention of the Western States instructed William D. Jones to correspond with the London Unitarian Society for the Promotion of Christian Knowledge and Virtue, requesting that they "communicate to us from time to time all interesting and useful matter which may come to their knowledge, respecting the increase of liberal principles, in the old world throughout Europe, Asia, and elsewhere, and all other matters which they may deem interesting to a society of people who are searching after truth."[8] Two years later Jones reported receiving books and pamphlets from this organization. In 1866 at Galesburg the General Convention received a communication from English Unitarian ministers expressing congratulations for the end of the war and hopes that peace would promote denominational success. A friendly reply was authorized. Occasional contacts with this group were maintained for some years.

Scattered throughout England and Scotland were lonely groups of Universalists.[9] At the Convention of 1872 much interest was aroused by an appeal from a Universalist of Scotland for aid to a group of Scottish churches, originally established by the followers of James Relly or their descendants. There were churches at Dunfermline, Glasgow, and Larbert. At least in the last community there was a church building and a minister. For some years the Convention supported a "Scottish Mission." Caroline

A. Soule was sent over in 1875 as an "accredited evangel" of the Women's Centenary Association. She went a second time in 1878 at the invitation of the Larbet church. While there she was ordained by the Scottish Convention, thus becoming, so it is claimed, the first women to be ordained in Europe. Connection with these churches was continued at least until 1894.[10]

We may also note here that there was an early Universalist movement in Nova Scotia[11] and that in 1956 communication was established with a group of Universalist churches in the Philippines.[12]

FRIENDS AND OPPONENTS IN AMERICA

From the beginning of our movement, relationships with other denominations in the United States have been variable, depending on place, time, and individuals. In 1790 in the Philadelphia area there was a friendliness manifested by some of the German sects, some Baptists, some Episcopalians, some deists. In Rhode Island and southeastern Massachusetts an occasional Baptist or Episcopalian pulpit would welcome Murray or Winchester. Cobb seems often to have been welcome to use Unitarian churches for an occasional service. Brooks in Cambridge promoted union meetings in which he was joined by both Unitarians and Methodists. Usually, however, the attitude was likely to be one of open opposition and attack.

According to denominational folklore there were even threats of violence. In Philadelphia the contra argument once took the form of beating on pans, throwing stones, and promised assassination. In New Orleans a mayor threatened the arrest of anyone preaching Universalism, except on shipboard. So on shipboard were the services held. Another form of opposition was to assert that such a belief as Universalism removed all restraint, made men bad and kept them so. Its adherents were said to be profane, licentious, immoral, without benevolence, unwilling to listen to preaching against the sins of the day. Universalism was thought to be a steppingstone to religious infidelity. Even the competence of Universalists to testify in court was challenged. The basis was an old English decision, about which American practice varied. It was reported in 1828 that in New York testimony of a Universalist had been admitted, that in Connecticut those who did not believe in future rewards and punishments (Ultra Universalists?) were excluded, and that in Massachusetts the credibility of a Universalist could be challenged.

More scholarly were the doctrinal challenges. It was puzzling to Andrew Croswell of Boston in 1775 that God permitted Murray to preach "in these parts," sowing his tares and delivering young rakes and old sinners from the qualms of conscience. The following year John Cleavland wrote, "an Attempt to nip in the Bud the unscriptural doctrine of Universal Salvation which a certain Stranger, who calls himself John Murray, has of late been endeavoring to spread in the First Parish of Gloucester." (An excellent collection of pamphlets on such themes may be found at the American Antiquarian Society in Worcester.) Universalists replied forcefully to all such accusations, asserting orthodoxy to be the real source of despair and degradation. Back and forth there was much citing of alleged statistics concerning criminals and the insane.

As the liberal gospel moved to the frontier, the battle became bitter, even unethical and unchristian. The partialists hoped to check the Universalist tide, whereas the Universalists sought to liberalize the theology of their opponents. The politest form of argument was either publishing a planned controversial correspondence or public debating. There were numerous instances of both. One of the last almost professional Universalist debaters was T. E. Ballard of Indiana. In a conversation about 1916 he expressed to me his conviction that public debate was the fairest form of theological discussion.

It is difficult to determine just when a more tolerant attitude arose. Perhaps it was after the Civil War that Universalists, at least in some communities, were able to cooperate with other churches in interdenominational activities. Yet this privilege was not always granted, as for example in membership requirements for the

YMCA. In some cities our ministers have been welcomed into ministerial associations; in some, not. For several years from about 1925 on the General Convention gave attention to cooperation and comity, appointing commissions and arranging conferences. The right of a local church to federate with a church of another denomination and to hold dual fellowship, and the similar right of a minister, was recognized in 1917.

The Convention occasionally expressed itself with respect to other denominations or interdenominational organizations. To the Free Religious Association (1867–1927) few Universalists were attracted. Representatives were sent to the New York City meeting of the Evangelical Alliance in 1873. From time to time fraternal delegates from other sects were welcomed by the Convention and accorded special privileges. Five representatives attended the Protestant Missionary Society of the United States and Canada in 1893. A committee on cooperation with other denominations was authorized. In 1921 delegates were appointed to a session of the New Thought Alliance. To the National Spiritualist Convention greetings, but not delegates, were once sent. Cooperation with the Federal Council of Churches and financial contributions for the council's work in industrial areas were reported in 1925. Increasingly aid was voted for projects not controlled by the denomination. Many of these are described by Lalone. Here we may note activities of the Social Service Commission, the setting aside of a yearly Sunday School Sunday, cooperation with the Fellowship of Reconciliation, and contributions for Near East Relief.

Increasing tolerance, growing urbanity, and advances in scholarly research gave pause to thoughtful Universalists. In 1880 John Coleman Adams wrote "New Problems in our Church Work," in which he expressed doubts about the future of our denomination.[13] Already among the educated, he said, it was no longer convincing to appeal to isolated random biblical texts. The study of biblical exegesis will continue to be modified. New interpretations of theological terms will be proposed. As churches of other denominations become less rigid, Universalists will feel more at home in them and be admitted to membership. Accompanying this easing of tensions is our disposition to proclaim Universalism merely as a hope rather than a conviction. Adams feared that our future was being rendered uncertain.

Several of our ministers participated in the New Thought movement of the early 1900's. Although respectfully listened to, they were unsuccessful in their effort to persuade the denomination to go along. After the emergence of Reform Judaism there was fraternizing in many cities between Rabbis and the Unitarian and Universalist pastors. Their example seldom led their congregations to do more than hold services together on Thanksgiving Day.

As we direct our story towards the merger, relationships with Unitarians must demand our chief attention. The discussion will first consider doctrines and then organizations. The classical over-quoted statement of the difference between the two sects is usually attributed to Thomas Starr King, although he once gave credit to an unidentified layman: Universalists believe that God is too good to damn man; Unitarians, that man is too good to be damned. George H. Emerson analyzed the difference as chiefly one of taste, rather than one of principle.[14]

THE MEANING OF UNITARIANISM IN 1800

In this study the word *Universalism* refers chiefly to a religious organization, the General Convention, with its constituent state conventions, associations, and societies. In the chapter on Universalist beliefs the same word refers to a profession or system of beliefs. In practice organization and doctrine are closely related, but in theory they may be discussed separately. Universalism as a doctrine is ancient. As an American organization it is recent.

So it is with the word *Unitarianism*. There is Unitarian doctrine and there is Unitarian organization. The former is ancient, the latter recent. As organization Unitarianism signifies (for our purposes) the American Unitarian Association and its affiliated bodies. As doctrine it signifies (in its inclusive sense) a denial of the doctrine of the Trinity and the affirmation of the unity of God. Thus it means *anti-trinitarianism*. But one who takes this position is expected by his opponents to offer some theory concerning the place of Jesus in the Christian scheme. If Jesus is not God, who is he? And what is his role in the drama of salvation?

Anti-trinitarianism expresses itself in several classic forms. Among these are Arianism, Socinianism, and (in its narrow sense) Unitarianism. In oversimplified terms these doctrines may be defined thus: Arianism holds that Christ, although of a similar nature to God, was a being intermediate between God and man. Socinianism teaches that Jesus was a true man, yet not a mere man, for he was born of a virgin, lived sinlessly, and performed miracles. Unitarianism (again, in the narrow sense) affirms that Jesus was a being of strictly human origin, either with or without a special mission to perform.

An easily overlooked fact about American Unitarianism is that the men who were on the liberal side in the nineteenth-century split within New England Congregationalism were not Unitarians in this narrow sense. In the more inclusive anti-trinitarian sense they were Unitarians. Better described as Arians, they felt themselves unfairly used when their opponent forced the Unitarian label upon them.[15] It was with reluctance that they accepted it.

Since that period the connotation of the word has so broadened that it is no longer restricted to matters of ancient theology. But if we are to understand the relationship of our two denominations, we need this much of a background of doctrinal positions. We shall now consider the prevalence of Unitarian beliefs among Universalists. When early Universalists affirmed Unitarian views, this was likely to mean Arian views. Gradually there was acceptance of a more specifically unitarian position. In what follows, however, exact shades of opinion will not be considered.

UNITARIAN BELIEFS AMONG UNIVERSALISTS

Among early Unitarians there were those who were silent about universal salvation or who even preached endless suffering.[16] Similarly there have always been Universalists who were not Unitarians in any sense of that word.[17] John Murray and Edward

Mitchell were among these. Their views were set forth in the *Berean,* a journal issued irregularly from 1802 to 1811. Elihu Palmer was denied fellowship by Philadelphia Universalists because of his Unitarian views. The opposite or Unitarian trend was expressed in Sargent's *Free Universal Magazine* (1793) and in the *Gospel Visitant* (1811 f.), a quarterly produced by Ballou, Turner, and others.

In 1792 the churches in New Jersey, presumably under the influence of Sargent, proclaimed that there was but one God, one person in the Godhead, and that the Mediator was "the man Christ Jesus." In a sermon three years later Ballou presented Unitarian views, which soon spread widely among his adherents. There were some who took offense, but there was no schism over trinitarian versus unitarian views. By 1816 probably the only trinitarian ministers were Mitchell and Paul Dean. This does not mean that in the years which followed every Universalist minister was antitrinitarian. But throughout our history outspoken trinitarians have been in the minority. I recall two in my youth who always showed up at YPCU conventions. My impression is that generally there was no widespread diversity in views about God and Christ between the two denominations. The fact that Unitarians became a separate denomination about 1825 perhaps diminished the responsibility which Universalists might otherwise have felt to battle against trinitarianism.

It was once argued by S. R. Smith that Universalists were earlier than Unitarians in affirming the common view about divine unity, denial of vicarious atonement, denial of man's moral depravity, and affirmation of the paternity of God. Neither denomination, he goes on to say, has anything to boast of in piety and practical morality.[18] However that may be, it is now generally agreed that Ballou's *Treatise on Atonement* was the first Unitarian book published in America.[19]

My own recollections offer only a hazy image of views concerning Jesus held by ministers whom I knew. My impression is that there was a lack of theological precision. I doubt if there were many trinitarians among them. They were inclined to stress the divinity, but not the deity, of Jesus and to look upon the Unitarian emphasis upon his humanity as too extreme.

Unitarians had scarcely established themselves as an independent denomination when they were troubled by internal controversy over transcendentalism. The subversives of that period have become the saints of today. At that time, however, conservative members of our two denominations shared a common acceptance of an inspired Bible, the saving moral influence of Jesus, and the historicity of miracles. Those few Universalists who were attracted towards transcendentalism were taken to task by their conservative brethren. Concern over their own Restorationist controversy blinded Universalists to the larger universalism of Emerson and Parker. Neither Emerson nor Universalists seem to have noticed to any great degree the existence of the other. In 1871, A. D. Mayo called attention to Universalist opposition to the Free Religious Association.[20] Yet both these movements must have contributed to the trend towards Universalist rationalism.

CONDITIONS WHICH KEPT THE TWO DENOMINATIONS APART

Charles Lyttle names four causes which kept the two denominations separate.[21] Unitarian inclusion in the Establishment together with traditions there generated was one cause. Class differences were another, for Universalists were frequently obscure people, whose ministers indulged in uncouth enthusiasms. The third cause was the early predominance of Ultra Universalism; Unitarians found this repugnant. And the fourth was political. New England Unitarians tended to be Federalists; Universalists, anti-Federalists or Jeffersonians. Politics may have also interfered with fraternizing between Boston Unitarians and Philadelphia Unitarians influenced by Jefferson and Priestley. It was not until 1850, says Lyttle, that Unitarians and Universalists began to recognize their theological affinity.

In Massachusetts until 1833 both Unitarians and Trinitarians were part of the Establishment. The only clear instance of a Universalist church becoming eligible to receive tax money from the state occurred in Malden.[22] Established churches tended to be arrayed against Baptists, Methodists, and Universalists, who had to appeal to the courts for their rights and who were thus opposed to the Establishment. In 1838 Whittemore attacked the Standing Order in his *Trumpet*.

The Establishment ceased; political parties changed; Ultra Universalism gave way to Restorationism. But the difference in social strata lingered. Universalism arose not out of the "schools" but out of the intense needs of common people. Its early members were often farmers, middle-class merchants, or even frontiersmen. Its first ministers, amazingly intelligent though they were, lacked formal education. Its first societies either had no buildings at all or else met in the humblest of structures. In Massachusetts in 1850 the average value of a Unitarian building was $14,000, of a Universalist $5,000.

Unitarianism arose in Harvard halls and hallowed pulpits of long-established churches in cultured centers. Its first societies had nearly two centuries of colonial background, with buildings of great beauty. Its early members were city folk, prosperous and pillars of the economic and professional life of their communities.[23]

Early Unitarians felt superior to Universalists, who in turn felt inferior. In some respects these feelings were factually justified, but in other respects they were baseless on both sides. Yet the feelings existed and hindered mutual understanding and decent neighborliness. Universalists felt that they were being snubbed by Unitarians, and perhaps they were, for often early Unitarians refused to pay the mark of ministerial courtesy of that period—an exchange of pulpits.[24] To Universalists, Unitarians seemed high-hat, patronizing. To Unitarians, Universalists lived on the wrong side of the tracks. Unitarians of Malden once quarreled over the proposal to permit Universalists to use their building. Channing, it was alleged, warned his colleagues against the Universalists, and in 1824 the *Christian Register* attacked and ridiculed them. But three years later Ballou praised Channing for his avowal of Universalism.[25]

The Unitarian movement, wrote I. M. Atwood, "had no infancy. . . . It had numbers, wealth, high social position, the strength of eminent names, and the fascination of the best culture of the period. . . . When the Universalists were humble, poor, unlettered, the Unitarians were rarely conscious of their existence." In unchristian fashion, he continued, the Universalists cherished the memory of this treatment, with the result that when at a later date Unitarians made friendly overtures, these were repulsed. If early there could have been mutual support, the outcome might have been better for both groups.[26] "Without representation, such as the Unitarians enjoyed, on bench and bar and boards of trade, its growth was slow, while the strong Separatist tendency within it prevented adequate ecclesiastical organization."[27]

Under frontier conditions barriers were less formidable. At Pittsford, New York, in 1813 the Universalist church was composed largely of English Unitarians. Universalists cooperated with Starr King in his Unitarian church of San Francisco, which in the sixties included many of that faith, including one clergyman, Alpheus Bull. Nearly a half century ago in San Diego I was told that the Unitarian church there had been established with Universalist aid.

On the other hand, Adin Ballou stated that in 1813 Unitarians showed dislike, even disgust, towards all Universalists, including his Restorationist associates. So strong was this feeling that when he forsook Ultra Universalism he could not think of joining them. However, he accepted the pastorate of the First Parish of Mendon (Unitarian) and was soon enjoying warm personal friendships with a few colleagues of his new allegiance, especially Bernard Whitman and Samuel May. When Whitman helped to ordain a Universal Restorationist, he was rebuked by colleagues for inducting an uneducated man into the ministry. Some forty years later conditions were so changed that Ballou gladly accepted membership in the Worcester Unitarian Conference. Yet in Boston in 1848 when Starr King, not a college man, moved from a Universalist to a Unitarian pastorate, the church which called him was criticized severely by other Unitarians.[28] In both denominations any cooperative gesture was likely to be condemned by conservative leaders and editors.

Of Lyttle's four causes of separation the most persistent was class difference. Or more accurately, it was a *tradition* of difference. For Unitarians sometimes forgot that their churches had not been composed exclusively of persons all equally competent to become president of Harvard College. Their publicized intellectualism, often justly deserved, sometimes became a boast based on borrowed merit. Yet between the two denominations there had been an elusive difference, operative through the years. Indeed, to some degree it is still operative in the new merged denomination, even though Universalists have steadily improved their economic, educational, and social status, and Unitarians tend to dwell somewhat remotely from the neighborhood of Boston and are less exclusive.

But it took a long time. Today the constituency of the "Uni-Uni" group is a roughly defined social class, unlike that of which either parent was a member. Its rural population has diminished to an estimated less than 4 per cent of its total. Unitarian preeminence in social respectability has declined. The descendants of those who supported Starr King in San Francisco, it is said, are now to be found in the Episcopalian Cathedral. Religious lines are now redrawn.

I have emphasized these formal social distinctions in order that they may be admitted historically as once relevant, but also that they may be recognized presently as inapplicable. Officers and committees of the Unitarian Universalist Association, in my judgment, have been extremely conscientious in remembering the Universalist strand in the new mesh.

FACTORS WHICH DREW THE TWO DENOMINATIONS TOGETHER

Although at first there were but few instances of cooperation, the conditions just described do not correctly picture the total situation, for there were many within each group who accepted the ideals and approved the activities of the other, who were conscious of no psychological barriers, and who felt happy and at ease in one another's society. It was in the Unitarian church of Philadelphia that Priestley made his public avowal of Universalism. By 1840 there were occasional pulpit exchanges. By 1854 there were even suggestions of group cooperation in small communities.

"We stand side by side on the same great plane of free thought with the Unitarian Church and the Christian Connection," wrote Universalist R. O. Williams in 1875. He marveled that these movements were "not able to come nearer together . . . and work earnestly in common accord for a great Christian structure."[29] Unitarian Livermore, president of Meadville Theological School, wrote to the General Convention of 1886, "I have . . . wished . . . that Unitarians and Universalists . . . might be brought into more helpful and cooperative union. And I see from afar that glorious day advancing. May it come soon!" These hopes were long shared by many.

The earliest advocacy of merger to come to my attention is reported by Alfred Cole, who asserts that in 1856 a writer in the *New York Evening Mirror* quoted from Unitarian sources the suggestion of fusion of the two denominations.[30] From then on the possibility was in the air, now praised, now condemned. What follows is the story from the Universalist side. It will not attempt to be the complete account of events but will rather present a sampling to indicate the course of our history.

The shift of Starr King to a Unitarian pulpit without ceasing his public avowal of Universalist convictions adumbrated events which were to come. May we not say that the merger first occurred over one hundred years ago in the mind and heart of that remarkable man? Let us recall a few incidents which mark the trail.

In 1853 G. H. Webster, in connection with a request to the General Convention for fellowship while he was still in fellowship with the Unitarians, offered a resolution favoring Christian union on other than a doctrinal basis. His unaccepted proposal led to the appointment of a committee of twelve to consider "the expediency and propriety of inviting the cooperation of Liberal

Christians throughout the world in the assembly of the World's Convention for the promotion of Gospel Truth and the unity of the Christian spirit, and strengthening the bond of peace among men." Two years later this committee reported that a world conference was then inexpedient.

At the Convention of 1873 there appeared for the first time an official of the American Unitarian Association, in the person of Frederick Hinkley, who was received and seated. Thereafter interchange of fraternal delegates occurred with increasing frequency. By them greetings were communicated in both directions. In 1880 Unitarians found Universalists engaged in "much the same battle as ourselves for the simple, practical gospel of Christ." "We reciprocate," replied the Universalists, "the expression of interest and sympathy from a sister church in a common world of religious enlightenment."

The World Parliament of Religions, held in Chicago in 1894, with subsequent sessions in 1895 and 1896, was regarded by the institutionalists as a threat to denominationalism. The only Universalist sponsoring group at the second session was the Illinois Convention. Any minister who acted as a "missionary" for the movement was in trouble. Yet out of the first meeting there emerged an American Conference of Religious Liberals, which included twenty-two rabbis, seventy Unitarian ministers, twelve Universalist ministers, and four Ethical Society leaders.

A similar movement, the National Federation of Religious Liberals, was instituted fourteen years later by Unitarian Charles Wendte. Member organizations included Universalists, Unitarians, Friends, and the Central Conference of American Rabbis. It held annual meetings for a dozen years or more. Among its goals was the promotion of closer cooperation between our two denominations. Meanwhile the Convention and the American Unitarian Association continued to exchange greetings and practice restrained cooperation. For example, Unitarians adopted a fraternal resolution in 1890 after an address by Universalist Perin urging teamwork in Japan.

DEFINITE GESTURES TOWARDS MERGER

When Universalist summer meetings were being held at The Weirs, they were in a Methodist grove. They were preceded by similar Unitarian meetings. Overlapping attendance made possible much fraternizing. Everett Rexford in 1890 delivered the same address to both groups. In it he pointed out that both denominations were preaching the same gospel and that "there might be a liberal national church ministering to the needs of the people." He advocated union. Unitarians, he says, responded somewhat more favorably than Universalists.[31]

In subsequent summers there were more informal discussions, culminating in an organization which, at the suggestion of Universalist Marion D. Shutter, took the name United Liberal Church. Unitarian E. B. Payne and Universalist L. H. Squires were chosen president and secretary respectively. Its purpose was cooperation, mutual assistance, expansion, and ultimate union.[32] On the national scale such movements were ineffective, but the impetus which prompted them produced People's churches, United Liberal churches, and a growing cohesion among Universalists friendly to Unitarians.

In spite of this surge of rebellion, in spite of repeated polite greetings, the relationship between denominational officials was one of friction and competition. At least this was the testimony of Universalist Frank O. Hall twenty-five years later. In 1899 Unitarians proposed a permanent joint committee on cooperation. When Universalist Sweetser sought to substitute a plan favoring cooperation with all Christians, his proposal was rejected and the original adopted 101 to 26. Universalist members of the first committee were Hall, Isaac M. Atwood, and John C. Adams. Hall said later that the move was successful, much of the friction being eliminated.

Below the national level there were continuing instances of a move towards fusion. Perhaps the first union of individual Universalist and Unitarian churches is reported for Chicago in 1836.

Unitarians supported the Universalist church of Cedar Rapids, where there might have been a merger if it had not been for official Universalist refusal to abandon the Winchester Profession. In Iowa five joint state conventions were held between 1911 and 1923.

The number of local mergers is believed to have been small. Somewhat akin were Federated churches, in which Universalists joined with Congregationalists or Methodists or others. There was Universalist support for the Community Church of Boston, organized in 1920 by Universalist Clarence Skinner and former Unitarian John Haynes Holmes. On the other hand, there were failures: an attempt to unite Universalist and Congregational churches in Roxbury was unsuccessful. But there were instances of merged conferences: the Canadian Conference of Universalists, Unitarians, and Kindred Religious Liberals, and a similar group in southern California. Ministerial associations sometimes combined.

Thus, for over a century there were those on both sides of the liberal fence who were trying to get acquainted and make friends. Their object was matrimony between their two churches.

CHAPTER 8

The Movement Towards Consolidation with Unitarians (1926-1961)

Merging was not a series of steady sailings towards the port of organic union with Unitarians. It was rather a zigzag and occasionally retrogressive course, influenced by frequent changes of helmsmen, shifting winds of general opinion, and not always clearly understood hailings from friendly churchmen on passing vessels. Moreover, the denomination did not give its attention unreservedly to this voyage alone: other matters demanded consideration. Thus the story is difficult to put together. I am too close in time to the events, and have been too remote in space, to depend on personal recollections. My friends who were caught up in the events likewise find it difficult to recall the details. Many have kept no records, or their records have been lost. Convention minutes, which always screen out what goes on behind the scenes, seem provokingly inadequate. Articles in the *Leader* are spotty and doubtless colored by prejudices. For these reasons, and because the complete story should include the view from the Unitarian lookout on Beacon Hill, this chapter does not pretend to tell all.

The events to be narrated occurred in a context of national and world events which followed their predecessors with ever-increasing acceleration. In international affairs this was a period of hot tempers and cold wars. Into domestic affairs desegregation of the Negro, retirement living for the elderly, and democracy on the college campus intruded themselves among the more conventional social and political problems. Conservation of what remained of wilderness beauty attracted a widening circle of supporters. Flight to the suburbs changed patterns of living and of church structure. Individual churches had to face new conditions, still in flux. These were the years which included not only the economic depression but a religious depression felt by all denominations, from 1920 on. Church attendance and Sunday-school enrollments declined. Interest waned in the social gospel and in liberal orthodox theology.[1]

A PERIOD OF REORIENTATION

These changes in social, educational, political, and economic life could not be ignored by Universalists. They were all too evident in their effect on the programs of individual churches, state conventions, and the national organization. Rural churches could no longer be depended on to serve as a denominational foundation. Ministers could no longer be content to deliver the traditional message. The tested methods of church extension could no longer be guaranteed to work. So it was that a sense of disease began to be felt. Universalists began to recognize that they were faced with unanticipated problems and to consider what might be done about them. A few looked back upon what had been happening over the years in an attempt at historical stock taking. More looked ahead, proposing various plans, sometimes vaguely, as to what course to take. Many became confused, increasingly so as the inconclusive series of hot and cold negotiations produced a sense of insecurity, especially among the younger ministers. Were we federating, or merging, or neither? Talk of actual merger was often at the unofficial level, with implications not clearly formulated. Merger was sometimes equated with "going out of business." This in turn led to a state of apathy. Walter MacPherson was dismayed by its extent. Leaders complained that we were still in "the lonely way of extreme individualism" and merely "a loose federation of rather touchy and cantankerous parishes." Ministers were withdrawing to transfer to other faiths or to enter business.

Self-examination and stock taking began about 1900. Lee McCollester found eight periods in our history: awakening and self-discovery, independency and fellowship, institutional and educational activity, moral and humane pronouncements, reorganization, adjustment to science, social and religious reaction, and self-analysis.[2] W. C. Selleck outlined the development of the altered situation as he saw it. Everything before 1870 was for him pioneering. Then biblical and evolution studies changed our outlook, Unitarians and Universalists became allies, Reform Jews and Friends were added, we undertook work in Japan. Now (1934) the new task was less with controversy and theology, more with tolerance and humanitarianism.[3] Alfred Cole summarized important developments since 1860 as reorganization and standardization, formation of the YPCU, alignment with evolutionary theory, acceptance of the Revised Version of the Bible, adoption of a new statement of faith, and an approach to responsibility.[4]

Internal structural changes, always a popular ecclesiastical sport, were not forgotten. The roles of the several conventions had become somewhat altered. Now the General Convention was exercising greater jurisdiction. State conventions were even being questioned as outmoded. Several midwest conventions entered into a new northwest conference.[5]

One outcome of the backward and forward looks is that committees gradually received more permanent status as commissions. Many of these entered upon their assignments with zeal, even though appropriations were often so meager that business had to be conducted solely by mail. There were commissions on churchmanship, church and education, church architecture, pastoral psychology, spiritual healing, denominational literature, liberal evangelism, faith and order, social welfare, and foreign affairs and world peace. There was also a Board of Foreign Missions. Some of these bodies were short-lived; others continued for several years. Their reports, although not earth-shaking, were occasionally excellent and always served to keep issues alive among ministers and laity. Annual conferences of state superintendents, called by the general superintendent, began to function in a manner which earlier would have been impossible. Thus the supervisory plans became increasingly efficient.

Another instrument which facilitated denominational advance was the summer institute. Increase in number, growing registrations, the wide variety of topics considered, and independence of Convention control constituted a denominational leaven. Not only were those in attendance moved and informed, but their enthusiasms were communicated to the people of their churches.

Expressions of social idealism, continuing the trend described in earlier chapters, were a major concern during this period. A Director of Service Projects was appointed. The Convention adopted a formal declaration of social principles. New fields of interest received attention: marriage counseling, birth control, mental health, funeral customs, rural churches, size of farms, the Scopes trail, freedom of the press, the Ku Klux Klan.

A new problem was the conscientious objector and the position which the denomination should take toward him. In 1917 the New York Universalist Convention had first adopted and then, after adjournment, illegally repudiated a resolution on conscientious objection, of which I was the author. It was not until 1925 that a positive statement went into General Convention records. It was then voted, 80 to 53, that the Convention "recognizes as being in accord with our fundamental principles the right of members of this church to refuse on conscientious grounds to participate in any warfare." Six years later this position was reaffirmed in the statement that it was a cardinal principle of the Universalist Church that allegiance to spiritual authority and leadership of Jesus was to be interpreted by each according to his conscience with reference to refusal of military service at any time. It was noted that this was in accord with the minority opinion of the Supreme Court. In 1935, by vote of the Convention, the secretary entered into correspondence with the government departments in an unsuccessful attempt to obtain a ruling on the wartime status of our conscientious objectors. Shortly afterwards a register was opened at headquarters in which objectors might enroll their names.

Practice in the social field did not always match pronounce-ments. Jeffrey Campbell, five-sixteenths Negro, graduate of St. Lawrence, was ordained and served acceptably as an interim minister but for many years could not find an opening as a permanent pastor.[6] Nor could Francis Davis, who married Campbell's sister. That Martin Luther King was once an honorary member of the Illinois Convention hardly compensates for these failures.

Communication with British liberals continued. World War I had interrupted this but on the other hand had promoted interest in English Universalism, especially with the church at 57 Caven-dish Road in London.[7] Arthur Peacock (1905–1968), its minister, became a frequent contributor to the *Leader*. As an outgrowth of correspondence between Joseph Fort Newton and the vicar of the parish church at Alton, in which John Murray had been christened, a memorial tablet was unveiled and dedicated there in 1925.[8] European sessions of the International Association for the Pro-motion of Liberal Christianity and Religious Freedom, formerly the International Congress of Religious Liberals, drew increasing attendance by American Universalists.[9] About 1931 good-will tours to the Association and to European shrines became popular.

A few other ventures may be briefly listed. Some Universalists in Los Angeles cultivated friendly relations with a Buddhist group. The number of merged Unitarian Universalist churches increased. More ministers were enjoying dual fellowship, either with the Unitarians or with the Congregationalists. Universalists began to organize fellowships in communities too small to support a minister. The first of these were at Silver Spring, Maryland, and Terre Haute, Indiana, in 1955. A boys' organization, the Knights of King Arthur, sponsored by Frank Lincoln Masseck, lost out to the Boy Scouts, in which Masseck was also active.[10] Stella Marek Cushing, talented musically and otherwise, was officially designated in 1930 as a bearer of good will to her own people in Czechoslovakia and to the peoples of Yugoslavia and Albania.[11] Many articles, both pro and con, discussed Buchmanism, now known as Moral Rearmament.

In 1940 the Convention board appointed an Emergency War Relief Committee which, working with the Red Cross and otherwise, was to minister to suffering peoples of Europe and elsewhere.[12] Lacking in specific aim and competing with other organizations, achievement was small; in four years only about twenty thousand dollars was raised. Then, under the leadership of Superintendent Cummins and of Carleton M. Fisher, the committee became the Universalist Service Committee. Personnel and policies were modified to provide for sending field workers to Europe under the initial guidance of the Unitarian Service Committee, already established there. Fisher sailed for France, whence he went to the Netherlands in charge of distribution of food and clothing. He next did similar work in Hungary, and child-care work in West Germany. Universalists supported work camps of the Friends and set up some of their own. Through the camp idea the service ideal spread to projects at home, including assumption of responsibility for Jordan Neighborhood House in Suffolk, Virginia. In 1949 service projects were initiated in Japan and later in Korea and the Philippines.[13]

THE SUPERINTENDENCY OF JOHN SMITH LOWE (1917–1928)

Since 1900 the tendency has been to look increasingly both to the general superintendents and to the presidents of the conventions for initiative, leadership, and acceptance of responsibility. Lowe took office in 1917, but here we shall be considering chiefly the closing years of his administration, in which he was associated with Frank D. Adams as president. During Lowe's earlier years in office the presidents had been Lee McCollester, Roger Galer, and John Murray Atwood. Galer was a layman; McCollester once a pastor and then dean of the theological school at Tufts; Atwood was once a pastor and then dean of the theological school at St. Lawrence. Both Lowe and Adams were ministers.

In his report for 1927 Lowe, admitting that many former churches were not cooperating, nevertheless asserted that fewer churches were accomplishing more than the many had done and that never before had we been so effectively organized and that a new campaign for funds was going well.[14] With some success during his superintendency there were crusades for a million-dollar drive, for a national memorial church, for new buildings in Japan, and for increasing pensions. Offices of all our national organizations were brought together in one building. Underlying these operations was a basic program to enrich the consciousness of the people, reinvigorate the church, and recommit Universalists to following Jesus more closely in their daily lives.[15]

Although the denomination was moving towards the position that a common spirit and purpose, rather than acceptance of theological pronouncements, was the true bond of union, this view did not quickly, if at all, affect rules of fellowship. Clarence Rice and Joseph Newton, highly respected Universalist leaders, motivated at least in part by ecumenical ideals of church relationship, applied for and received ordination in the Episcopal Church. Because that denomination did not accept them on the basis of their former ordination with us, both lost their Universalist status. By a vote of 25,000 clergymen Newton has been included as one of the twenty-five most influential ministers in the United States. Of him Congregationalist George Gordon wrote this description: "beloved by the whole ministerial profession, a man as brilliant as he is generous, of whom I can never think but with grateful affection."

THE SUPERINTENDENCY OF ROGER F. ETZ (1928–1938)

After experience in the parish ministry Etz became secretary of the Convention in 1921. He continued in that office after Lowe retired, performing also some of the duties of the superintendency, until he was advanced to that office in 1930. Associated with him as presidents were Adams; Victor A. Friend, a layman; and Walter Macpherson, minister at Joliet.

Etz had the misfortune to shoulder the burden during a period of denominational decline. Revenues were falling, headquarters staff had been reduced, churches were in trouble, ministers in distress. The great depression was placing its mark on Universalists. Although general and trust funds were reported as increasing, operational costs showed growing deficits. Between 1924 and 1934 receipts from quotas assessed to the churches were reduced by one half. Convention delegates frequently demanded a balanced budget, yet persisted in appropriating more than the annual income which their churches provided. The low point was reached in 1937.[16]

In contrast to this tendency Etz reported that letters were being received from churches abroad requesting fellowship and that five hundred ministers of other denominations were wishing to join us.[17] In 1934 he was sent on a round-the-world good-will trip, which included a visit to the Japan Mission.

By vote of the Convention of 1935 there was set up at headquarters a Council of Executives, composed of staff members representing the Convention and affiliated organizations. Such steps towards centralized management were urged by those who continued to feel that we were still burdened by individualism, inefficiency, and anarchy. Areas of responsibility, they claimed, were undefined. Standards were lacking. Under such pressures improved methods began to produce more acceptable results.

The long effort to erect a memorial church in the national capital, first proposed in 1868 and, by Louis Ames, revived in 1921, came to fruition in a dedicatory service on April 27, 1930. Containing memorials contributed by widely dispersed Universalists, it was adorned with a peace tower in honor of Owen D. Young.[18] Support of this project had been withheld by many of those expected to contribute. Nevertheless, it was regarded as the greatest cooperative effort yet carried through by the denomination.

Other endeavors of this type, although not especially connected with the Etz administration, may be mentioned here. Attempts to create a similar shrine in Boston were disappointing. About 1914 fire had destroyed the building on Columbus Avenue, home of the old Second Society. At this time Boston real-estate values were declining. After an interval of several years the society erected a magnificent building at another location, neglecting, however, to set aside adequate funds for its maintenance. Although the Massachusetts Convention came to the rescue, the property became a heavy financial burden and was sold. The Society united with the Arlington Street Unitarian Church. In 1948 the Massachusetts Convention established in Boston a new base of a different sort: the Charles Street Meeting House, which, under the leadership of Kenneth Patton, has experimented in new forms and aids for worship.

The churches at Gloucester, Massachusetts, and Murray Grove, New Jersey, both connected with the work of John Murray, have often been thought of as national shrines. Another is the birthplace of Clara Barton at Oxford, Massachusetts, supported by Universalist women.

While the denomination was thus experiencing these ups and downs of internal welfare, the conviction was spreading more and more widely that "merges are in the air; we can't do it alone." Great expectations were aroused when at its 1927 session the Convention received two proposals—one from the Unitarians and one from the Congregationalists.[19] Friendly relationships with the Congregationalists had been developing for some time. The two national organizations had often exchanged greetings. Ministers had met together. The Boston Universalist Club had sponsored joint meetings. A writer in the *Leader* had proclaimed, "I hope to live to see Congregationalists, Unitarians, and Universalists all in one free church."[20]

Now the Congregationalists, stimulated by their own churches in northern California and by Maine Universalists, proposed a joint commission to consider practical steps towards closer fellowship. At the same time Unitarians asked for a council of representative liberal Christians to promote sympathy and cooperation. Neither overture suggested organic union. Universalists had previously approved closer relationships with all liberal Christians, based not on uniformity of belief but on community of ideals and purposes.

Friendly interchanges with Congregationalists now grew to

the extent that the editor of the *Christian Register* accused Universalists of ignoring Unitarians. Some Universalists agreed. Enthusiasm for threefold cooperation mounted. Churches in and about Lowell were one nucleus of this movement. A conference of the three denominations in that city in 1930 voted unanimously for organic union.

Such sentiment was not without exceptions. There were those who were indifferent, those who preferred the Congregationalists whether the Unitarians were included or not, and those who preferred the Unitarians. (All through the subsequent years of negotiations, opinions within each of the denominations were divided.) Much of what went on did not percolate down to individual churches and their members, who for some years were given no opportunity to express their preferences. At one session of the Convention, opponents of a resolution which would have endorsed continued negotiations looking to union with the Congregationalists prevented it from being presented to the delegates for a vote.[21]

In 1931 Unitarians renewed overtures for a study of possible union. This led to the appointment of a new commission by each group. Three alternatives presented themselves to the commission: continue the status quo, merge completely, or find some middle ground. The decision was to propose a Council of the Free Churches of America, to which they hoped other denominations would be drawn. This report disappointed those who had hoped for merger. Indeed, it had been understood that plans for a merger were what the commission was directed to prepare. When it failed to do so, the charge was made within both denominations that it was composed largely of denominational officials who, prior to appointment, were already on record as being opposed to merger and that the commission had given no serious thought to its assigned task.

To such objections the commission replied that it was necessary to consider the wishes of minorities, both radical and conservative, that to a limiting extent the plan involved merging, that churches had been consulted, and that with their plan there was hope that

Ethical Culture societies would join. Nineteen areas of possible federated work were suggested. The new council was incorporated in April, 1933, under the name Free Church Fellowship.[22] In October the Convention voted to become a member.

One spokesman for the opposition was Vincent Tomlinson, who listed several practical difficulties: the plan was a disguised merger, no real effort has been made to include other denominations, it was not clear what the Free Church was to stand for, and individual churches were given no opportunity to accept or reject the plan. Another objection was that the name implied that other churches were not free. Modifications in the plan quieted some objections, and it was adopted by the Convention.

Meanwhile, Frank Adams and others attacked the opposition for its inconsistency. For years, they said, we had been seeking to convince Christendom of the truth of our doctrine, only to meet bitter denunciation; but now, when at last others were willing to accept us as a part of the fold, we turned away in righteous isolation.

Some of the opposition to, or neglect of, a more inclusive organization came from churches and ministers. But the accusation was made that it was official Universalism which had saddened the Unitarians by blocking every movement towards union. The Rhode Island Convention, for example, went on record in 1928 as opposed to any merger. Although J. Murray Atwood strove for tolerance, the basis of much opposition was a fear of Unitarian humanism. There was even a desire for an official statement of faith that would keep humanists out. Even the most enthusiastic advocates of union sometimes entertained second thoughts. Perhaps, they said, our destiny after all was to maintain a separate denomination. After four years of experimenting with Congregationalists, Tomlinson had once said, and after failing to respond to Unitarians, nothing happened. Would not going our own way be more successful?

Growing humanist sentiment among Unitarians had dampened Congregational ardor, but three of their number were elected to the Council of the Free Church Fellowship. Unitarians and Uni-

versalists were in it as denominational bodies. Individual churches
from both, along with a scattering of Community, Methodist, and
Independent churches, began to join. The first individual church
to come in was the Universalist church of Salem. A Methodist
was elected to the council. At the first annual meeting in
Brooklyn in 1935, devoted largely to discussion of possible plans,
Methodist Bishop Fred B. Fisher replaced Unitarian Louis Cornish
as president. Study commissions composed of professional persons were provided for.

The 1936 session, held at the Methodist church in Detroit,
was attended by 650 "delegates," including Jews and Roman
Catholics. Against the background of the economic situation at
home and the persecution of Jews in Germany, a sense of world
crisis pervaded the meetings. There was much enthusiasm but no
challenging plan for action. The 1937 session in Chicago, although provided with a good program, drew small attendance. In
addition to these national gatherings, there were occasional regional
programs, as in California in 1938. But gradually, for reasons
which are partly obscure, the whole movement was allowed to
die, without friends and with no memorial service. Among Universalists there was much indifference and preoccupation with
internal problems.

THE SUPERINTENDENCY OF ROBERT CUMMINS (*1938-1952*)

The vigor and enthusiasm of Cummins enabled the denomination to slow down its decline to a stop and to start the climb
towards new courage and new life. Associated with him as presidents were Louis Ames and Harold Latham, businessmen of New
York City, and clergymen Ellsworth Reamon and Brainard
Gibbons of New York and Wisconsin respectively. Gibbons had
been a practicing attorney prior to his ministerial career. Ames
had a long history of church activity, going back to the early
days of the YPCU. Before becoming a Universalist and entering
our ministry, Cummins himself had been in military service in

World War I, had served as director of interfaith activities in a
state university, and had worked in the tropical Orient.

The new superintendent devised a four-year plan for increasing finances and growth. Under the slogan "Forward Together"
what had formerly been ten separate appeals were combined into
one. Work at headquarters was further systematized. Ministerial
pensions were increased to four hundred dollars annually. Philip
Giles later summarized the situation. During the depression there
was a period of inactivity, even retrogression. Etz managed to
hold the organization together. Under Cummins the tide was
turned and the denomination again took heart.[23]

Visiting churches, state conventions, and auxiliary groups,
Cummins presented his conviction, shared by other youngish men,
that Universalists must stress "the universals and unities essential
to building One World" and become aware that they were
potential leaders towards this goal. Upon his recommendation
the official statement of purpose was altered to read, "To promote
harmony among adherents of all religious faiths, *whether Christian or otherwise.*"[24]

He also promoted another constitutional change. Prior to
1942 the name General Convention (or similar designation) had
had a dual reference. It meant both a legal corporation and
an annual or biennial legislative gathering. But in that year the
corporation became the Univeralist Church of America (UCA);
the gathering became the General Assembly. These changes, together with the three professions of faith, were included in a new
charter.

In connection with World War II, as already stated above,
the UCA board appointed its Emergency War Relief Commission
and appropriated money for the Red Cross. This became the
Service Committee, which cooperated with Unitarians in relief
work among impoverished and homeless European peoples.
Money was raised for Armenian relief. Meanwhile at home current tendencies in foreign affairs were studied at summer institutes, especially at Ferry Beach.

One of the outstanding projects of Cummins' administration

was application for membership in the Federal Council of Churches in America, later known as the National Council. Although Unitarians of 1908 had been instrumental in its original formation, neither they nor the Universalists had been included in invitations to membership. But Universalists had cooperated individually and institutionally in the work of the Council. At the time of application we were recognized as full members of eight state interdenominational councils, for some of which we had been initially responsible, and of many county and city councils of churches. We were members or participants in several other national interdenominational bodies and had contributed workers and money to departments and commissions of the Federal Council.

The decision to apply for membership was arrived at with friendly encouragement by liberal leaders within the Council and by the desire of Universalists to cooperate more fully in the excellent work of the Council in a war-torn world. Support may have come also from those Universalists who wished to maintain closer identification with traditional Christianity.[25]

Unable to accept an invitation to attend the 1940 session of the Council, Cummins sent Frederick Perkins, who was given a most cordial reception. Stanley Manning and Mrs. Irving Walker, also present, were of the opinion that had an application been presented, it would have been accepted. Hence the General Assembly of 1941 voted power to the board to make such an application; this the board decided to do. The purpose of the council, as stated in the preamble to its constitution, was (in part) to "more fully manifest the essential oneness of the Christian churches of America in Jesus Christ as their divine Lord and Savior, and to promote the spirit of fellowship, service and cooperation among them." Given freedom to interpret, Universalists found the first clause no stumbling block, but it was upon the second that they based their eligibility.

Early informal negotiations uncovered a difference of opinion within the Council between those who sympathized with the Universalist dream of church unity founded on a common purpose and those who could conceive of unity only in terms of acceptance of a common creed which must contain an affirmation of the deity of Christ. Although we were given advance promises of support, doubts of the outcome were soon evident. Informal conferences with influential persons gave encouragement but not assurance. Liberal members of the Council welcomed the opportunity to obtain a categorical decision on an important issue.

Our tentative application, thought too lengthy by some who were consulted, was shortened (and later thought too brief) for formal presentation. In spite of support promised by friends within the Council, the application was ignored at its session of 1942. The issue continued to be pressed until 1944, when the Council took action by rejecting it. Churches voting for our admission were Congregational-Christian, Disciples of Christ, Friends, Seventh-Day Baptists, Colored Methodist Episcopal in America, and African Methodist Episcopal. Churches voting against us unless we accepted "Jesus Christ as Divine Lord and Savior" were Northern Baptists and Protestant Episcopal. Churches voting unconditionally against us were National Baptist Convention, Church of the Brethren, Evangelical and Reformed in America, Reformed Episcopal, Lutheran, Methodist, United Brethren, United Presbyterian, Presbyterian USA, and United Church of Canada.

Among those who spoke in favor were Douglas Horton and Theodore F. Herman. Some others became timid because Lutherans threatened to withdraw if we entered. The negative Methodist vote drew editorial criticism within that denomination. The rejection aroused widespread indignation against the Council and sympathy for Universalists. Thus encouraged, the General Assembly voted in 1946 to reapply. Again the Council refused to accept us. Four denominations voted to accept, eight were opposed, three wished further information, and one abstained. Our Assembly of 1947 resolved to continue support in these words, "Whereas the Federal Council of Churches of Christ in America is the only existing agency of united Protestantism, and the Universalist Church of America finds itself not at variance with the broader aims and principles of this body, be it resolved that the UCA lend its support to the program of the Federal Council of Churches in such matters as are compatible with the liberal tradition and outlook of the Universalist Church."[26]

Negotiations with Unitarians were not entirely forgotten. The possibility of merger had again been proposed in 1947 by Frederick Eliot, president of the American Unitarian Association (AUA). It is difficult to keep in mind all the commissions—there were at least five—which were involved in the several steps toward merger, especially since there were variant names in popular use for each of them. In 1949 one of these commissions conducted a plebiscite on "federal union" of the two denominations. Seventy-two per cent of Universalist churches and 75 per cent of Unitarian churches recorded a strong affirmative majority for studying and considering such union. In 1951 another Commission on Church Union reported favorably on federal union and proposed still another commission: the Joint Universalist Unitarian Commission on Federal Union. There was a concurrent committee on bylaws, which found it convenient to become absorbed into the commission. After instructions from Cummins and Eliot, this commission began to prepare a precise plan. The immediate goal was a new corporation to which would be assigned the functions previously performed by the UCA and the AUA with respect to publications, public relations, and religious education. It was believed that other functions could be transferred later.

Many unexpected problems arose at commission sessions. Criticisms of its work and of the whole idea were received. It seems to have made a commendable effort to keep the two publics well informed of such matters, as well as of its decisions. William Lewis, its chairman, pointed to some causes of the failure of previous attempts: not proposing a real program, lack of conviction in leaders, substitutions of our own denominational programs in place of proposals, vested interests, supposedly irreconcilable operational difficulties, not conducting an exploratory study of plans. One operational obstacle was that Unitarians were subgrouped into regions without regard to state lines, where

Universalists were divided into state conventions, independent of the UCA. These were sometimes trustees of endowments, whereas Unitarian regional groups seldom were.

In spite of such considerations another favorable vote of churches was obtained. Bylaws of the new corporation were written. In the summer of 1953 the new Council of Liberal Churches was incorporated. In that same summer the two denominations met jointly at Andover. Universalists voted for federal union 257 to 12; Unitarians unanimously.

THE SUPERINTENDENCY OF BRAINARD F. GIBBONS (*1952-1956*)

In 1952 Gibbons moved from the president's chair to take charge of the superintendent's office. A layman, Alan Sawyer, was president during approximately the same four years. Some saw our internal situation as still fragmented. This view was common among our younger ministers. In 1950, for example, Albert Ziegler found eight varieties among us: trinitarians; those who see no difference between Universalists and other Christians; the off-centered cross group who see Christianity as included within but not central to Universalism; non-Christians; emergent Universalists (neo-Ballouists); emotional Humanists; rational Humanists; and social activists.[27] Although this may be an exaggeration, there certainly was room for an approach to closer unity in thought and in action.

The Council of Liberal Churches proved cumbersome and expensive. There were now three corporations and sets of officers to support in place of two. In 1955 a new Joint Interim Commission of Federal Union was instructed to study and report on the working of the council and to suggest the next steps—perhaps the addition of two more departments. But it was found that the only really successful achievement had been the uniting of the two departments of education. After due study this joint commission recommended still another: a Merger Commission. This recommendation was strengthened by facts.

More and more individual Universalist and Unitarian churches merged their activities at the local level. The conviction became general among well-informed members of both denominations, both those who were enthusiastic and those who were hesitant, that merger in some form was the only possible policy for the foreseeable future.

In this situation the aim of Superintendent Gibbons was to place the legal and financial affairs of the UCA on as sound a basis as possible, in order that it not be hopelessly outclassed by the more affluent AUA. As already mentioned, the greater part of the AUA's funds were under centralized control, whereas Universalist assets were only in part with the UCA. Some state conventions controlled large endowments. Tactful negotiations were needed to secure their cooperation. Some UCA funds had been established so many years earlier that no authoritative records could be discovered which stated the purposes for which they had been given. But after a long and careful analysis perhaps 90 per cent of them were clarified.

During the lean years of the period with which this chapter deals the Universalist board, in conformity with common practice among non-profit corporations and in expectation of successful campaigns for increased giving, drew upon invested non-restricted capital funds to support ongoing projects. Gibbons sought, so far as possible, to check this habit and to prepare an accurate statement of current assets. At the same time the board transferred such funds as were invested in real estate to a more liquid form, employing a professional adviser from outside the organization. Also, a professional survey was made of Universalist potential for giving. Professional aid was employed to bring annual contributions into closer approximation with what could reasonably be expected.

The youth groups of the two denominations, YPCU and YPRU, came together in 1954. Since 1897 they had been advocates of cooperation.[28] In 1933 they set up a joint committee on social responsibility. They promoted discussion groups in colleges, fraternized with European youth, and arranged work camps

at home and abroad. One of these was at the Universalist center in
Royhill, England.

A youth merger was discussed and even planned in 1934
and 1935, but officials of the UCA dissuaded the YPCU, without,
however, extinguishing the desire and drive. Cooperation with the
YPRU continued at the local and national level. In 1953 the
two groups dissolved their organizations, uniting to form Liberal
Religious Youth (LRY). In a personal letter to a friend one
attendant on that occasion writes: "It was the singingest convention 'ever I seen'—the rafters were always ringing with song.
. . . Emotions were at a high pitch for both the banquet and
the installation service which followed. . . . 'Twas difficult to
look down on the sea of tear-filled faces."

In 1961 a new development entrusted youth of college age
to Student Religious Liberals and concentrated LRY upon the
activities of those of high-school age.

THE SUPERINTENDENCY OF PHILIP R. GILES (*1956-1961*)

The final legal steps and internal adjustments for full consolidation were successfully carried through to completion under
the superintendency of Philip Giles and the presidency of Carleton
Fisher. Both were ministers, ordained in 1942 and 1935 respectively, and both had had pastoral experience. The General Assembly adopted the proper authorizations for merger at its
sessions in Atlantic City and Syracuse, with a final session in
Boston in 1961. At Syracuse the Universalist vote for complete
consolidation was 238 to 33, the Unitarian 518 to 43.

Final debate was not limited to matters of legal structure
and finances but dealt also with formulating a statement of purpose, about the wording of which humanist and theist contended.
The chief question was: Shall reference to Jesus and the Judeo-
Christian tradition be included? It was decided to include the
latter but not the former. A further point was insistence upon
safeguarding the tradition of congregational independence. The

new corporation, the Unitarian Universalist Association (UUA), was formally organized in May, 1961.

Some Effects of the Merger

In spite of copious publicity there was, and still is, ignorance and misunderstanding as to what was merged and what the merger meant. The two consolidating bodies were the UCA and the AUA. The UCA ended its period of 167 years as a distinct religious body and legal entity. The AUA ended its career of 136 years. Now the original tasks and purposes of both organizations, adjusted to a changed and changing world, are being carried forward by the UUA. It is the responsibility of this organization to see that they are carried forward. It would be incorrect to say the UCA has gone out of business; or if one insists upon saying this, one should also say that the AUA has gone out of business. There is a special responsibility resting upon those who feel themselves bearers of the historic Universalist tradition to see to it that the UUA is continuing to engage in the business of the UCA.

There were some in both camps who did not accept the merger. At least one Unitarian church and several Universalist churches refused to go along. On the other hand, several Universalist state conventions and Unitarian regional districts worked out ways to combine their interests by consolidating in districts with new geographical boundaries. Some auxiliary organizations have not adopted the new name. One home for the aged uses solely the Universalist designation, whereas others use the Unitarian also, or neither. Independent Universalist conventions still exist. The two historical societies continue separately. Revised provision for theological education has not been completed.

The merger did not require internal changes of any sort in individual churches. In accordance with the traditional congregational (democratic) form of government to which they had been accustomed, these were left free to conduct their affairs in their own ways. They might adopt any name they

wished. They were free to adopt any creed or covenant or profession which they might elect, or to adopt none. They were free
to call any person they might elect as minister, with the single
restriction that if they wished their minister to be listed in the
denominational yearbook, he must satisfy the standards set by
the fellowship committee of the UUA.

At the time of the merger there were two service committees,
the Universalist under UCA control and the Unitarian, an independent corporation. Rival opinions about how this situation
should be met delayed decision, but eventually a plan was worked
whereby the two were combined into a single Service Committee.

By consulting the final issue of the Universalist Year Book
prior to merger, I sought to determine how many of our churches
which were eligible to vote on the merger issue had been established
in the early days of the denomination. Remembering that church
statistics are often of questionable reliability, I concluded that
there were perhaps 147 such churches which had been first
organized before 1850, of which 130 were classed as "active." I list
below those which were in existence when the Winchester Profession was adopted in 1803; there are sixteen:

1649	Malden, Mass.
1737	Saugus, Mass.
1744	Stoughton, Mass.
1779	Gloucester, Mass.
1781	Milford, Mass.
1785	Oxford, Mass.
1793	Portsmouth, N. H.
1796	Barre, Vt.
1798	South Strafford, Vt.
1798	West Chesterfield, N. H.
1799	Norway, Maine
1800	Southbridge, Mass.
1802	Barnard, Vt.
1802	Hartland, Vt.
1803	Andover, Vt.
1803	Turner, Maine

I like to think that the merger of Universalist and Unitarian thought occurred over one hundred years ago in the mind and heart of one man. He looked upon Jesus as a poet, few of whose statements were literally true. The core of his message is the Divine Paternity. The task of the church is to proclaim that message and its implications. One test of a religion is what it can do for men. Can it meet their needs? Can it educate their spiritual nature? Want, suffering, and oppression need to be studied under the law of brotherhood. Cheap garments should not be bought at the price of child labor, nor cheap coal at the expense of miners' manhood and comfort. Men have a community of interest in friendship, in the family, in the state, and in civilization as a whole.

If one has great purpose, and if one acts on Christian principles, he has something of eternal life. A man is saved to the degree to which his spiritual faculties are developed. There is no other salvation than a Christ-like spirit, no other damnation than an evil heart.[30] So wrote Thomas Starr King.

Part III

EPILOGUE: THE HERITAGE

"We should be careful to get out of an experience only the wisdom that is in it."

Mark Twain, quoted by ARTHUR SCHLESINGER, JR.

"No one ever pioneered in behalf of a tradition."

FRANK D. ADAMS

"We are not bound by it; it is ours to use."

MAX D. GAEBLER

"All we have willed or hoped or dreamed of good shall exist;
Not its semblance, but itself; no beauty, nor good, nor power
Whose voice has gone forth, but each survives for the melodist
When eternity affirms the conception of an hour."

ROBERT BROWNING

CHAPTER 9

A Critical Evaluation
of the Universalist Church

The Search for a Usable Past is the intriguing title of a recent collection of essays by Henry S. Commager. It would seem equally well to describe my effort to find my way through the mass of data available about Universalism in America, so large as to arouse both challenge and despair. Can this tale illuminate the roadway ahead, along which churches of the future must travel? Is there a Universalist past usable in any denominational future? Is it usable by others? I now address myself to this question, offering an evaluation of past achievements. The final chapter envisions new interpretations for the future.

UNIVERSALISM AS PROTESTANTISM

By all Universalists of early days and by many of today, Universalism has been held to be a form of Christianity, diverging from the traditional interpretation of Protestantism only with respect to doctrines concerning the character of God and the destiny of man. By this allegiance they became involved in weaknesses as well as strengths of the Protestant movement. When Universalists attacked, it was the beliefs of other Protestants which they attacked. When they acted, they sometimes (but not always) imitated the action of other Christian bodies.

UNIVERSALISM AS A FOURTH FAITH

Even in pioneer days there was a sensing that although American Universalism had been derived historically from

Protestantism, it had become something different. Such intimations developed into the conviction that Universalists and Unitarians, together with liberal Congregationalists, Ethical Culturists and others, constituted a new genus, to be called Liberal Christianity or, more recently, a Fourth Faith, in distinction from Catholics, Protestants, and Jews.

Writing for a Unitarian clientele over ten years ago, Henry Nelson Wieman named four mistakes of earlier liberalism,[1] which may now be read as applying to Universalists: (1) failure to formulate clearly the problem which religion tries to solve; (2) failure to distinguish between two contradictory propensities in religion—striving to give oneself into the power of a creative, saving, transforming reality, and cultivating certain beliefs for their psychological effect; (3) failure to distinguish between realms of transcendental being and the realm of space and process; and (4) failure to offer a fruitful theory to guide inquiry.

UNIVERSALISM AS AMERICANISM

The General Convention became the Universalist Church of America. Today writers are stressing the view that Protestantism is a culture religion. This is not a new idea, for, as Adin Ballou put it, "If it be said that, according to my own showing, I mixed up my religion with politics, patriotism, and warlike reveries, it was in the same way that nominal Christians have been doing for sixteen hundred years—in the same way that a vast majority are doing now."[2] In our America there has been a "growing identification of religious mores with those prevailing in the society at large."[3] For example, there was an identification of northern piety with the Union cause and of southern piety with the Confederacy, some of whose generals were distinguished Christian leaders. Similar identifications occurred pretty generally during both world wars. Our civilization has often been called a Christian civilization; with it the American way of life is easily confused.

Universalism as Humanism

Although our founding fathers stressed theological views of the future life, their motive for preaching was to bring comfort, happiness, and peace to men and women on this earth. Increasingly there appeared leaders who rejected conventional approaches and who spoke against the sins of society. For them Universalism was a social critique and a social gospel. They insisted that a high religion must be an ethical religion, offering analysis, protest, reconstruction, and leadership.

Internal Criticism

Internal criticism, that is, criticism by Universalists themselves, appeared as early as 1848, and it has never ceased. If we group some of these reflections topically instead of chronologically, they form this composite pattern: In general outlook many early Universalists, it is said, were disinterested in knowledge, in education, and in an educated ministry. Their movement was drifting and purposeless. In communities where there were enough believers, they often failed to maintain religious societies or to form churches where they had secular societies, to arrange for public worship, to attend these services when provided, or to promote church membership. Their early clergy were preachers rather than ministers, engaging in too much controversial preaching. After Hosea Ballou no comparable leader appeared among them.

Both early and later Universalists failed adequately to support forward-looking decisions of conventions with respect to church extension and reform movements. They were unable to secure the number of ministers needed. Pastorates were often brief, separated by long vacancies. They long lacked proper standards for ordination. In rural areas they failed to organize or maintain permanent circuits. There was too long a delay in formulating a denominational policy. No general superintendent to coordinate the work assumed office until the organized movement was over a hundred years old.[4]

These harsh criticisms were offered by loyal Universalists. Some parts of the indictment are obviously applicable chiefly to the periods of gathering and growing. Some in varying degree perhaps apply to the whole period of our history. It may be admitted that in early years and in the melting pot of the Ohio Valley, adherents were often superficial, uneducated, and even unreligious. Yet this gives no true picture of convinced and conscientious believers and solid supporters of the movement then and subsequently. Constantly they were under attack. Even if a man prided himself on fighting back fairly, it was difficult to maintain this stance. "I was in the midst of a polemical war with vast hosts of bitter antagonists whose watchword was 'No quarter to Universalists of any school.' I neither asked nor expected any, and fought accordingly. The whole denomination of which I had become a member was at that time in the same combative sphere—one not very conducive of personal and social piety of the constructive type."[5]

Forced out of the Christian Connection in 1822, Adin Ballou was unwavering in his conviction of universal salvation. But he was unhappy about some of his new associates. They were "strongly opposed to the idea of any future disciplinary punishment; they explained away, often by far-fetched interpretations, all the passages of Scripture which teach retribution after death; they ridiculed revivals of religion; they held all spiritual experience to be superstitious or fanatical; and they expended nearly all their effort in proving, argumentatively, the naked tenet of universal salvation, as if that were the whole gospel of Christ."[6] Of his brief pastorate in New York City Ballou writes: "With the exception of a few choice spirits, it was difficult to tell what the majority of professed Universalists believed or were aiming at—only that they had cut loose from the endless-misery sects and were adrift somewhere on the high seas of liberalism, with less of sound faith than volatile skepticism. Of fraternal unity, fellowship, and cooperation, there was little."[7]

Presumably analogous criticisms could be made against other denominations. Theodore Parker took Unitarians to task for losing their opportunity in 1834. When the newly constructed railroads were bringing young men to the cities, "Unitarians ought to have welcomed such to their churches, to have provided helps for them and secured them to the Unitarian fold. . . . But they did no such thing. . . . They were aristocrats and exclusive in their tastes, not democratic and inclusive."

Adverse criticism directed against the quality of our Sunday schools was undoubtedly well taken. They shared the short-sightedness of other religious groups. Yet a plausible claim may be made that Shippie Townsend and Oliver Lane (Boston friends of Murray) and Benjamin Rush of Philadelphia "sustain the same relation to Sunday Schools in America that Robert Raikes sustained to those of England and Europe."[8]

"BOYS, WE HAVE SIMPLY GOT TO DIG IN, EVERY ONE OF US"

In his address as president of the Convention of 1929 Frank D. Adams delivered perhaps the most incisive indictment to which a group of Universalists ever listened.[9] Perhaps he knew that there was precedent for such an attack, for William A. Drew in his Convention sermon of 1836 had condemned belligerent attitudes, hasty ordinations, and hasty resolutions. Adams pointed to an "almost unceasing barrage of criticism levelled at officials . . . for trying to carry out the instructions which you have given." The Convention voted for a memorial church in Washington, prorating the cost among the churches. Protesting the project, "two-thirds flatly refused to pay." Similarly, many refused contributions to the Japan Mission.

As to proposals for comity with other denominations: "I need not rehearse the history of these three years. If you have read the reports . . . you know exactly what has been done. And you know how little that is, how harmless, how innocuous. A few meetings of joint commissions, at which the utmost possible action was a discussion of the obstacles to be overcome before we can even work as friendly and understanding allies, to say nothing of actually merging our several forces. That, and writing reports about it."

What was the trouble? Who was to blame? "We of this day," he continued, "have lost or failed to recapture the spirit of adventurous daring which was in the hearts of our fathers. . . . Our ministers are none too brave, God knows; but the chief inertia is among the laymen. The majority of men and women who are supporting our churches today honestly do not want them any different. . . . And this is the attitude, conservative, reactionary, almost bellicose, that is rendering us helpless today. . . . Boys, we have simply got to dig in, every one of us."

His hearers were somewhat shocked. But they didn't throw him out. The address, spoken by a man of recognized sincerity and ability, may have produced some changes of heart. But the habits of years persevere. Over twenty years later Gibbons could complain about the "quibblers at Portland."[10]

SUMMARY OF CRITICISMS

Let me now summarize and restate the items in this unfavorable picture in my own manner. First, I shall restate Wieman's general charges in a form to apply specifically to Universalism:

1) The Universalist Church never made up its mind as to its proper function. Was it to develop a strong independent denomination? Or was it to liberalize other denominations? When statistics were favorable, speakers extolled the first; when unfavorable, they consoled themselves with the second.
2) It failed clearly to distinguish between making men acutely aware of the love of God and insisting upon the intellectual belief in universal salvation.
3) It failed clearly to distinguish between heaven beyond and heaven here, or at least to balance interest in future life with social reform.
4) Although it did well in adjusting to biblical criticism and to evolution theory, it failed to develop a philosophic method of supporting, extending, and proclaiming its fundamental tenets.

I now restate the total unfavorable picture:

1) The years have left us a heritage of extreme, sometimes pathological, individualism, which has retarded the formation of an effective denomination and sabotaged its implementation.
2) Under the label of liberalism a restricted and narrow-minded emphasis on a single doctrine has permitted the neglect of other important segments of religious life.
3) There has been a partial failure to attract, or to retain, those potential leaders who were seeking a broader concept of Universalism. We did not attract Rush and his friends. We did not retain Turner or Kneeland or Brownson. Adin Ballou left us.[11] Starr King departed, lingeringly. We could find no place for Joseph Fort Newton.
4) Leaders have often been poor planners. We have planted too many churches at the wrong places at the wrong times.[12]
5) We failed to resolve the conflict between two conflicting goals: building a strong denomination and leavening the thought of others.
6) Many convention sessions were dull and unworthy of a great body—"the kind whose going was more welcome than its coming." They showed more reverence for Robert's *Rules of Order* than for the spirit of the New Testament.
7) We failed to meet the nineteenth-century fundamentalist challenge by continuing to proclaim the original biblical message in the Bible belt.
8) We indulged in a growing self-satisfied smugness.

Criticisms 7 and 8 are related to each other. Most Universalist churches, especially those in cities, thrived in regions where the upper and middle-class denominations had become less traditionally dogmatic and more tolerantly "liberal." Universalists, perhaps deservedly, gave their own denomination credit for this. But hearing fewer and fewer affirmations of hell, they decreased their denials of it. Thus they neglected those regions where the old emphasis on eternal damnation was still accepted gospel. They ignored the new fundamentalist denominations. Some of the sociological and political situations associated with this surviving doctrine of hell are described in Erskine Caldwell's *Deep South* and Sally Carrighar's *Moonlight at Midday*, especially the chapter "The Missing Spirit," where she describes parts of Alaska as a "religious wilderness."

REPLY TO CRITICISMS

If the reader will glance through these charges again, he may possibly decide that many of them can still be brought by analogy against other denominations and against the Unitarian Universalist Association and its constituents—perhaps that not all of them apply exclusively to the Universalist side of the family. If some early Universalists failed to establish churches, so do some Unitarian Universalist fellowships today express antagonism to becoming a church or even to being thought religious. If our forebears sometimes met in uninspiring quarters, so do our contemporaries. One fellowship is thus frankly described by an otherwise sympathetic attendant: "They meet in an incredibly dingy room of a very shabby hotel downtown. The bare lights hanging from the ceiling illuminate a depressingly decrepit display of furniture. People come into this harsh environment, perch on uncomfortable chairs, and in this depressing scene manage magically to explore their visions of God and the universe."[13]

With respect to the charge that no general superintendent was appointed until 1899, it should be remembered that the standing clerk performed some coordinating duties from 1811 on and that more specifically from 1867 to 1876 the office of convention agent was filled successively by E. G. Brooks, Asa Saxe, and J. M. Pullman.[14]

SOME NEGLECTED FACTORS

In bestowing either praise or blame on Universalists of the past it is well to avoid extreme judgments, for in addition to their degree of wisdom and devotion there were probably other factors whose existence can only be suggested here as possibilities.

Why did Universalism flower in New England and not in eastern Pennsylvania and New Jersey? Why did it prosper in the Mohawk Valley, western New York, and the original "west" of Ohio, Indiana, and Illinois? Why did it not prosper in the old South, and the states to the west? Why did no native leaders appear in these regions, comparable to those of New England, to hold the movement together? Why did New England clergymen who came to Philadelphia not succeed well enough to remain? Admittedly the seed was sown extensively. Churches were established in the Carolinas, Virginia, Georgia, Kentucky, and even in Louisiana and Texas.

Was there something peculiar about New England temperament or society which made Universalism more acceptable there than in the South? Should we take account of health and disease, of the early yellow-fever epidemics which made life precarious in New York and Philadelphia and more southerly cities?

Was it perhaps that the intellectual atmosphere emanating from Philadelphia, with its scent of deism, Ephrata doctrine, and the preachings of De Benneville, had softened the theological climate to the point where Universalism had no shock value? Did it not challenge sufficiently to arouse an emotional response? Was the preaching of Winchester and the lesser men too lowbrow for the widely read and widely traveled national leaders living there?

Scott suggests that Universalism contains two strains.[15] The one springs from the more mystic leaders of the Reformation, becoming more evident among us in the middle colonies, where it stressed the primacy of persons, freedom, and Christian humanism. The other, developing more fully in New England, is characterized by an emphasis on organization, institutions, and conformity. Although Irwin does not specifically refer to this distinction, she reinforces it by her emphasis on the pietist origins of Universalism in the middle colonies. Such environmental, cultural, and social factors, not only south of the Hudson River but in other regions, deserve further study. Later immigrations changed the climate of regions receptive to Universalism.

Whenever and wherever slavery had become firmly established, Universalism could not readily be accepted, because its anti-slavery implications were too obvious. The doctrine of a classless future heaven was especially appealing on a classless frontier, but it was not a comfortable conviction in a slave society.

SOME POSITIVE ACHIEVEMENTS

A *Leader* editorial once summarized our contributions in the realm of concepts: no literal hell, God a universal father, God's love and power limitless, universal brotherhood of man, a moral theology which insists that man rather than God needs to be reconciled, the moral worth of every man, and man's responsibility to develop an ethical society.[16] Neither the spread of these beliefs nor the idea of universal salvation is to be attributed solely to our denomination, for expressions of them are to be found among churches of the Old Catholic faith, of the Methodists, of the Mormons, and in Bahai.[17] Many in other denominations share them also.

Positive credit can certainly be assigned in the field of education. Efforts to establish schools and colleges of their own for general education and for ministerial training met with considerable success, for which due acknowledgement should be made, especially since the founders were usually men and women lacking in formal education themselves. As to one of their colleges, a speaker at the Second Society in Boston once reported: "Tufts College owes its beginnings, largely to the time, money, effort, given by members of this society. Through pioneer days, through the hard years of the Civil War, the Second Society carried the burden."[18] Libraries, laboratories, and instructional levels were forward-looking for their times. Many faculty members were able, dedicated, and inspiring.

Much influence and interest was directed, especially between 1830 and 1860, toward cutting off state aid to denominational schools, to keeping religious ceremony and indoctrination out of public schools, and to what would now be called academic freedom. Orthodox attempts at carrying out opposite policies, whether open or in the form of clandestine proselyting, were resisted. The record which Universalists themselves established in colleges and schools is good. It was provided at Tufts, for example, that there should be no religious tests for appointees to the faculty or for entering students. Universalists of this period tended willingly to accept moral training, and indeed perhaps some non-sectarian religious training, in the schools, although they were skeptical of plans by Horace Mann for achieving these goals. There were occasions when public feeling was deeply aroused over religion in education. At one time there was a wave of anti-Catholicism; Universalists advised non-violence and calmness. Their role has been described as that of "trustees of education" until the public-school system was established.[19]

CONTRIBUTIONS TO AMERICAN LIFE BY INDIVIDUALS

In earlier chapters a few persons were mentioned who made some special contribution to the life of their times, especially in education. We recall Charles Tufts, Benjamin Lombard, John Buchtel, and Amos Throop. But there has been no attempt to compile a complete list of outstanding people, either ministers or laymen. Nor is such a list to be offered now. But the *Dictionary of American Biography* includes several to whom attention may be directed.

Among the ministers included there and about whom some information has already been given these may be noted: the three Ballous—Hosea the preacher, Hosea 2nd the educator, and Adin the reformer; Ebenezer Fisher of St. Lawrence; Abner Kneeland the conscientious; John Murray the pioneer; Starr King the orator; T. J. Sawyer the educational administrator; Thomas Whittemore the editor, legislator and president of bank and railroad; and Edwin Chapin the prophet of New York City.

Among other ministers given space in the *Dictionary* are two women. Olympia Brown (1835-1926), who graduated from St. Lawrence in 1863, became the first woman to be ordained by a regularly constituted ecclesiastical body. Active in the cause of woman suffrage, she held pastorates in Massachusetts, Connecticut, and Wisconsin. Phoebe Coffin, later Mrs. Hanaford (1829-1921), was probably the first woman to serve as chaplain of a legislative body of men, in this case the legislature of Connecticut. She was minister of churches in that state, Massachusetts, and New Jersey.

To the roster of male clergymen the *Dictionary* adds other names. Sylvanus Cobb (1798-1866), zealous for temperance and the abolition of slavery, served as legislator in both Maine and Massachusetts. Elmer H. Capen (1838-1905), after serving churches in Gloucester, St. Paul, and Providence, was for many years the president of Tufts College. Charles Hudson (1795-1881), in addition to ministerial positions, held several offices in the governments of Massachusetts and the United States. Charles Spear (1801-1863), having early developed a sympathy for condemned and discharged criminals, was active in the Society for Abolition of Capital Punishment and editor of the *Prisoners' Friend*. He and his Universalist brother, John Murray Spear, were instrumental in introducing into Boston a sensitivity to humanitarian treatment of criminals. John Coleman Adams (1849-1922) was known as the Dean of the Hartford Ministry. Some of these names also appear in the new *Schaff Herzog Encyclopedia of Religious Knowledge*.

The index of the *Dictionary* does not facilitate identification of Universalist laymen. But I have noted the following, many of whom were lifelong Universalists. All were associated with the movement at some period of their lives.

James Mitchell Varnum (1748-1789), judge of Ohio Territory
Winthrop Sargent (1753-1820), secretary of the Ohio Company
Charles Tufts (1781-1870), donor to the college named for him
Phineas T. Barnum (1810-1891), showman and impresario
Horace Greeley (1811-1872), editor, reformer
Sarah Edgarton Mayo (1819-1848), writer
Mary Rice Livermore (1820-1905), feminist
John R. Buchtel (1820-1892), industrialist

Alice Cary (1820-1871) and Phoebe Cary (1824-1871), poets
Corlis P. Huntington (1821-1900), industrialist
Clara Barton (1821-1912), humanitarian
William D. Washburn (1831-1912), industrialist and philanthropist
Charles L. Hutchinson (1854-1924), business executive
Thomas M. Osborn (1859-1926), penologist
Philip G. Wright (1861-1934), economist
Arthur Nash (1870-1927), practitioner of the golden rule
Orlando F. Lewis (1873-1922), penologist

Very likely there are other names which I did not recognize. But this list will indicate that the denomination, in spite of its humble origins, can boast of its men and women who have shown social responsibility and wielded influence.

Success in Applying Universalism

From that day in 1790 when Philadelphia Universalists with the assistance of Benjamin Rush proclaimed their version of applied Christianity, the implications of Universalism for public morality have never been lacking. At some periods the formulations of these implications have been repressed by preoccupation with denominational organization and expansion; at other times they have been dominant. In rural communities, both in New England and on the later western frontier, such moral problems as existed were easily recognized by everyone—alcoholism, sharp business practices, political corruption. These were considered individual rather than social problems; consequently not much was said about applied Christianity except in terms of temperance and personal morality. Merely to free men's minds from their belief in an orthodox hell—in itself a kind of social achievement—was enough.

After 1834 Universalists became increasingly aware of moral problems in city life and at all levels of government. From that date until 1860 more and more thought was given to the meaning of life on this earth. These were the years of dominant reform sentiment among Universalists. These were the years in which they placed themselves at the front of Christian thinking about decency and justice. Whittemore thundered through the *Trumpet* against capital punishment and for education and for legally accepting testimony from witnesses who were not conventionally religious. He even condemned Kneeland's prosecution and imprisonment, defending his right of religious liberty. Cobb, thinking Whittemore too conservative, issued his *Christian Freemen,* steadily overcoming objections that it was too radical. Spear tackled prisoner problems. T. B. Thayer and Abel C. Thomas initiated an adult education movement for young members of their congregations who worked in the mills of Lowell. This was the most glorious period of American Universalism. It all culminated in the work of the Reform Association. It was all interrupted by the Civil War.

After the war emphasis shifted to organization and expansion. But this regression did not go long unchallenged. In 1878 George Harmon, whom I recall in his later days as still a fiery little man, awakened the sleepers to what life was like among immigrant laboring people. George Emerson, Levi Powers, Frederick Bisbee, Ellen Johnson, Marion Shutter, Frank Hall, Lee McCollester, George Perin, and many others joined the agitators. They joined it not merely to talk. Under their influence came everyday churches, settlement houses, residences for young women, collegiate adult-education lectures, work with prisons and prisoners, developments in other fields of social responsibility. It all culminated in the Social Service Commission led by Clarence Skinner. It was all interrupted by World War I.

After the war emphasis shifted to erecting an ecclesiastical shrine in the nation's capital. But this second regression did not go long unchallenged. About 1937 there was a revival of social interest. Although Universalists were no longer leaders in applied Christianity, they were preaching and implementing the social gospel. Without forsaking their belief in the universal fatherhood of God, they often preferred to speak of the universal brotherhood of man. Again the name of Clarence Skinner stands out, with Emerson Lalone as another devoted advocate. Hardly had this revival gained momentum when it was interrupted by World War II. After the war dedication to the ideals of applied Universalism continued to express itself through the old channels, finding new outlets in European relief projects. But organizational problems arising out of the merger movement prevented any great advances in sensitivity to social responsibility for social action.

Here, then, are condensed data from which to evaluate faithfulness to the ideal of the kingdom of God on earth. It rose and fell as a tide, cresting at shortening intervals, dedicated and pioneering in its early surge, still committed to the task in its latter days, when the breakwaters against which it pounded were recognized as far more resistant than the founding fathers had known.

JUDGMENTS BY NON-UNIVERSALISTS

Many books are written about American history which ignore religion. Some which mention religion ignore Unitarians. Some which mention Unitarians ignore Universalists. But there are exceptions. In colonial times, it is said, "a quiet current flowing from mind to mind became a torrent through the preaching of Murray." In comparison with Unitarians, "the seminal influence of Universalism . . . has been far less appreciated."[20] As to recent years: "The message of modern Universalism to American life is inspired largely by its fidelity to the cause of reformed social morality. . . . It is not merely a social creed, nor a protest against what it regards as past errors of orthodoxy, but a unifying and reconciling faith."[21]

One specific contribution to national life may be mentioned. Blau credits the Universalists of 1828 as being the most outspoken against the effort of Ezra Stiles Ely to establish a Christian political party in American public life. He names two of Ballou's Restorationist group, Pickering and Morse, and also Zebulon Fuller.[22]

Leonard Bacon asserts, "The record of their fidelity, as a body, to the various interests of social morality is not surpassed by that of any denomination."[23]

George Gay quotes a paragraph from Unitarian *Unity* of about 1920:[24] "The Universalists have been notable for a high degree of intellectual candor and courage. They have believed in education, and nobly fostered it. Their interpretation of God and his Universe in terms of moral values constitutes a priceless contribution to religion. Above all, Universalists have understood the common heart, have known how to reach the common man, and thus have even been in close sympathy with the common people."

George Willis Cook, Unitarian historian, describes Universalism as "part of the humanitarian awakening of the time, the new faith in man, the recognition that love is diviner than wrath." Chad Smith asserts that it was part of the American Romantic movement, indeed of a world-wide movement. England's Gordon Smith is reported to have bestowed high praise: "The only important contribution to Christian life credited to America is the Universalist Church. If it should disappear its influence would remain forever in the religious consciousness of humanity." A recent syndicated column by Lester Kinsolving, without mentioning the denomination, affirms that universal salvation is accepted by many scholarly leaders of Protestantism today.

An appraisal by Whitney Cross is most generous. He credits Universalists with social vision and action in many causes. In failing to record these efforts he criticizes other scholarly writers. "Students of American Culture and church historians," he writes, "alike have quite neglected the Universalists, and the oversight seems to be a serious one. They greatly exceeded the Unitarians in their area of influence. . . . Their impact upon reform movements and upon the growth of modern religious attitudes might prove to be greater than that of either the Unitarians or the freethinkers, and their less sophisticated, more homely, warfare upon the forces fettering the American mind might be demonstrated to have equalled the influence of the transcendentalist philosophers."[25]

SUMMARY OF ACHIEVEMENTS

Remembering that the movement has been carried on by people who have shown weaknesses and errors of judgment, what positive outcomes can Universalists claim for their two hundred years of denominational life? What has the movement accomplished?

1) It has brought release from fear; it has brought comfort, inspiration, and a basis for right living to the many thousands of men, women, and children who have welcomed its message.

2) It has increasingly offered an opportunity for deeper insight, spiritual growth, and broader vision to those who have associated themselves with its work, as children in its Sunday schools, as youths in its discussions, as worshipers in its pews, as officers and members of committees, as ministers in its pulpits. How many have availed themselves of this opportunity? To what level has their development attained? Although there are no measurements, it is possible to think in terms of large numbers and increasing maturity.

3) It has offered a context in which the extreme individualism of early adherents was distilled into an attitude compatible with a group spirit. When fellow Universalists encountered each other for the first time, it was like a meeting of congenial friends. It steadily developed among its members a loyal cohesiveness and a commitment to social responsibilities.

4) It established several educational institutions, in which thousands of young men and women received much of their education.

5) It made its contribution to thinking and action in the domain of social ethics under various names: social service, social action, reform. Early Universalism was "an ethical movement and a revolt against spiritual oligarchy."[26] "Universalism did begin as a protest . . . but it was a moral protest, theological in form."[27] It has supplied agitators and skilled leaders in work for temperance, anti-slavery, woman suffrage, peace, prison reform, labor relations, and other goals.

6) It has contributed to the calmer theological atmosphere of our day. If the nightmare preaching of Edwards and his

revivalist imitators be compared to the present general mood of Christianity, the contrast is striking. True, there are still preachers of everlasting torment, but belief in hell no longer dominates public life and private thoughts. Credit cannot go solely to Universalists, but they were a powerful influence.

7) It worked out an original solution to the problem of creed. With the exception of the unfortunate attempt at uniformity in 1870, for which little acceptance was ever secured, it has never had a creed in the sense of a statement of beliefs to which literal assent is required of members and ministers. Instead it adopted a cumulative series of professions. These were useful as acceptable public statements but were not literally binding upon individuals.

8) It vindicated in America what early Unitarianism had demonstrated in eastern Europe, namely that support of liberal religion is not confined to an educated elite class. Under intelligent and devoted leadership common folk established and long maintained a movement whose basic tenets time has shown to be more widely acceptable among educated Christians than the views of their orthodox opponents.

A MEMORIAL AND A PROPHECY

Should the Universalist Church ever be in need of an epitaph for its gravestone, perhaps some poet among its children will compose a modification of that once proposed for an English statesman:

Richard Bacon Westbury
Lord High Chancellor of England.
He was an eminent Christian,
An energetic and merciful Statesman,
And a still more eminent and merciful Judge.
During his three years' tenure of office
He abolished the ancient method of conveying land,
The time-honored institution of the Insolvent's Court,
And
The Eternity of Punishment.
Towards the close of his earthly career,
In the Judicial Committee of the Privy Council,

He dismissed Hell with costs,
And took away from orthodox members of the Church of England
Their last hope of everlasting damnation.[28]

As a new generation of Unitarian Universalists contemplates
the two hundredth anniversary of Murray's first sermon on American soil it may be well to recall the outlook one hundred years
ago. In preparing for the 1870 Centennial, the committee permitted itself to estimate the performance of the first hundred
years. We can read their words with mixed approval and regret.

A hundred years, enriched by the labors of self-sacrificing and
consecrated men, on whose work God has approvingly smiled,
have not only secured us a place and power as a recognized
branch of the Church of Christ, but have also witnessed such a
spreading influence of the great truth peculiar to our faith, that
no Christian sect now exists in our land, whose dogmas it has not
changed or modified. Poetry receives its noblest inspiration from
the prospects of the glorious future assured by Universalism; Civil
Government attests its wide-felt power in every claim and demand
put forth for liberty and protection, based on the manhood of our
race; Philanthropy finds here alone its incitement, hopes and
consolation; Moral Science demonstrates its worth in its theories
of obligation, conscience, justice, and benevolence, and in all
which it presents as the highest motive to moral action; while
the more subtle philosophies, and the discoveries of Natural
Science, whether taught in popular story or in labored treatise,
demand the "Perfect Harmony of the Universe," as the only
satisfactory solution of the problems of life, and the possibilities
of Almighty Wisdom and Love.[29]

In contrast to these backward glances the 1928 testimony of
Robert Whitaker, California Baptist, independent, and reformer,
sounds a prophetic note: "The religion of the future will be
Universalism, in the broadest sense of that word. . . . Its emphasis will be upon the unlimited in time and space, and upon a
beneficent unity as over-ruling and guiding all, and manifesting
through all as one vast incarnation of an infinite Wisdom and
Power and Love."[30]

CHAPTER 10

Universalizing Universalism

Up to this point the account has dealt with facts concerning a segment of church history. Even when I have offered interpretations, these have been based on supposedly actual historical events. In this chapter I will no longer be limited by such a restriction. Facts will be referred to, but often facts of a different sort. These will be woven into what may be thought of as a dream far removed from the theological nightmare with which this book began.

The word *Universalism* has been used to refer either to an organization or to a set of doctrines. That organization has ceased to exist, probably never to be revived. Those doctrines in the form they were promulgated two hundred or even one hundred years ago are no longer relevant to human needs. But the thesis of this chapter is that the word *universalism* has a broader meaning than our founding fathers imagined and that in this broader connotation it is deeply relevant.

Stephen Pearl Andrews once told an audience, "You Universalists have squatted on the largest word in the English language. You ought to improve the property or get off the premises." What follows is an attempt to accept this advice. It is addressed not only to those who adhere to what is now called Unitarian Universalism but also to all those who are concerned about the place of religion in the modern world.

NEW MEANINGS FOR OLD WORDS[1]

Let us play with a few familiar words. Consider the possibilities of *Unitarian* as an adjective. Ignoring the fact that some

Unitarians have been great poets and some have been great
political and social leaders, let us stipulate that, for the moment,
the Unitarian element in religion is the intellectual or rational
element. The first law for this element is: In judging the truth
or falsity of assertions in religion, thou shalt respect thine intelligence. The unforgivable sin is to be identified with prejudice
against ideas and with censorship of the intellect. Every man has
the privilege and the duty of thinking for himself. William
Montague put it thus: "For the irreligious freethinking would be
optional, but for the religious it would be compulsory. A church
member who refused to allow his belief to be tested in the light
of reason would be expelled as one of little faith."

Similarly we may consider *humanist*. Ignoring the artistic and
the rational traits often found in humanist individuals, let us
stipulate that, for the moment, the humanist element in religion
is the active element. The first law for this element is: Wherever
there is need and possibility of human betterment, thou shalt act
and persuade others to act with thee. The unforgivable sin is
then identified with lazy sentimentalism and lazy intellectualism.
History, as Croce once said, "is what we make it." To the humanist, conventional churches resemble athletic teams warming
up for games which are never played.

And then there is *Universalist*. Ignoring Universalist thinkers
and Universalist activists, we may stipulate, for the moment,
that this word refers to the emotional, or better, to the feeling,
element in religion. Its first law is: Thou shalt love the Lord thy
God with all thy heart, and thy neighbor as thyself. Its unforgivable sin is prejudice against people and suppression of sympathy. It looks to the brotherhood of man both as a personal goal
and as a social goal. It springs from a feeling to be cultivated
towards all other human beings.

To those who are in churches or fellowships affiliated with
our continental Unitarian Universalist Association, perhaps this
superficial play with words will give meaning to a suggestion that
the merger of a few years ago has left some factors incompletely
merged. We have merged corporations but not backgrounds,

traditions, and insights. The several chapters of this book are offered as material to be considered in a marriage of thought and ideals. For some years we may expect that our churches will continue to be composed of persons of varying opinion, persons who will differ among themselves in their convictions, their sympathies, and their plans of action. To discover that such differences exist in a church should give not concern but rather satisfaction, for they are necessary, though not sufficient, evidence that the church is indeed liberal. It is illiberalism which, in the words of Croce, stifles "the diversity of impulses, spontaneous developments and the formation of individuality."

Too often the church unity which is sought is a mathematical unity, a unity measured by absence of multiplicity of beliefs and temperaments. It should be the aim of liberal churches to strive for organic unity, a unity whose achievement is measured by the intensity of a unifying spiritual power to bring together in one harmoniously cooperative project of worship and work men of widely divergent temperaments and convictions. For a church to concentrate on a narrow selection of interests implies lack of faith in its unifying power. The wider the range of interests represented in a congregation, the greater the evidence for the presence of that unifying power.

To suggest that Unitarianism and Universalism are as yet incompletely combined is not to ask that the old professions and slogans be revived. It is rather to ask that the Universalist past be remembered, appreciated, and interpreted. It is to ask that the word Universalist be retained as more than a polite gesture. It is to hope that the word will take on new and expanded meanings.

To those who are in other churches, or in no church at all, this little exercise in possible word meanings may be turned to some practical application in their own thinking. No matter what one's beliefs, no matter what one's affiliations, in any individual life which shows religious quality, and in any institution which is vitally religious, these qualities of feeling, intellect, and action must be wisely integrated. Indeed, I might claim that it was such an ideal that Plato had in mind when he wrote of the just man and the just state.

UNIVERSALISM AS A CONCEPT IN SCIENCE[2]

The temporary stipulation about the meaning of Universalism has hopefully served its purpose and may be forgotten. The purpose of the remainder of the chapter is to indicate a sampling of more inclusive meanings which the word universalism now enjoys or might easily enjoy. There is no pretense of compiling an exhaustive list of disciplines where the term fits. The discussion now begun is but a quick and superficial scouting of the territory. The reader is invited to develop the idea further for himself.

First let us note that the word actually describes significant aspects of contemporary life and thought. This is true in at least three types of discourse: science, ethics, and education. It is commonly asserted that natural laws apprehended by scientists are universal in space and time, at the moon and the distant stars as on the earth; for example, the Maxwellian equations have been supposed to hold throughout all space. Second, science is universal in that it ignores national boundaries; what is true of studies for peaceful uses of atomic energy in the laboratories at Los Alamos is true also in those at Munich, Frascati, Jutphaas, and Novosibirsk. Third, science is universal in that it sometimes claims the ubiquity of process, the unreality of a region where nothing at all is happening, and the reality of the presence everywhere of everything at all times. Without the assumption of a genuine universe it would seem that pure science, or even some of our technology, would lack theoretical foundation.

Logic also rests upon an assumption of universalism. It affirms that although expressions of truth are local, truth is universal. This is assumed in every logical effort to convince an opponent that his opinions are incorrect. It is assumed that if he were aware of the same facts as the speaker and that if he freed his mind of all preconceptions and prejudices, these facts plus a universal set of logical principles would compel him to agreement.

It must be granted that universalism in science has not been demonstrated with certainty. After years of endeavor there is no single system of laws which applies to the whole body of scientific data. There is not yet a unity of science. There is doubt among some students that the laws of physics and chemistry will adequately explain the behavior of living things and of social groups.

Moreover, there are doubts about the oneness of our world. We are not so sure as our ancestors were that ours is genuinely a universe. What men once believed to be laws holding throughout all time and space may actually describe what is happening during merely the human era in our region of space. We may be living in what Bertrand Russell once called a "higgledy-piggledy" world. Even logic is challenged.

Nevertheless, logic and scientific theory are still forms of universalism. The assumptions made are universal assumptions. Logical dialogue demands that participants employ the same regulative principles of sound thinking. Imaginative scientific research, if it is to be above the level of humdrum detail, must rest on a belief (a faith?) that there is an order of nature to be discovered. If the supposedly universal order of nature is found to change from one moment to another, separated by light-years of space and eons of time, then scientific-minded men will assume that this change occurs in accordance with some inclusive, universal natural law of a higher order.

UNIVERSALISM AS A CONCEPT IN PRACTICAL AFFAIRS

Many of our daily concerns are associated with technologies arising out of scientific achievement and in that sense have a universalist base. But the several disciplines have additional universal assumptions. Consider psychology. Admittedly psychology is a science, but it is convenient here to think of it as the foundation of various segments of practical affairs. In spite of all the proper emphasis on individual differences there is a quiet assumption that in basic needs all men are alike. If they were not universally alike in some respects, there could be no science of psychology. Thus psychology reinforces the independent claims for universality made with respect to several other disciplines, three of which will now be mentioned.

Humanistic universalism proclaims the ideal of a union of all individuals and tribes and nations into a single world-wide community. Older than Christianity, it expresses itself today in such organizations as the World Federalists. Called by various names, it is definitely labeled universalism by Sir Arthur Keith.

Ethical universalism asserts that every man, no matter upon what theoretical basis, should treat all other men according to a single moral code. Illustrations of such a prescription are the Jewish commandment quoted by Jesus about loving one's neighbor, the assertion that all men ought to act so as to bring about "the greatest good to the greatest number," and Kant's "act so as to treat man . . . always as an end, never merely as a means." Such is the dominant note of our ethical tradition. In the words of William James, it is the faith that there is "a genuine universe from an ethical point of view."

Educational universalism in its simplest form is the claim that all men should be educated. It sometimes asserts also that the curriculum for all persons should in some sense or to some degree be in many respects the same. For example, it leads to the demand for general education, for the humanities, for philosophy. Educational universalism also expresses itself in the idea of a university, an institution, where all sources of knowledge are brought together and made generally available. Thus in theory every university is dedicated to educational universalism.

OBJECTIONS TO UNIVERSALISM IN PRACTICAL AFFAIRS

The most obvious objection to universalism in human affairs is that in the face of insistent facts, it is preposterous. The world is so full of misunderstandings, enmities, clashing ideals, tribal and national wars, mental illnesses, ethical failures, unrealized dreams, as to suggest that sensible men should turn either partialists, striving to save a remnant here and there, or nihilists, prophesying doom for all.

Consider Sir Arthur Keith and his humanistic universalism. In spite of its loftiness and its antiquity and in spite of there being few in whom the universalist feeling is altogether lacking, Keith asserts that the ideal has never been really welcomed. He himself regards it as unfeasible and utopian.[3] For there is a counterforce working against it, the force of evolution, which has entrenched in man's nature a double code of morals. One code is for home affairs, the other for foreign affairs. One is allied with the core of cooperation, the other with the crust of antagonism. They are Spencer's rival codes of amity and enmity. Universalism negates evolution. Consequently Keith abandons it and its heaven for evolution and hell. He accepts what he calls limited universalism, that is, nationalism.

This position has been discussed by Russell. Tribal cohesion began as loyalty to a small group reinforced by fear of enemies without. Today it is fear of an external enemy which supplies the cohesive force holding individuals together in a national life. If a world state could be established, it would have no enemies to fear, and hence it would lose cohesion and fall apart.[4]

A pragmatic objection to universalism is that all practical attempts to bring men together into any kind of universal organization have failed. Caesars have sought to conquer the world, only to fall short and to have their limited empires disintegrate. Too frequently among Christians universality has signified merely that many other denominations and perhaps all non-Christians are to be excluded. Other world religions have similarly traveled the trail of isolationist fragmentism. As a Jew, John the Baptist limited salvation to those who might heed his call to come to an obscure river in an obscure corner of the empire. Paul, occasionally more universalist, never outgrew his conviction that God had written an only-favored-nation clause into his covenant with the Jews. Even Jesus, whose parables call up the vision of a possible universal religion, presented his gospel through "cultural localisms," translatable only with difficulty into the languages of other times and places.

A moral objection to universalism is that even if it could ever be attained, it is undesirable and not a goal to be striven for. This used to be expressed in criticism of the conventional picture of heaven as a dull and monotonous region, and in such remarks as "heaven for climate, but hell for company." "After man had transferred all pain and torments to hell," wrote Schopenhauer, "there then remained nothing over for heaven but ennui." Currently, however, it is expressed in the idea that universalism implies uniformity and that uniformity implies a planned society and that a planned society will take all the novelty, originality, and variety out of life. Or more cynically, there is the feeling that "life would lose its savor if there were no one to hate."[5] To many, humanistic universalism means totalitarianism, dictatorship, a police state.

These, I take it, are the three chief objections to universalism: it is logically unthinkable; it is practicably impossible; and it is ethically, esthetically, and politically undesirable. Any proponent of universalism, and especially a proponent of universalized universalism, must recognize these objections.

UNIVERSALISM AS A POSTULATE OR FAITH FOR LIVING

These and other objections may be raised against two other types of universalism, namely those which were promulgated by men and women of the Universalist Church. One, theistic universalism, asserts that there is one God, and one only, whose creatures all men are in every time and place. In His sight all are equally entitled to the same ethical treatment. The other, finalistic universalism, asserts a "far-off divine event, towards which the whole creation moves."

A simple, doubtless inadequate, reply to objections against universalism in the practical or theological realm is that they too rest upon unproven assumptions. But since we are here considering possibilities rather than arguing for a completely formulated position, no refutation will be offered.

Instead, what is being stressed is the idea that universalism is a concept actually at work in many fields. It is therefore plausible to build these various types of universalism into an unrestricted or universalized universalism and to adopt it as a working hypothesis or faith for living. It brings together the several types of lesser universalisms into a comprehensive way of looking at the human predicament. It asserts a common humanity permeating all individuals. It asserts a common educability which permits each to approximate a mature wholeness. It visualizes a capacity for cultural development towards a truly ethical society. It postulates that our universe hangs together as a logically consistent whole, whether it be studied by scientist, historian, theologian, artist, or philosopher.

Universalism in every area of thinking is first of all a postulate or rule. Consequently, if one is to live one's universalism, the quest for certainty must be replaced by a quest for commitment without certainty. Within the field of the practicably achievable, universalism assumes that the following are sufficiently possible to serve as humanistic goals: universal peace, universal ethics, universal maturation of personality, universal education. These are interrelated goals, each being a means to the other.

The possibility of psychology, religiously universalizing or integrating human lives, and at the same time preserving the unique individuality of each personality, has been convincingly developed by Gordon Allport. The current plea for education in the humanities re-emphasizes an old idea: the need for a universal element in the curriculum as well as an inclusive scope for education. To adopt the universalist assumption in education or social work is to recognize that there are no persons who are ineducable, none who are incorrigible. To be sure, a teacher or a social worker may say, as the people of Ephrata said two hundred years ago, "I don't see how it is possible for these people to be 'saved,' " that is, for this retarded child to be educated or for that stubborn criminal to be restored. But this is not a statement about the nature of the child or the man. It is a statement about the speaker. What it means is, "I do not have the knowledge and the tools and the will and the patience to succeed. Given more research, more cooperation, more vision, we might succeed. Meanwhile I must do what I can. I must not set up artificial blocks with such words as *ineducable* and *incorrigible.*"

There is no magic in labels. There are several words which refer to totalities, and there is more than one kind of wholeness. *Totalitarianism* and *universalism* might conceivably signify the same kind of whole, but actually they do not.[6] Totalitarianism connotes war, dualistic ethics, dictated partialism in education, and denial of personal individuality to all but a few. It is thus an antithesis of universalism, in aim, in method, and in promise.

It is because universalism joins other postulates with its assumed possibility of a world peacefully organized that the biological and sociological objections become not insurmountable. Bergson, recognizing these obstacles, nevertheless proclaims that some new leader, some mystic element of human nature, some dynamic religion, may render possible the apparently impossible.[7] James urges the development of a moral equivalent for war. Russell suggests the need for substituting in place of fear a consciousness of unity of culture.[8] The uncertainties of the twentieth century need occasion no retreat from the mature conclusion arrived at by Kant at the close of the eighteenth: nature guarantees lasting peace, not to the extent of enabling us to predict it with absolute certainty, but the certainty suffices for practical purpose and makes it one's duty to work towards it.[9]

The ideal of the universal brotherhood of man at the factual level refers to whatever evidence there may be that mankind is one in origin, nature, and needs. It refers to whatever friendly relations may have existed, or may now exist, between individuals or between groups. Beyond the factual it refers even more to a goal for me, for us, for all, so far as man may determine the outcome of history.

A universal ethics or conscience at the factual level refers both to the agreement concerning fundamental ethical principles which underlies the diversity of details in morals and to the agreement concerning fundamental ethical principles as stated by the great ethical teachers. As a goal it refers to the progressive elimination of that ancient partialism according to which every man must employ two codes, one for friend, the other for enemy. Indeed, it looks to an ethically classless society, in which, *so far as they imply ethically differentiated treatment,* the distinctions of Jew and Gentile, Greek and barbarian, American and alien, we and they, shall have withered away.

Occasionally philosophers have spoken for universalism. I would not contend that Leibnitz was theologically a universalist. But I find him writing: "God will have the greatest care for spirits and will give not only to all of them in general, but even to each one in particular, the highest perfection which the universal harmony will permit." And again: "A single spirit is worth a whole world."[10] With a similar reservation Rousseau is and quoted; the religion of man, he says, "acknowledges all the human race as brothers, and the society which unites them dissolves not even at death."[11] Santayana suggests that we may well think of God as the active good of the universe, which involves the love of every creature.[12] "It is pleasant to think," he writes, "that the fertility of the spirit is inexhaustible, if matter only gives it a chance, and that the worst and most successful fanaticism cannot turn the moral world permanently into a desert."

James speaks more positively. Admittedly he does reject what he calls universalistic supernaturalism in favor of occasional injections of the supernatural into the natural. But that does not contradict finalistic universalism. Most religious men believe, he writes, "that not only they themselves, but the whole universe of beings to whom the God is present, are secure in his parental hands. There is a sense, a dimension, they are sure, in which we are *all* saved, in spite of the gates of hell and all adverse terrestrial appearances. God's existence is the guarantee of an ideal order that shall be permanently preserved." And again: "If the hypothesis were offered us of a world in which . . . utopias should all be outdone, and millions kept permanently happy on the one simple condition that a certain lost soul on the far-off edge of things should lead a life of lonely torture, what except a specifical and independent sort of emotion can it be which would make us immediately feel, even though an impulse rose within us to clutch the happiness so offered, how hideous a thing would be its enjoyment when deliberately accepted as the fruit of such a bargain?" That finalistic universalism need not mean a completely determined universe, he argues by the analogy of a chess game, in which God does not know what moves are to be made by His opponents or by Himself. Of one thing, however, God may be certain: "and that is that his world was safe, and that no matter how much it might zig-zag he could surely bring it home at last."[13]

Choosing One's Dream

All systems of philosophy, James tells us, spring from preferences.[14] To what postulates shall one give preference? Why the postulates of universalism, rather than those of partialism or nihilism? For one who takes them seriously they add to the burden of life. They multiply our responsibilities and call upon us to extend our conscience to include the whole world and our love to those whom we shall never see.

Although postulates are chosen by preference or perhaps intuition, one may seek to justify the preference. The choice of universalist postulates may be justified, first because philosophy is basically a search for the most general and the most inclusive truths. Investigation may disclose facts which require revision of postulates, but at the beginning anything less than universalism is a prediction of failure. Second, because universalism is more adventurous and more challenging than the cautions or negations of its rivals. Third, because in some of its forms at least, universalism has justified itself pragmatically.

Our forebears, in selecting Universalist as their name, thereby attached themselves to a concept which they and their successors have interpreted in far too restricted a sense. For in science, in ethics, in logic, and in other fields of knowledge, there is almost universally a tendency to universalize. To be a philosopher in any sense is to be a universalist in some sense. This suggests universalized universalism as a basic position, both in philosophy and in religion. If the generalizations of such universalism are stated as rules for thinking, for discovery, for interpersonal relations, for life in all its phases, they lose their otherwise dogmatic character and offer to minds with diverse philosophical emphases a common intellectual faith.

If the Universalist past seems futile, if present Universalist ideals are out of tune with contemporary moods, if this closing chapter points to future goals unrealistically, I can only quote a verse which came to me forty years ago in a student's paper and which has been with me ever since:

> Only the dream is real. There is no plan
> Transcending even a rose's timid glory,
> A cricket's summer song. The ways of man
> Are stupors of the flesh, and transitory.
> There is no truth but dreams; yet man must spend
> His gift of quiet days in storm and stress,
> Unheeding that a single breath will end
> With one swift stroke the hoax of worldliness.
> Only the dream will last. Some distant day
> The wheels will falter, and the silent sun
> Will see the last beam leveled to decay,
> And all man's futile clangor spent and done.
> Yet after brick and steel and stone are gone
> And flesh and blood are dust, the dream lives on.[15]

Bibliography

The same abbreviations are used as in Footnotes.

I. Location of collections of Universalist material consulted by me:
Universalist Historical Library, Tufts University, Medford, Mass.
Starr King School for the Ministry, Berkeley, Calif.
Meadville Theological School of Lombard College, Chicago, Ill.
Iliff School of Theology, Denver, Col.
Historical Society of Philadelphia
Library Company of Philadelphia
American Antiquarian Society, Worcester, Mass.
Various state and historical libraries
Some city libraries, e.g., Los Angeles
(The collection of material on De Benneville near Philadelphia was not consulted.)

II. Other Bibliographies
Eddy, Richard: see below under III. In Vol. 11 consult pp. 485-589 for books, pp. 589-599 for periodicals. Use the latter in connection with *Union List of Serials.*
McCloy, Frank D., "The History of Theological Education in America," *Church History* XXXI (1962), 449-453.
Mode, Peter G., *Source Book and Bibliographical Guide for American Church History,* pp. 390-408 Menasha, c. 1920.
Smith, James Ward, ed., *A Critical Bibliography of Religion in America.* 4 vols. Burr, 1961. Esp. IV, 210-218, 1028, Index.

III. Standard Histories of American Universalism
Allen, Joseph Henry, and Eddy, Richard, *A History of Uni-*

tarians and Universalists in the United States ("American History Series"). 1894.

Adams, John Coleman, "The Universalists," in *The Religious History of New England.* 1917.

Cummins, Robert, "The Universalists," in *The American Church of the Protestant Heritage.* Philadelphia Library, 1953.

Eddy, Richard, *Universalism in America.* 2 vols. Boston: Universalist Pub. House, 1891.

Lalone, Emerson Hugh, *And Thy Neighbor as Thyself.* Boston, 1959.

Scott, Clinton Lee, *The Universalist Church in America, A Short History.* Universalist Historical Society, 1957.

IV. Encyclopedia Articles
Encyclopedia Americana, "Universalism." 1939.
Encyclopedia of Religion and Ethics, "Universalism" by James Hastings, 1922.
New Schaff Herzog Encyclopedia of Religious Knowledge, "Apocatastasis" and "Universalists."

V. Historical Studies—Books
Adams, John G., *Fifty Notable Years.* Boston, 1853.

Anonymous, *The Columbia Congress of the Universalist Church.* Boston, 1894.

Anonymous, *The Winchester Centennial 1803-1903.* Boston, 1903.

Bisbee, Frederick A., *A Miniature History of the YPCU.* 1914.

Cole, Alfred S., *Our Liberal Heritage.* 1951.

Cone, Orello, ed., *Essays Doctrinal and Practical.* Boston, 1889.

Crispin, William Frost, *Universalism and the Problems of the Universalist Church.* Akron, 1888.

Dean, Paul, "Restorationists," in John Hayward, *Religious Creeds and Statistics.* 1836.

Gorrie, P. Douglass, *Churches and Sects of the United States,* art. 43, 44. 1856.

Miller, Russell E., *Light on the Hill.* Beacon Press, 1966.

Miner, A. A., "The Century of Universalism," in Justin Winsor, *Memorial History of Boston.* 1881.

Pink, Louis H., and Delmage, Rutherford E., eds., *Candle in the Wilderness.* 1957.

Robinson, Elmo A., *The Universalist Church in Ohio,* Ohio Universalist Convention, 1923.

Rugg, Henry W., *Our Word and Work for Missions.* 1894.

Skinner, Clarence R., *The Social Implications of Universalism.* 1915.

Spanton, A. I., *Fifty Years of Buchtel.* 1922.

Sutton, Katherine A., and Needham, Robert F., *Universalists at Ferry Beach.* 1948.

VI. Historical Studies—Journal Articles and Pamphlets

Bailey, Ralph C., "Theological and Social Aspects of American Unitarianism and Universalism," *JLM,* VII (1967), 31-48.

Ballou, Hosea, 2nd, "Dogmatic and Religious History of Universalism in America," *UQ,* V (1848), 79-103.

Bassett, Joseph A., "History—The Local Dimension in Religious Education," *UC,* XXIV (1968), 15-21.

Bogue, Mary E., "The Minneapolis Radical Lectures and the Excommunication of Harman Bisbee," *AJUHS,* VII (1967-8), 3-69.

Bradley, A. C., "Pacific Coast Universalism," *UL,* XXXIX (1936), *passim.*

Cassara, Ernest, "The Effect of Darwinism on Universalist Belief," *AJUHS,* I (1959), 32-42.

Cummins, Robert, "The General Superintendency of the Universalist Church in America," *AJUHS,* III (1962), 14-29.

——, *Parish Practices in Universalist Churches.* 1946.

——, *Excluded* ("Beacon Reference Series"). 1943.

Folsom, Ida M., ed., *A Brief History of the Work of Universalist Women.* Boston, 1955.

Kapp, Max A., and Parke, David B., *109 Years: An Account of the Theological School of St. Lawrence University, 1856-1965.*

The Maine Book on Universalism.

MacPherson, David H., and Woodman, Richard M., "The Decline of Universalism, 1900-1950," *AJUHS* VI, (1966), 5-45.

Miller, Russell E., "Universalism and Sectarian Education Before 1860," *AJUHS,* III (1962), 30-53.

Morris, Carol, "A Comparison of Ethan Allen's *Reason the*

Only Oracle of Man and Hosea Ballou's *A Treatise on Atonement*," *AJUHS*, II (1961), 34-69.

Robinson, Elmo A., "Universalism in Indiana," *Indiana Magazine of History*, XIII (1917-1918), 1-19, 157-188.

——, "Universalism a Changing Faith," *AJUHS*, II (1961), 1-21.

Scott, Clinton Lee, "Universalism in New Hampshire," *AJUHS*, I (1959), 1-10.

Whitney, G. W., "Doctrinal Phases of Universalism During the Past Century," *UQ*, XXIX (1872), 314-334.

Williams, George Hunston, "The Attitude of Liberals in New England Towards non-Christian Religion, 1784-1885," *CR*, IX (1967), 59-89.

Wescott, Scharf, *History of Philadelphia*, II, 46 ff.

VII. Theses

Brown, J. Alden, "The Social Applications of Universalism." Tufts, 1947.

Canfield, Mary Grace, "Early Universalism in Vermont and the Connecticut Valley." Ms., UHS.

Carpenter, P. Elton, "John Murray and the Rise of American Liberal Thought." Columbia, 1937.

Collier, Charles A., "Aspects of the Growth of American Universalism." Harvard Honors thesis.

Irwin, Charlotte, "Pietist Origins of American Universalism." Tufts, Master's, 1966.

Richardson, Peter Tufts, "The Dynamics of Unitarianism in Boston." St. Lawrence, 1964.

Sawyer, Alan F., Jr., (1) "The Detrimental Effects of Creedal Limitation in Universalism"; (2) "The Restorationist Controversy among Universalists Re-examined." Harvard Divinity School, 1955.

Scott, Peter Lee, "A History of the Attempts of the Universalist and the Unitarian Denominations to Unite." St. Lawrence, 1957.

Swanson, James A., "A History of Lombard College." Western Illinois State College, 1955.

Tucker, Elva L., "The History of the Universalist Church in Iowa." Univ. of Iowa.

Vickery, Charles N., (1) A Century of Rapprochement between the Universalist Church of America and the American Unitarian Association (Tufts, 1945); (2) "History of the Service Projects of the Universalist Service Committee (digest only in pamphlet, n.d.).

VIII. Biography

Adams, J. G., *Memoir of Thomas Whittemore*. Boston, 1878.

Ballou, Hosea Starr, *Hosea Ballou 2nd*. Boston, 1896.

Bell, Albert D., *The Life and Times of Dr. George De Benneville*. 1953.

Elbridge Streeter Brooks, *The Life-Work of Elbridge Gerry Brooks*. Boston, 1881.

Brown, Olympia, "Autobiography," *AJUHS*, IV (1963), 1-19.

Cassara, Ernest, *Hosea Ballou; The Challenge to Orthodoxy*. Beacon, 1961.

Cobb, Sylvanus, *Autobiography*. Boston, 1867.

DeBenneville, George, "The Life and Trance of Dr. George De Benneville," *AJUHS*, II (1961), 71-87.

Ferriss, Walter, *Book of Sketches, Records, Etc.* Reproduced by UHS.

Goodman, Nathan G., *Benjamin Rush*. Philadelphia, 1934.

Greeley, Horace, *Recollections of a Busy Life*, chaps. "My Faith" and "Reform." New York, 1868.

Hanaford, Phoebe A., *Daughters of America*. N.d.

Hicks, Granville, *Part of the Truth*, chaps. 2-6, 1968.

Hunt, James D., "The Social Gospel as a Way of Life, a Biography of Henry Clay Ledyard," *AJUHS*, V (1964), 31-63.

McGehee, Charles White, "Elhanan Winchester; a Decision for Universal Restoration," *AJUHS*, I (1959), 43-58.

McGlauflin, William H., *Faith with Power*. Boston, 1912.

Manford, Erasmus, *Twenty-five Years in the West*. Chicago, 1867.

Miller, Russell E., "Hosea Ballou 2nd: Scholar and Educator," *AJUHS*, I (1959), 59-79.

John Murray, *Records of the Life of Rev. John Murray*. Boston, various ed., 1816-1869.

Elmo A. Robinson, "Jonathan Kidwell, a Pioneer Preacher in the West," *UL*, XXI (1918), 104 f.

————, "The Universalist Connections of Thomas Starr King," *AJUHS*, V (1965), 3-29.

Rogers, George, *Memoranda of . . . a Universalist Preacher* (1845).

Seaburg, Alan, "Clarence Russell Skinner: A Bibliography," *AJUHS*, V (1965), 65-77.

Scott, Clinton Lee, *These Live Tomorrow: Twenty Unitarian and Universalist Biographies*. Beacon.

Sawyer, Thomas J., *Memoir of Stephen R. Smith*. Boston, 1852.

Smith, S. R. *Historical Sketches and Incidents*. . . . Buffalo, 1843.

Stacy, Nathaniel, *Memoirs*. Columbus, Pa., 1850.

Thomas, Abel C., *Autobiography*. Boston, 1852.

Winchester, Elhanan, Preface to *The Universal Restoration*. 1831.

NOTE: There are many other biographical accounts, some in book form, some scattered through the files of the *Quarterly, Leader,* and other periodicals.

IX. Religion in America—a few of the many studies

Abrams, Ray, ed., "Organized Religion in the United States," *Ann. Amer. Acad. Pol. and Soc. Sci.*, Vol. CCLVI (1948).

Bates, Ernest Sutherland, *American Faith*. 1940.

Billington, Ray Allan, *Westward Expansion, 1834-1864*.

——, *The Protestant Crusade, 1800-1860*.

Bowers, D. F., ed., *Foreign Influences in American Life*. 1952.

Bainton, Roland H., *Christian Unity and Religion in New England*. 1964.

"Religion in America," *Daedalus*, Winter, 1967.

Gaddis, Morrill E., "Religious Ideas and Attitudes in the Early Frontier," *CH*, II (1933), 153-170.

Gaustad, Edwin Scott, *Historical Atlas of Religion in America*.

——, *A Religious History of America*. 1966.

Goen, C. C., *Revivalism and Separatism in New England, 1740-1800*. 1962.

Handy, Robert T., "Christianity and Socialism in America, 1900-1920," *CH*, XXI (1952), 39-54.

Heimert, Alan, *Religion and the American Mind*.

Hudson, Winthrop S., *Religion in America*. 1965.

Littell, Franklin H., *From State Church to Pluralism*. 1962.

Meyer, Jacob C., *Church and State in Massachusetts.* 1930.

Miller, Perry, *Life of the Mind in America.* 1965.

Persons, Stow, *Evolutionary Thought in America.* 1950.

Rowe, Henry Kalloch, *The History of Religion in the United States.* 1924.

Schlesinger, Arthur M., and Fox, Dixon Ryan, eds., *A History of American Life,* espec. Vols. V-VIII.

Schneider, Herbert W., *Religion in Twentieth Century America.* 1952.

Smith, Chard Powers, *Yankees and God.* 1954.

Smith, Elwyn A., "The Forming of a Modern American Denomination," *CH,* XXXI (1962), 74-99.

Smith, H. Shelton, Handy, R. T., and Loetscher, L. A., *American Christianity.* 1960.

Sperry, Willard B., *Religion in America.* 1940.

Sweet, William Warren, *Religion in the Development of American Culture.* 1952.

Notes

The following abbreviations are used:

AJUHS = Annual Journal of the Universalist Historical Society
CH   = Church History
CR   = Crane Review
JLM   = Journal of the Liberal Ministry
UC   = Unitarian Christian
UHS   = Universalist Historical Society
UL   = Universalist Leader (1819-1897; 1926 ff.) or Christian Leader (1897-1926)
UQ   = Universalist Quarterly. With volume 21 a "new series" numbering system was begun, but without discarding the old system. The old system is used here.

Eddy *I* and Eddy *II* = Richard Eddy's two-volume *Universalism in America*
Lalone   = Hugh Emerson Lalone's *And Thy Neighbor as Thyself*
Ohio and *Indiana*   = Elmo A. Robinson's book and essay dealing with these regions. See Bibliography.
Scott   = Clinton Lee Scott's *The Universalist Church in America*

See Bibliography for dates of publication. As stated below under Chapter Three, note, 38, the authority for many statements is the original minutes of the General Convention. Since the approximate date is indicated in the text, specific references are omitted.

CHAPTER ONE

[1] This section is paraphrased biography as if it were autobiography. The quotations are genuine, except that many words and phrases have been omitted without conventional indications of where the omissions occur. The sermons may be found in *The Works of President Edwards* (New York, 1830), Vol. 3, Sermon No. 7; Vol. 7, Sermon No. 7.

[2] Charles Chauncey, in Craven, *A Documentary History of the American People* (Blaisdell Pub. Co., 1865), p. 80.

3 Joseph Priestley, *Unitarianism Explained and Defended* (London, 1796), pp. 40 f.; *Memoirs* (London, 1806), Appendix No. 5.

4 P. T. Barnum, *Why I Am a Universalist* (pamphlet) (n. d.).

5 Quoted by Joseph Fort Newton, *The Mercy of Hell* (Boston, 1917), p. 5.

6 H. W. Dewey, "Some Personal Recollections," *UL*, Jan. 25, 1930.

7 From a letter to a friend quoted by Mary P. Mann, *Life of Horace Mann* (Boston, 1865).

8 Quoted in *Ohio*, p. 72, from William A. Venable, *A Buckeye Boyhood*.

9 Andrew D. White, *Autobiography*, II, 519 f.

10 "Dogmatic and Religious History of Universalism in America," *UQ*, V (1848), 79-103.

CHAPTER TWO

1 *The Life of John Murray*, written by himself and Judith Murray (Boston, 1816 and several later eds.). There was another John Murray; see *UL* CXXIV (1942), 463.

2 Clarence R. Skinner and Alfred S. Cole, *Hell's Ramparts Fell* (Boston, 1941), pp. 172 ff.

3 Albert D. Bell. *The Life and Times of Dr. George de Benneville* (1953).

4 *UL*, XXVII (1924), 21; XXXI (1928), 909; Vol. XXXV (1932).

5 Albert D. Bell, "An Introduction to Pennsylvania German Universalism," *UL, CXXXV* (1953), 10 ff.

6 Elhanan Winchester, *The Universal Restorationist* (1831); Edwin Martin Stone, *Biography of Rev. Elhanan Winchester*.

7 Other information and references on Winchester will be found in Chap. Seven.

8 W. S. Balch, "Caleb Rich," *UQ*, XXIX (1872), 58-78.

9 Ernest Cassara, *Hosea Ballou* (1961).

10 Ferriss' own *Book of Sketches*; but see also Eddy, *passim*.

11 W. S. Balch, "Random Sketches," *Universalist Union*, V (1840), 337-340.

CHAPTER THREE

1 Andrew J. Drummond, *The Story of American Protestantism* (1951), p. 71.

2 Julius Friederich Sachse, *The German Sectarians of Pennsylvania*, II, 83; see also pp. 95 ff. For a study of the European origins of Universalist ideas among German colonists in Pennsylvania see Charlotte Irwin, "Pietist Origins of American Universalism" (Tufts, Master's thesis).

³ Thomas Butler, "Universalist Beginnings in America," *UL,* CXXII (1940), 672; also his notebook, "Universalism in Pennsylvania" (in Historical Society Library, Phila.). Herman M. Gehr, "Our Philadelphia Story," *UL,* Vol. CXXXVIII (1956). See also *UL,* CXX (1938), 332 f.

Good Luck was the old name for the present Lanoka Harbor, a few miles south of Toms River, New Jersey. It is the oldest settlement in Lacey Township, Ocean County. Originally called Good Luck, it was changed to Cedar Creek, then to Lanes Oakes, and finally to Lanoka Harbor. The old Potter church is still there—not the original, built in 1766 by Thomas Potter, but a replica built in 1841. The church and surrounding ground are now called Murray Grove. There is a large rock with an appropriate marker, indicating the spot where Potter and Murray first met.

Here John Murray preached what has officially become known as the first Universalist sermon on this continent.

⁴ G. Adolf Koch, *Republican Religion,* p. 59.

⁵ Clinton L. Scott, "Universalism and Free Thought in America," *UL,* CXXXIII (1951), 332 f.

⁶ For more information on some of these men, see Eddy, *passim,* and/ or the following:

Davis Ballou: *UQ,* VI (1849), 185 f.; XI (1854), 185 ff.
Davis: *UQ,* XXXV (1878), 239-241; XXXVIII (1881), 431 ff.
Farwell: *Univ. Union,* V (1840), 337-340
Rich: *UQ,* XIX (1872), 58-78; XXXIV (1877), 162 ff.
Richards: *UQ,* XXIX (1872), 162 ff., 275 ff,; XXXII (1875), 11 ff.
Turner: *UQ,* (?) (1871), 151-180
M. Winchester: *UL,* XXXVIII (1935), 526 f.
Wright: *UQ,* VI (1849), 11 ff.
A. and Z. Streeter: *UQ,* XXXVIII (1881), 431 ff; *UL,* CXX (1938), 719 f.

Sketches of men entering the movement somewhat later may be found in the *Quarterly:*

Sebastian Streeter: XLVI (1879), 5 ff.
Thomas Whittemore, XXXIV (1877), 261 ff.
Walter Balfour, XXXII (1875), 133 ff.
Hosea Ballou 2nd, XXXV (1878), 386 ff.
Henry Bacon, XIV (1857), 75 ff.

⁷ *Ohio,* pp. 12-17; Eddy *I, passim.*

⁸ Winthrop S. Hudson, *Religion in America* (1965), p. 22.

⁹ D. F. Bowers, "Hegel and Darwin in American Tradition," in his (ed.) *Foreign Influences in American Life* (1952).

¹⁰ In describing general characteristics of American life I have used

Notes 249

extensively the relevant volumes of *A History of American Life,* ed. by John Allen Krout and Dixon Ryan Fox (New York, 1944).

11 Percy H. Epler, *The Life of Clara Barton* (1917).

12 Some years later my future paternal grandmother was employed in a mill at Lowell.

13 Adin Ballou's *Autobiography,* chaps. 1 and 2, pictures rural life in Rhode Island at this time.

14 *UL,* Vol. XXVIII (1925), Feb. 14.

15 C. C. Goen, *Revivalism and Separatism in New England Churches, 1740-1800* (1962).

16 Lawrence R. Craig, *Three Centuries of Religious Living* (1966); A. J. Patterson, "A Hundred Years," *UQ,* XXXI (1874), 70-96; E. A. Robinson, "The Universalist Connections of Thomas Starr King," *AJUHS,* V (1964), 6 f.

17 Peter Tufts Richardson, "The Dynamics of Unitarianism in Boston" (thesis).

18 *An Account of the Celebration of the 75th Anniversary of the Second Society of Universalists in Boston* (Boston, 1893). This was the church which I attended in my student days. It was still legally known by its original name. It had long before moved from School Street to Columbus Avenue, near the Back Bay station. Portraits of Ballou and his successor, Alonzo Miner, hung in the vestry. When the church was burned, these portraits were rescued by the sexton, a Mr. Lang.

19 Elbridge S. Brooks, *The Life of Elbridge Gerry Brooks,* p. 52.

20 Richard Eddy, *Universalism in Gloucester, Massachusetts* (Gloucester, 1892).

21 *The Centennial Book of the First Universalist Society in Providence, Rhode Island.*

22 Abel C. Thomas, *A Century of Universalism in Philadelphia and New York* (Philadelphia, 1872); S. R. Smith, *Historical Sketches* (Buffalo, 1843).

23 Allen and Eddy, *A History of the Unitarians and the Universalists in the United States,* p. 377.

24 Gehr.

25 Joseph L. Blau, *American Philosophic Addresses* (New York, 1946), pp. 548 f.

26 Anson Titus, "Universalism in Maine Prior to 1820," *UQ,* XLII (1885), 430-453. Levis Buck, *Memoir of Rev. Thomas Barnes* (1856).

27 Elsewhere it is stated that Barnes preferred to spell his name Barns.

28 Allen and Eddy, p. 377.

29 Harold A. Lerusder, "The Meetinghouse of the Second Religious Society of Oxford, called Universalist," *UL,* CXXV (1943), 439; Don C. Seitz, "The Universalist Church at Oxford, Massachusetts," *UL,* XXXIV (1931), 331 f; also *UL,* XXXIV (1931), 1324 ff.

30 Sylvanus Cobb, *Autobiography*, p. 362.

31 *Christian Ambassador*, Feb. 11, 1860.

32 Thomas J. Sawyer, *Memoir of Stephen R. Smith* (Boston, 1852); Nathaniel Stacey, *Memoirs of the Life of Nathaniel Stacey* (Columbus, Pa., 1850); Frederick W. Betts, *Forty Fruitful Years* (n. d.).

33 *Universalist Theological Magazine* (London), VI, 26 ff.; *New York Universalist and Philadelphia Magazine*, IV, 14; Clarence Gohdes, *Some Notes on the Unitarian Church in the Ante-Bellum South* (Durham, 1940), pp. 327-366.

34 Eddy *I*, 206 ff; G. W. Skinner, "Universalists as a Christian Sect," *UQ*, XXI (1864), 103-111; W. S. Balch, *op. cit.*

35 Available to me was *The Convention Book* in longhand. Eddy may have had another record of these same sessions. He wrote a series of articles for *UQ* on "Universalist Conventions and Creeds," which runs through Vols. XXXI-XXXVII. See also footnote in *UQ*, LXXI (1874), 334.

36 The Plan was published by Thomas Dobson of Philadelphia (1790). It is reproduced in Lalone Appendix.

37 Nathan G. Goodman, *Benjamin Rush* (Phila., 1934), p. 319.

38 From this point on I have relied chiefly on the original minutes of the Convention. At the present time three longhand volumes and additional printed volumes are in the library of the Universalist Historical Association. More recent records of Convention and Board are at 25 Beacon St. I have supplemented information from this source by material from Eddy. It has seemed unnecessary to continually refer to these sources by footnotes.

39 Sanford H. Cobb, *The Rise of Religious Liberalism in America* (New York, 1902); J. G. Adams, *Memoir of Thomas Whittemore*, pp. 49-53.

40 T. J. Sawyer, "Universalism in America," *UQ*, XLIV (1887), 271 f., describes difficulties of these trips.

41 For an example, see Edwin Davis, *UQ*, XLV (1888), 223-231.

42 Brooks, p. 35.

43 Richard Eddy, "The Universalist Origin of American Sunday Schools," *UQ*, XXXIX (1882), 448-459.

44 Ray Allen Billington, *Westward Expansion* (1949). See also Sidney E. Mead, "The American People: Their Space, Time, and Religion," *J. Religion*, XXXIV (1954), 244-255.

45 I have made use of my *Ohio*.

46 Minutes of this organization are preserved by UHS.

CHAPTER FOUR

1 Data from Eddy *II*, *passim*.

2 Data from *Ohio*, *passim*.

[3] Peter Cartwright, *Autobiography* (1856).

[4] For longer list of Ohio ministers see *Ohio,* pp. 164-224. There have been many biographies published of western ministers. See also James H. Tuttle, *The Field and the Fruit* (1891); Robert H. Nichols, "The Influence of the American Environment on the Conception of the Church in American Protestantism," *CH,* XI (1942), 181-192.

[5] See, e.g., Menzies Rayner, *Six Lectures on Revivals of Religion* (1834).

[6] *Alta California,* Aug. 7, 1853; June 21, 1860; May 5, 1874.

[7] As in the previous chapter, much of the information has been taken from Convention records, with some dependence on Eddy.

[8] Brooks, *The Life of Elbridge Gerry Brooks,* p. 213.

[9] John G. Adams, *Fifty Notable Years,* p. 75.

[10] For one assessment of the present conservatism of a once Universalist school, see "Academic Freedom and Tenure: Dean Junior College," *AAUP Bull.,* LIII (1967), 64-69.

[11] E. G. Brooks, "Hosea Ballou 2nd," *UQ,* XXXV (1878) 389-410; Hosea Starr Ballou, *Hosea Ballou 2nd* (Boston, 1896).

[12] Melvin C. Van de Workeen, "The Universalist Historical Society," *UL,* CXXXVI (1954), 201 f.

[13] H. S. Ballou.

[14] See, e.g., G. H. Emerson, "Our Late Publisher," *UQ,* XIX (1862), 318-323.

[15] *Indiana.*

[16] See Richard Eddy's two essays on "Denominational Polity" in *UQ,* XXXVII (1880), 5-24, 389-400; also Hosea W. Parker, "Denominational Organization and Polity," in *Columbian Congress of the Universalist Church* (1894).

[17] Lalone; John G. Adams, pp. 51-56; Horace Greeley, "The Christian Spirit of Reform" in *The Religious Aspects of the Age* (New York, 1858), pp. 54 ff.

[18] *Trumpet,* Aug. 18, 1846.

CHAPTER FIVE

[1] Alfred S. Cole, "Historical Backgrounds of the Universalist Movement," *UL,* CXIX (1937), 1420 ff; Harry A. Hersey, "Rochester Before and After," *UL,* CXXXII (1950), 24; Charles A. Collier, Jr., thesis.

[2] E. S. Brooks, *Life of Elbridge Gerry Brooks,* pp. 227 f.

[3] William J. Wolf, *The Religion of Abraham Lincoln* (1963).

[4] Albert Nevins, *The Emergence of Modern America* (Macmillan, 1927), p. 345.

[5] G. L. Demerest, "The General Convention and Missions," in Henry W. Rugg, *Our Word and Work for Missions* (1894); also Lalone.

[6] *The Columbia Congress of the Universalist Church, passim.*

[7] Don C. Seitz, "Horace Greeley, Universalist," *UL*, XXXIV (1931), 650 f.

[8] E. S. Brooks, pp. 162-167.

[9] William McGlauflin, *Faith With Power.*

[10] Robert Cummins, "The General Superintendency of the Universalist Church," *AJUHS*, III (1962), 23-29.

[11] Eddy *II*, 475 f.

[12] Fannie Shaw Fisher, *Fifty Years of Work by Universalist Women in Illinois; The Columbian Congress of the Universalist Church*, address by Cordelia A. Quinby, "The Woman's Centenary Association."

[13] Ida M. Folsom, *A Brief History of the Work of Universalist Women.*

[14] *Centennial Celebration of the First Universalist Church of Rochester, New York*, 1946; also my personal recollections.

[15] James D. Tillinghast, "The Young People's Christian Union," in *The Columbian Congress of the Universalist Church.*

[16] In my account of the schools and colleges I have drawn on these books. See also *UL*, May 17, 1921.

[17] Max Kapp and David Parke, *109 Years.*

[18] Tilden, a former high-school teacher, was discovered working in a plumbing shop and recruited by Henry A. Niven, then agent for Lombard. Niven, a friend and contemporary of mine, was a Universalist from Rochester, N.Y.

[19] McGlauflin.

[20] Asa M. Bradley, "Pacific Coast Universalism," *UL*, XXXIX (1936), *passim;* also Bradley mss. at Starr King School and UHS.

[21] *Indiana.* Joshua Smithton (1792-1861) was born in North Carolina and was a long resident of Vevay, Ind.

[22] Scott, pp. 75-82; Eddy *II*, 437.

[23] Eddy *II*, 571-589, 598 ff.

[24] McGlauflin.

[25] C. E. Nash, "Possibilities," and R. A. White, "Our Work in the West," in Rugg. In Arkansas, e.g., there were once five churches and a state convention. The lone survivor is at Mt. Ida, with one Universalist left in what is now a community church.

[26] Among others who served the mission are: Mr. and Mrs. Ayers; Mr. and Mrs. Harry Cary; Mr. and Mrs. Harry Cary, Jr.; Mr. and Mrs. Nelson Lobdell; Miss Agness Hathaway; Kideon Keirn; Hazel Kirk; M. Louise Klein; Edgard Leavitt; Catherine Osborne; Mr. and Mrs. Clifford Stetson. I had intended to recount and evaluate the work in Japan in greater detail, but found the task to be a project in itself. See *UL*, XXXVII (1934), 1219, 1416; CXXXI (1949), 135; CXXXIII (1951), 26; CXXXIX (1957), 71.

[27] Eddy *II*, 359.

28 McGlauflin, pp. 73-85; *The Maine Book on Universalism; UL,* CXXIV (1942), 593; *UL,* XXXIII (1930), 542.

29 Elmo A. Robinson, "Philosophy Teaching, California, 1857-1957," *J. Hist. of Ideas,* XX (1959), 369-384.

30 Children's Sunday was instituted by Charles H. Leonard in Chelsea, Mass., in 1856. He adapted an earlier custom of John Murray.

31 John G. Adams, "The Vestry and Its Uses," *UQ,* XXVII (1870), 320-334.

32 For one man's comparison of church buildings in 1812 with those of 1848, see *Ohio,* p. 70.

33 Elmo A. Robinson, "Country Church Conference at Cornell," and "Country Life Institute at Canton," *UL,* XVI, (1913) 303, 312.

34 G. M. Harmon. "Social Reform and the Churches," *UQ,* XXXVI (1879), 179-186.

35 E. A. Perry, "Workingmen's Rights," *UQ,* XLIII (1886), 75-84; R. O. Williams, "Monopoly, Labor Combinations, Strikes, Boycotting," *UQ,* XLIV (1887), 69-84.

36 After the death of Mr. Nash we heard nothing more of his project; I was unable to obtain information about its abandonment.

37 Scott, pp. 83-86.

CHAPTER SIX

1 Herbert W. Schneider, *A History of American Philosophy* (New York, 1946), pp. 37, 226; Ralph H. Gabriel, *The Course of American Democratic Thought* (New York, 1940), p. 14, *passim.*

2 Eddy *I,* 401; Eddy, *UQ,* XXXIV (1877), 162-179; XXXV (1878), 34-46; also *An Appeal to the Impartial Public* (Boston, 1785).

3 Eddy *I,* 297, 302, 307.

4 Eddy, *UQ,* XXXV (1878), 44.

5 The following account is taken chiefly from Ferriss' *Book.* See also *UL,* XXIX (1926), 4, 9, 19, 21.

6 Huntington was an orthodox clergyman whose Universalist views were made known after his death.

7 J. S. Cantwell, in *The Winchester Centennial, 1803-1903,* pp. 18-29; W. S. Balch, "Caleb Rich," *UQ,* XXIX (1872), 58-78.

8 T. J. Sawyer, "Universalism in America," *UQ,* XLIV (1887), 268.

9 Eddy *II,* 55 f.

10 For variant statement see Eddy *II* and Eddy, *UQ,* XXXIII (1876), 149-160.

11 *Statement of Faith Delivered to the Saints* (Keene, N. H., 1817).

12 Robinson, *Ohio,* p. 79; *The Maine Book on Universalism.*

13 Thomas Whittemore, *The Plain Guide to Universalism* (1840).

14 I. D. Williamson, *The Universalist Church Companion* (1855).

15 Moses Marston, *Sermons of the Rev. Franklin S. Bliss* (1878).

16 Cantwill.

17 John C. Adams, in *The Winchester Centennial.*

18 Frederick Perkins, *Beliefs Commonly Held Among Us* (1940), p. 40.

19 Norris C. Hodgden, *A Denominational Offering* (1871), p. 27.

20 Sylvanus Cobb, *Autobiography*, pp. 107 f.

21 E. G. Brooks, "Edward Turner," *UQ*, VIII (1871), 151-180, 265-289.

22 For Eddy's account see *II*, 260-342.

23 Brooks, *loc. cit.*

24 Ernest S. Bates, *American Faith.*

25 For Adin Ballou's account, see his *Autobiography, passim.*

26 In later years Whittemore and Ballou "made up": J. G. Adams, *Memoir of Thomas Whittemore*, p. 343. Whittemore's version of the controversy is said to be found in his memoir of Ballou.

27 Adams, *loc. cit.*

28 Original minutes of Charlestown Universalist Society.

29 Frank H. Foster, "The Eschatology of the New England Divines," *Bibliotheca Sacra*, XLV (1888), 669-694.

30 Lyman Abbott, Eric Waterhouse, and William G. Tousey, "The Problem of Human Destiny as conditioned by Free Will" (Boston, c. 1900).

31 The treatment of Darwinism which follows is taken from my "Universalism, a Changing Faith," where specific references to source material may be found. An excellent summary is Ernest Cassara's "The Effect of Darwinism on Universalist Belief."

32 Stow Persons, "Evolution and Theology in America," in his *Evolutionary Thought in America* (1950), pp. 450 ff.

33 Arthur M. Schlesinger, in *Mass. Hist. Soc. Proceedings*, LXIV, 526.

34 Howard MacQueary, *Univ. Monthly*, VI (1892), 7 f. See also Orello Cone, *Essays, Doctrinal and Practical* (1899), and essays in *The Columbia Congress of the Universalist Church.*

35 Max Kapp, "Orello Cone," *UL*, XXXIII (1930), 724 ff.

36 *Univ. Monthly*, VI (1892), 10 ff. For a general account see John C. Adams, "The Spiritual Harvest of Fifty Years," *UL*, XXIV (1921), 990 ff.

37 Many allusions to the situation are found in the rationalist *Universalist Monthly.*

38 G. M. Harmon, "The Restoration of Humanity," *UQ*, XXXIX (1882), 328-338; E. C. Sweetser, "The Necessity of a Change in the Language of Our Creed," *UQ*, XL (1893), 34-42.

39 John C. Adams, *Universalism and the Universalist Church* (1915), pp. 111 f; Perkins, p. 46.

40 *UL*, XXXVI (1933), 661.

41 John M. Atwood, "The Church and the Humanist Controversy," *UL*, XXXIII (1930), 75.

42 *UL*, CXXXIII (1951), 232.

Notes

text.

Notes 255

[43] Clarence R. Skinner, *A Religion for Greatness* (Boston, 1945).
[44] *UL*, XXXVII (1934), 68.
[45] "The Liberty Clause, a Symposium," *UL*, CXXXIII (1951), 49.
[46] Alan F. Sawyer, "The Detrimental Effects of Creedal Limitation in Universalism" (thesis).
[47] Mary F. Bogue, "The Minneapolis Radical Lectures and the Excommunication of Harman Bisbee," *AJUHS*, VII (1967-68), 3-69.

CHAPTER SEVEN

[1] Wayne K. Clymer, "The Life and Thought of James Relly," *CH*, XI (1942), 193-216; Irwin, pp. 98 ff.
[2] *Universalist* (London), Vol. III (1927), May.
[3] William Vidler, *A Sketch of the Life of Elhanan Winchester* (London), 1797.
[4] *Encyclopedia of National Biography;* also Irwin, *passim.*
[5] *Encyclopedia of National Biography.*
[6] Cf. Harmon Gehr, "Elhanan Winchester," *UL*, CXXXII (1950), 165 ff., with Vidler and with *Universalist Theological Magazine* (London), Vol. VIII (1903).
[7] *Encyclopedia of National Biography.*
[8] *Ohio*, p. 91.
[9] *UL*, XXXIII (1930), 19.
[10] Ida Folsom, *A Brief History of the Work of Universalist Women,* pp. 5 f; A. G. Laurie, "Universalism in Scotland," *UQ*, XXIV (1867), 455-467.
[11] Costello Weston, "Universalism in Halifax," *UQ*, XXXVI (1879), 320-328.
[12] *UL*, CXXXVIII (1956), 190; CXLI (1959), 18.
[13] John C. Adams, "New Problems in our Church Work," *UQ*, XXXVII (1880), 461-474.
[14] For a general statement of relationships from the Unitarian side see Earle M. Wilbur, *A History of Unitarianism in Transylvania, England, and America* (Cambridge, 1952).
[15] For the drift towards Arian views see essay by John Winthrop Platner in *The Religious History of New England* (1917).
[16] John Wesley Hanson, *Biography of William Henry Ryder* (Boston, 1891).
[17] Eddy *I*, 304.
[18] Norris C. Hodgdon, *A Denominational Offering* (Boston, 1871).
[19] Wilbur, p. 409.
[20] A. D. Mayo, "Free Religion in the West," *UQ*, VIII (1871), 389-412;
[21] Chas. H. Lyttle, *Freedom Moves West* (Boston, 1952), p. 13.
[22] Sylvanus Cobb, *Autobiography,* pp. 186-208. For other possibilities

see his reference to South Weymouth and recall Winchester's assertion about Attleboro. There may be other instances.

23 Jacob C. Meyer, *Church and State in Massachusetts.*
24 Hanson.
25 Alfred S. Cole, *Our Liberal Heritage,* p. 41.
26 I. M. Atwood, *Walks About Zion* (Boston), 1882.
27 Ernest Sutherland Bates, *American Faith,* p. 403.
28 Elmo A. Robinson, "The Universalist Connections of Thomas Starr King," *AJUHS,* V, 3-29.
29 R. O. Williams, "Our New Departure," *UQ,* XXXII (1875), 281-300.
30 Cole.
31 E. L. Rexford, "Union Between Universalists and Unitarians," *Univ. Monthly,* I (1891), 8 f.
32 *Ibid.,* VII (1893), 11 f.

CHAPTER EIGHT

1 Robert T. Handy, "The American Religious Depression, 1925-1935," *Church History,* XXIX (1960), 3-16.
2 L. S. McCollester, "The Genius of American Universalism," *UL,* XXXIII (1930), 614 ff.
3 W. C. Selleck, "Our Altered Situation," *UL,* XXXIII (1930), 716.
4 Alfred S. Cole, "Historical Backgrounds of the Universalist Movement," *UL,* CXIX (1937), 1320 ff.
5 *UL,* CXXXIII (1951), 65; CXXXVII (1955), 202.
6 Jeffrey W. Campbell, "Personality Not Pigmented," *UL,* CXXII (1940), 180 ff.
7 Robert Cummins, "Universalism in England and Holland," *UL,* CXXX (1948), 53 ff.
8 *UL,* XXVIII (1925), 22.
9 *UL,* CXX (1938), 884.
10 *UL,* XXXIV (1931), 175.
11 *UL,* XXXIII (1930), 1460.
12 *UL,* CXXII (1940), 535 ff.
13 Charles N. Vickery, "History of the Service Projects of the Universalist Service Committee," in *About the Unitarian Universalist Service Committee* (mimeographed, 1967).
14 *UL,* XXX (1927), 1357.
15 *UL,* CXXXIII (1951), 189; XXVII (1924), 11.
16 *UL,* CXXXV (1953), 156.
17 *UL,* XXXII (1929), 1363 f.
18 *UL,* XXXIII (1930), 587, 645.
19 *UL,* XXX (1927), 1254 ff.
20 *UL,* Vol. XXVII (1924), Feb. 9.
21 Scott, p. 109.

[22] *UL*, XXXVII (1934), 34.

[23] *UL*, CXXXV (1953), 156; CXXXIX (1957), 267.

[24] Robert Cummins, *Excluded* (pamphlet; "Beacon Reference Series," 1966), pp. 4 f.

[25] My account is taken chiefly from *Excluded* but also from Charles S. Macfarland, *Christian Unity in the Making* . . . (1948). See also Carl McIntire, *Twentieth Century Reformation* (1945), pp. 75 ff.

[26] Cummins, p. 28.

[27] *UL*, CXXXII (1950), 240.

[28] *UL*, XXXVI (1933), 1014, 1110; CXXXVI (1954), 64.

[29] Abstracted from my "Universalist Connections of Thomas Starr King," *AJUHS* V (1965), 22-24.

CHAPTER NINE

[1] Henry Nelson Wieman, "Neo-Orthodoxy's World Without Science, Liberalism's Challenge," *Christian Register*, CXXXV (1956), 16 ff.

[2] Adin Ballou, *Autobiography* (Lowell, 1896), p. 33.

[3] Franklin H. Littell, *From State Church to Pluralism*, pp. 59 ff. See also *Daedalus*, "Religion in America," Winter, 1967.

[4] I. D. Williamson, *The Universalist Church Companion;* William Frost Crispin, *Universalism and the Problems of the Universalist Church;* A. J. Patterson, "A Hundred Years," *UQ*, XXXI (1874), 70-96; R. O. Williams, "Our New Departure," *UQ*, XXXII (1875), 281-300; Henry Blanchard "The Power and Progress of Universalism," *UQ*, XXXVIII (1881), 180-194; Charles A. Collier, "Aspects of the Growth of American Universalism," (thesis).

[5] A. Ballou, p. 113. Eddy consulted Ballou; Ballou, p. 507, thought Eddy's account very fair.

[6] *Ibid.*, p. 89.

[7] *Ibid.*, p. 148. Ballou's pastorate in New York was unsuccessful.

[8] L. L. Briggs, "Our Sunday Schools," *UQ*, XXVII (1870), 194-202; Richard Eddy, "The Origin of American Sunday Schools," *UQ*, XXXIX (1882), 448-459.

[9] Frank D. Adams, "Address," *UL*, XXXII (1929), 1390 ff.

[10] *UL*, CXXXIII (1951), 335.

[11] It is reported that Tolstoy rated Adin Ballou as the greatest man America had produced.

[12] See Scott on why churches die, *UL*, CXXXIX (1957), 22, and Gibbons on the same theme, *UL*, CXXXI (1949), 383 ff.

[13] Personal correspondence.

[14] G. L. Demerest, "The General Convention," *UQ*, XXXV (1878), 102.

[15] Scott, p. 3.

[16] *UL,* CXX (1938), 458 f.

[17] F. E. Meyer, *The Religious Bodies of America* (1961), pp. 516-519.

[18] J. A. Cousens, "Great Start in Boston," *UL,* XXXI (1928), 1579 ff.

[19] Russell E. Miller, "Universalism and Sectarian Education Before 1860," *AJUHS,* III (1962), 30-53.

[20] James Ward Smith, ed., *A Critical Bibliography of Religion in America,* IV 210 ff.

[21] *Ibid.,* p. 218.

[22] Joseph L. Blau, ed., *American Philosophic Addresses* (1946), pp. 548 f.

[23] Leonard W. Bacon, *A History of American Christianity* (1897), p. 227.

[24] *UL,* XXVIII (1925), 11.

[25] Whitney Cross, *The Burned-Over District* (Cornell Univ. Press, 1950). Used by permission of Cornell Univ. Press.

[26] Lalone.

[27] Robert Cummins in V. Ferm, *The American Church of the Protestant Heritage,* p. 335.

[28] This document is mentioned, although not quoted entire, in *Dictionary of National Biography.*

[29] Eddy *II,* 358.

[30] "Universalism and Unitarianism," *UL,* XXXI (1928), 840 f.

CHAPTER TEN

[1] This section is based on my "A Trinity for Religious Liberals," *Crozer Quarterly,* XXIV (1947), 207-213.

[2] This and following sections are from my "Unrestricted Universalism," *Crozer Quarterly,* XXIX (1952), 158-172. Additional meanings of *universalism* may be found in *Oxford English Dictionary,* in *Century Dictionary,* in Nicolas Berdyaev, *The Russian Idea,* chap. 2.

[3] Sir Arthur Keith, *Evolution and Ethics,* pp. 52, 59, 109, 113 f.

[4] Bertrand Russell, *Authority and the Individual,* pp. 16, 19.

[5] *Ibid.,* p. 20.

[6] Elmo A. Robinson, "Universalism or Totalitarianism," *Christian Century,* LIX (1942), 978 ff.

[7] Henri Bergson, *The Two Sources of Morality and Religion,* pp. 255 ff.

[8] Russell, p. 38.

[9] Immanuel Kant, *Eternal Peace,* 1st ed.

[10] Leibniz, *Discourses on Metaphysics,* para. 36.

[11] Rousseau, *The Social Contract,* Book 4, chap. 8.

[12] See Robinson, "Unrestricted Universalism."

[13] *Ibid.*

[14] *Ibid.*

[15] Anderson M. Scruggs.

Index

Note: Names of places (states, cities, etc.) usually refer to Universalist activities therein.

Huntington, Joseph, 133, 147
Huntley, George, 126
Hymnals, 51, 63, 121

Indiana, 60, 70, 73, 75-77, 86, 114, 116, 155, 169
International Conference of Religious Liberals, 186
Iowa, 75, 86, 155, 181
Irwin, Charlotte, 148, 215
Israel, Israel, 49, 51

James, William, 121, 158, 231, 236f.
Japan Mission, 102, 118-120, 155, 179, 189, 211
Jefferson Liberal Institute, 105
Jefferson, Thomas, 43, 174
Johnson, Ellen, 220
Jones, Thomas, 41, 43, 51
Jordan, Joseph, 113
Jordan Neighborhood House, 187

Keith, Sir Arthur, 232
Kendall, Paul R., 74, 110
Kidwell, Jonathan, 72f., 86, 114, 155
King, Thomas Farrington, 40, 42, 45, 56, 62f., 83f.
King, Thomas Starr
 family and friends, 56, 75, 82
 sermons, 84, 217
 Unitarian Universalist, 145, 171, 176-178, 203, 213
Kinsolving, Lester, 222
Kneeland, Abner
 active in convention, 63
 defended by Whittemore, 220
 disciplined for blasphemy, 56f., 154f., 162, 213
 ordained, 56
 pastorates, 42, 45, 59
 reformer, 160, 217
Knox College, 112
Korea, 187

Labor relations, 89f., 99, 125
Lalone, Emerson H., 90, 96, 106, 127, 145, 170, 220
Latham, Harold, 103, 193
Legality of testimony by Universalists, 169
Leibniz, G.W., 236
Leonard, Charles H., 111
Liberal Religious Youth, 200
Lincoln, Abraham, 75, 95, 109
Lombard, Benjamin, 110
Lombard College, 74, 82, 86, 101, 105f., 109-113
Loveland, S.C., 58, 98
Lowe, John S., 187f.
Lutherans, 76, 196
Lyttle, Charles, 174, 177

McCollester, Lee S., 111, 128, 184, 187, 220
McCollester, Sullivan H., 110, 127, 152
MacPherson, Walter H., 183, 188
Maine
 associations and conventions, 59, 76
 churches and societies, 44, 54, 115, 202
 description, 34, 67
 faith, 137
 overtures to Congregationalists, 192
 See also Ferry Beach; Westbrook Seminary
Manford, Erasmus, 74, 86, 155
Mann, Horace, 9, 217
Manning, Stanley, 195
Marriage and divorce, 124
Maryland, 30, 35, 46, 95
Massachusetts
 churches and societies, 18f., 30, 44, 47, 54, 58f., 114, 202
 Massachusetts convention, 87, 107